LONDON CANARY WHARF
AND DOCKLA

Professor S K Al Naib
University of East London

Building the Future of Great Britain

CONTENTS

PREFACE

Preface

Welcome to 'London Canary Wharf and Docklands' - an independent research publication on London's great urban regeneration and the people who build, live and work in Europe's fastest growing new city within a city. The book reports and reflects the developments over the past few decades in the 8.5 square miles of London's waterside. Prior to regeneration, the area was a decaying leftover from a glorious trading post, which was a depressing and dying monument.

In July 1981, the Government set up London Docklands Development Corporation (LDDC). Coupled with outstanding international finance and enthusiasm, it has turned the eyes of the world once again on the area extending east of Tower Bridge. New dramatic skylines of Canary Wharf have emerged with more plans in the pipeline. Homes and offices have been built alongside converted warehouses, while tracts of land, historic squares and Dickensian cobbled roads have been revitalised. In a traditional part of London brimming with completely new ideas, the book aims to reflect this cosmopolitan district through in-depth analysis and coverage. As far as possible, each article is written as free standing and self-contained. The locations of the colour illustrations had to be in accord with the printing requirements.

The towers at Canary Wharf are the most visible buildings on the London skyline and the tallest in Britain. The project has aroused strong feelings and has been the subject of much media attention. Such is the importance of Canary Wharf, both for East London Docklands and London as a whole, it is appropriate to reflect in details on this project and its considerable impact on the successful development of the rest of Docklands. Despite the private sector led development in Docklands, Canary Wharf represents a subsidy by Central Government on a large scale and reorientation of the planning process. The development when fully built during the first decade of the 21st century will be the world's largest office building complex, consisting of many millions-sq. ft. of office and commercial floors of space. Located in the Isle of Dogs, former Enterprise Zone, it is the centrepiece of the new London Docklands. Canary Wharf also occupies a highly significant space being near to the City of London, currently the world's pre-eminent financial centre.

This book has four main themes in unfolding the story of Docklands and Canary Wharf. The first outlines the background and significant events in the history of the area. The second concentrates on the formation of the London Docklands Development Corporation that helped bring Canary Wharf in existence. The third theme is the construction of the largest project in Europe and its impact on the London property and financial markets. The fourth theme is concerned with a variety of physical, environmental, social and economic changes, which were derived from the regeneration to benefit the whole of London and Docklands area.

"London Canary Wharf & Docklands"	ISBN 1 874536 988
First Printing	June 2003

Internationally Acknowledged Books by Professor Naib

"London Canary Wharf & Docklands"	ISBN 1 8745 36 988
"London Water Heritage" A Portrait	ISBN 1 8745 36 406
"London Millennium Guide" Ed., Ent., & Asp.	ISBN 1 8745 36 201
"London & Docklands Walks" The Explorer	ISBN 1 8745 36 252
"London Dockland Guide" Heritage Panora.	ISBN 1 8745 36 031
"London Illustrated" History, Current & Fut.	ISBN 1 8745 36 015
"Discover London Docklands" A to Z Guide	ISBN 1 8745 36 007
"London Docklands" Past, Present & Future	ISBN 1 8745 36 023
"European Docklands" Past, Present & Future	ISBN 0 9019 87 824
"Dockland" Historical Survey	ISBN 0 9089 87 800
"Encyclopedia of London Docklands"	ISBN 1 8745 36 333
"Fluid Mechanics, Hydraulics and Envir. Eng."	ISBN 1 8745 36 066
"Applied Hydraulics, Hyd & Envir. Eng."	ISBN 1 8745 36 058
"Jet Mechanics and Hydraulic Structures"	ISBN 0 9019 87 832
"Experimental Fluid Mechs & Hyd Modelling"	ISBN 1 8745 36 090

The author is Professor of Civil Engineering and Head of Department at the University of East London, Longbridge Road, Dagenham, Essex RM8 2AS, England.
(Tel: 020 8223 2478/2531, Fax: 020 8223 2963)

PLEASE ORDER THROUGH:

RESEARCH BOOKS, P O. BOX 82, ROMFORD, ESSEX, RM6 5BY, GREAT BRITAIN.

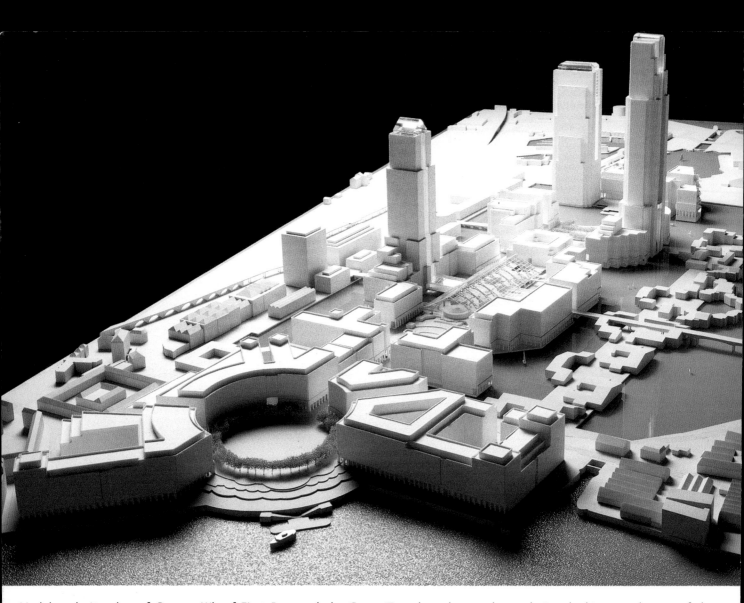

Model and site plan of Canary Wharf First Proposals by Grant Travelstead - an elevated view looking north east of the buildings showing three tall towers and the crossing of DLR with its glass roofed station, c1986. That was before the Canadian developers Olympia & York stepped in with their grandiose second scheme for a heady mix of Wall Street and Whitehall on water.

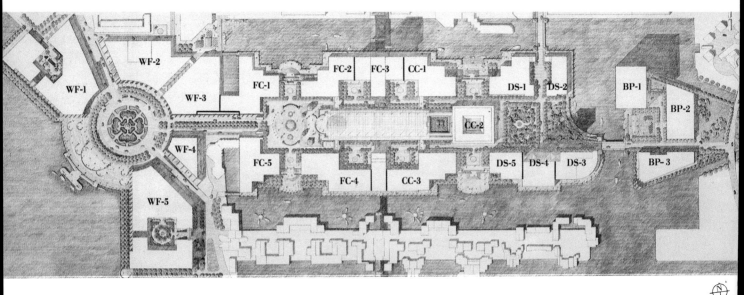

0   100 Metres

SITE PLAN

West Ferry Circus			Founders Court			Canary Concourse			Docklands Square			Blackwall Place		
Parcel Designation	Parcel Size (g.s.f.)	Buildable Area (g.s.f.)	Parcel Designation	Parcel Size (g.s.f.)	Buildable Area (g.s.f.)	Parcel Designation	Parcel Size (g.s.f.)	Buildable Area (g.s.f.)	Parcel Designation	Parcel Size (g.s.f.)	Buildable Area (g.s.f.)	Parcel Designation	Parcel Size (g.s.f.)	Buildable Area (g.s.f.)
WF-1	124,235	870,000	FC-1	77,280	541,000	CC-1	56,004	392,000	DS-1	45,833	320,000	BP-1	44,605	1,100,
WF-2	136,207	954,000	FC-2	56,004	392,000	CC-2	31,484	300,000	DS-2	42,462	297,000	BP-2	40,219	281,
WF-3	94,114	659,000	FC-3	43,244	1,238,000	CC-3	68,431	479,000	DS-3	46,217	324,000	BP-3	50,777	355,
WF-4	75,643	530,000	FC-4	68,431	479,000				DS-4	48,126	1,143,000			
WF-5	151,134	1,058,000	FC-5	68,529	480,000				DS-5	29,665	208,000			

4

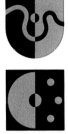
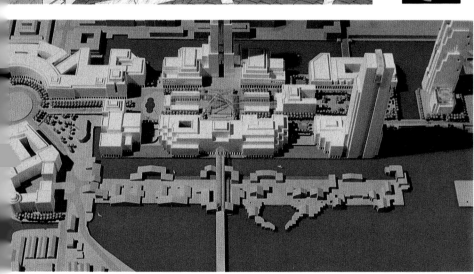

The original artists impressions for a speculative new financial centre to be built on the site of old banana warehouses called Canary Wharf, c 1986.

International Business Centre

The Docklands and Canary Wharf Story has become familiar to everyone who knows London. The glory of London's past as a major port, the gradual decline and the seeming closure of the area followed the rise and fall of the British Empire, which in its heyday controlled a quarter of the surface of the earth. Then came the boom of the 1980s and 1990s bringing new conquering spirits to Docklands and London, where the pioneers cut swathes of mirrored glass and bright painted steel through the old docks. Suddenly here new careers and lives were created. A thrilling combination of buildings was constructed, with warehouse renovations standing next to post modernist blocks in the shadows of Canary Wharf skyscrapers all on the edge of the ever changing Thames and its docks. The East London Dockland spirit emerged once again. Now, Canary Wharf is internationally recognised as the great district in London. As a business community it is rivalling the City. Newspapers, international banks, oil companies, advertising agencies and many other professions are amongst those companies who appreciate the space and freedom offered by the new development.

Canary Wharf stands on the Isle of Dogs, 2.5 miles east of the City of London, on the site of the former West India Docks. The Isle of Dogs is the name of the area surrounded by a loop in the Thames opposite Greenwich. The name probably is derived from the time when sailing ships had to track around the river's bend and heard the barking of dogs on the island. The island was for centuries the centre of London's thriving maritime trade and in the 19th century became a shipbuilding and engineering centre for the world. With the arrival of major international companies, Canary Wharf has become the centre of London's third business district. The high quality office accommodation enables companies to be competitive internationally and that is important for the future of the capital. Full provisions for shops, services and entertainment, have been developed. London has traditionally been built around squares and gardens and Canary Wharf is no exception. 25 of the 71 acres of Canary Wharf are squares, gardens, water courts and dockside promenades.

The Canadian Developers

Olympia & York is one of Canada's largest corporations with three principal divisions including manufacturing, investment and development. It is one of the largest developers and property owners in North America, and their properties include First Canadian Place Toronto, World Financial Centre, New York and other buildings in 21 cities. Canary Wharf together with adjacent sites of Port East to the North and Heron Quays to the South is their largest development to date.

Canary Wharf Tower at One Canada Square, was designed by Professor Cesar Pelli; it is 800 ft high, contains 50 storeys and is clad in stainless steel. The four cut-away corners soften the contours of the building and allow extra natural light into its centre. The pyramid roof completes the tower. By night it is lit from within and by day it is recognisable for miles around London. A symbol of the growth and vitality of Docklands, the Canary Wharf tower has changed the skyline of the capital.

Golden Corridor

As more people choose to make their offices and homes here, the facilities have grown to meet their demands. Superstores, such as Asda and Savacentre and other major retailers have emerged, with their attendant flexibility but in the intimacy of the various pretty docks, old pubs, which have been renovated and diverse restaurants. Pretty houses around Canary Wharf provide the shells for museums and winebars. The London Arena plays host to international sporting and entertainment events. The Millennium celebrations and Dome added to the regeneration of the area and with the vast improvement in public transport completed, it is certain that Docklands will never look back again. The Government has proclaimed its confidence in the future of Canary Wharf and Docklands, following the recent publications of plans to create a "golden corridor" development eastwards along both sides of the Thames from Docklands to Tilbury and Sheerness. It will be a vital economic growth area for London starting from Canary Wharf and extending to about 30 miles down the Thames.

Great Success Story

These days, the vast regeneration of London's famous Docklands has become the most widely known inner city development success story in the world. Every one knows of it or has read of it, yet few have more than a vague idea of what has happened in this enormous 8.5 sq. mile area of London. Within a short distance of the City, the unique riverside areas of Wapping, Isle of Dogs, Royal Docks and Surrey Docks provide an unrivalled setting for visitors. Spectacular new office and housing developments, historic churches, conservation areas and 19th century spice warehouses fuse together along the 55 miles of Thames waterfront to provide a breathtaking cityscape. This book attempts to give an insight into this constantly evolving scene with an in-depth knowledge of the history and regeneration of the whole area.

History of Isle of Dogs

London has always been a major international centre for commerce from its inception as a Roman settlement in 50AD. Despite the enormous changes over the centuries the City's function is still thriving, albeit further eastward at Canary Wharf, on the Isle of Dogs. The history of the Island has always been intimately linked with the River Thames and City of London. The river itself created the distinctive U-shape over millions of years in its sweeping course to the sea and by the building of the Embankment during the 18th century. The growth of London's population in the 17th and 18th century created a parallel growth in the demand for fresh meat. The Isle of Dogs became famous at City banquets for the quality of cattle fattened on its grass fields. At the beginning of the 19th century the island gave way to the bustle of industry, where the West India Docks were opened in 1802, to meet the needs of City merchants for secure storage and shipping facilities for their costly cargoes of rum, spices, hardwoods and sugar. They included the central part of Canary Wharf, named by the Port of London Authority after the Canary Islands trade of vegetables and fruit that arrived in ships with exotica of all kinds. Many innovations in shipbuilding were tried in the new yards, which opened up along the foreshore of the island in the first half of the 19th century.

Later on in the 1870s the island became an attractive site for more investors, one of the best known of these was William Cubitt, master builder and Lord Mayor of London who gave his name to the island's eastern district, Cubitt Town. His works were established in the late 1840s and other firms were set up to produce steel tanks, bridges, cranes, wire ropes, anchor chains, ships propellers and boilers. Many of these companies became famous worldwide. These giant companies supported a host of smaller industries, making ropes, sacks, kegs, drums, nails, horseshoes and cables. Other goods were manufactured here by firms, which became household names including Morton's jams, Maconochie's pickles, MacDougalls flour and Price's candles. The Millwall football club was first formed by workers in the Morton's factory. There were factories for car oil, paint, chemicals, lead and varnish works, manufacturers of prams and all supporting transport storage and catering services.

The island was heavily bombed during World War II and the Home Guards were based on the Mudshute Farm of today. Much of the Isle of Dogs and London's East End was destroyed by German bombers. They flew up the Thames, turned right at the McDougall's flour mills at the centre of the Isle and dropped their bombs on a line between there and the spire of St Anne's Church, Limehouse. Canary Wharf's sheds and vaults full of spirit burned for two weeks. During the post war period, new blocks of flats were built and trade and industry prospered for a brief period. But with investment in modern technology and a revolution in ship handling the island began to decline. Firms closed down or moved away, and finally the docks were closed in 1980.

The regeneration of the island was started with the setting up of the London Development Dockland Corporation and the Enterprise Zone in 1981. Now giant buildings and waterside studios stand mirrored in the still waters, where once exotic cargoes were unloaded and luxury and private houses cover the remains of the old slipways. New communication links have brought the Canary Wharf on the island close to the City and the world of international banking.

Docklands 200th Anniversary

Year 2000 marked the 200th anniversary of the laying of the first stone of London West India Docks on the Isle of Dogs, a ceremonial pronouncement of the City's high hopes for world domination of British trade in the years to come. It would have been hard for anyone to have imagined that the Isle would, before the end of the 20th century, have acquired a spectacular new skyline grandly reminiscent of Manhattan on Water. The Canary Wharf Tower, Britain's tallest building and its surrounding multi-storeyed modern architecture established and provided London with an imposing financial gateway in time for the third Millennium. With these came improved offices, housing and public transport including a modern light railway, wide new highways, extensive landscaping and modern telecommunication technology to match anything in the world.

Worldwide Interest

The development of London Docklands has created considerable interest in North America, Europe, Far East, Australia and other parts of the world. Many people have visited the new city over the past few decades eager to find out how the regeneration has been achieved.

Opinions have varied considerably about the way it has been handled but there is no doubt of the successful completion in 1998 by the LDDC's remit from central Government to secure the regeneration of the derelict Docklands physically there for all to see. There may have been other ways in which the redevelopment could have taken place. It is certain that the strategy of the 1970s Committees on Docklands would possibly had not achieved the right improvements in East London.

Policies to dramatically increase the amount of council/social housing, which then represented a high disproportionate percentage of the existing stock compared with other parts of London, would surely have placed substantial additional pressure on the local authorities' resources which are already straining under the existing pressure. Similarly, to build factories and low level warehouses on the Wharf for renting to maintain a low wage economy by only supporting initiatives which would provide unskilled and semi-skilled jobs for local people would have excluded the possibility of providing the wider range of employment opportunities for Londoners that are now available. It would certainly have reduced the chances of London as to maintain its status as the financial centre of the world in the 21st century.

Canary Wharf 1992 - The superb achievement shone forth in all its splendour, a remarkable testament to vision and determination of all those involved. The creation of a new city in four years is without doubt the most ambitious feat of building and engineering during the 20th century.

THE ISLANDERS PAST AND PRESENT

Anxiety and Strong Sense of History

Growth of Population and Industry

The Island's population grew with its industry. The few cattle farmers and windmill labourers of the 18th century expanded with the construction migrants from all parts of the British Islands. They formed a mixture of skilled artisans, labourers, dockworkers, shopkeepers and employers during the first half of the 19th century. The famous Scottish engineer, David Napier, who had boatyards on the island also lived in Napier House at his shipyard in West Ferry Road. In the late part of the 19th century, better off workers left the island for less crowded districts such as Barking and Essex. The population, which reached 21,000 by 1900, became almost entirely working class of dockers, stevedores and other manual workers. As the docks were isolated from the rest of London, the environment gave those who lived there a special sense of identity with the island as a unique place. It was a hard working environment with crammed community, where living conditions were alleviated by mutual support and self-sufficiency, despite the people being extremely poor. A lifestyle which in spite of material poverty is still remembered with pride for its simplicity and neighbourliness by those original islanders who still live there. The numbers have decreased considerably over the past three decades with substantial numbers from the Docklands area migrating to Essex and Suffolk areas.

Fred Olsen's Canary Wharf

Fred Olsen Line's 36 years association with Canary Wharf at West India Docks ended in 1970. Their last ship the 4,000 tonnes Braque finished loading with general cargo on 25 January and sailed for the Mediterranean. All Olsen's trade was then concentrated at their new centre and P, J and K berths of the former Millwall Docks. The new centre included an amenity block for the dockers, passenger terminal and offices for the importers and exporters, one of which was later occupied by the LDDC when they were first established in 1981. From 1970 until the closure of the docks ten years later, the PLA took over Canary Wharf. The first vessel to be worked was the Transupilo which was loaded with exports to Yugoslavia. Olsen's first took over the lease of Canary Wharf in 1933 and their ships brought fruit and vegetables from the Canary Islands. In the 1970s they operated a regular passenger cruise to the Canary Islands with their two ships, the Black Prince and the Black Watch. They had a dock labour force of around 240 mainly from the Island, who worked a two six-hour shift a day system. The men on the ships were paid a basic £39 a week. Quay workers were paid £34 a week. This agreement, argued other dockers, should be the type of arrangement throughout the port!

Island History Trust

A strong sense of history was still an unquestioned part of community life in the early 1980s, reinforced rather than undermined by the regeneration process on the island. It was not until the last few years that history seemed in any danger of being lost. In the 1980s and 1990s came the final break with the past, the physical evidence of the island's great trading history began to vanish altogether beneath the new and costly apartment buildings and shining facades of the new era. The stories and memories which had reinforced that evidence became legends. The old traditions no longer seemed to have any connection with the present. Because of this, the Island History Trust came into being as part of a community education project, funded through the urban aid programme in April 1980. The aim of the project was that, with the active help of the islanders, it should recover and preserve the history of the island and make that history publicly accessible, thus bridging the gap between the old and new communities and helping to provide a stable viewpoint from which to look into the future.

World of Two Factions

For the indigenous islanders, however, a different story can be told. Many had never been inside the walled docks but no sooner had they become familiar with the stretches of water and disused warehouses that surrounded them, a rapid change began in the mid 1980s. Within five years the dock area with its colourful new office complexes, expensive private housing estates and brand new railways had altered almost beyond recognition. Today the island remains an uneasy world of two factions: the old streets, churches and pubs and the last handful of traditional industries appear alongside the glittering printing works, telecommunications satellites and the financial and business centre of Canary Wharf. New housing contrasts sharply with the Council flats and maisonettes, many of which are in a neglected state of repair. A new population has moved in to fill the luxury homes and work in the modern offices and in the period of rapid change and the uncertainty that followed, the voice of the island community continued to be heard and sometimes had to be raised.

Opportunity for Future

The main anxiety is that any changes should benefit the existing population as well as bringing investment and new population into the area. Through training schemes, self-build housing, pressure on local Council, grass root actions and publicity campaigns to draw attention to local needs remain a feature of island life still today. Investment in providing new transport systems in Docklands has been substantial. It is now well accessible and provides a range of housing and employment opportunities as wide as any other part of London. However, the dramatic pace of change that has occurred has inevitably had its impact and stress on the lives of the residents of Docklands. The concern expressed about the new developments and the way they have changed the lives of these people is understandable and it is regrettable that they did not share the resulting benefits fully. It is probably too early to reach any final assessment of the success of the LDDC's work as the renaissance is likely to continue for another three decades. The opportunity is now available for Docklands Local Authorities and residents to adjust and accommodate their evolving needs to live and work together.

CANARY WHARF

The Global Marketplace

GREENWICH 1620

"As of the Manor of East Greenwich": In Tudor and Stuart times, the Royal Palace at Greenwich was the seat of power, affecting the future development of the country. Its strategic location at the neck of London's river dominated the approaches from sea and land. It was the birthplace of Henry VIII, Edward VI and Elizabeth I.

"On Thames's banks in silent thought we stood,
Where Greenwich smiles upon the silver flood:
Pleas'd with the seat which gave Eliza birth,
We kneel and kiss the consecrated earth."

Henry VIII

Dockers handling sugar bags at Canary Wharf, circa mid 1950s.

MILLWALL

Sir Francis Drake

Millwall takes its name from the seven windmills which stood on the wall built here to keep the Thames from overflowing at high tide.

The area is steeped in naval history: Columbus and Cabot came to petition Henry VII for support for their voyages to the New World; Sir Francis Drake was knighted by Queen Elizabeth I on board his ship, the "Golden Hind"; Peter the Great of Russia learned about navigation here; Captains Cook and Bligh lived here, as well as Sir Walter Raleigh; Lord Nelson's state funeral procession sailed around the Isle of Dogs, and Cleopatra's Needle travelled the same route on its last few miles from Alexandria, Egypt, to its present location on the Embankment.

THE ISLE OF DOGS

The Isle of Dogs is a peninsula, jutting south into the Thames, bounded by Limehouse, Greenwich and Blackwall Reaches.

It is believed that the origin of the name comes from the fact that Charles II kept the Royal Kennels in this marshy area, away from the Royal Palace at Greenwich.

Hanging Sign, Lombard Street

successor, Henry Addington, in 1802.

The Dock Company was composed of West India merchants and the City Corporation. The docks comprised of two parallel wet docks, each half a mile long, connecting with the Thames by basins and locks at either end, providing accommodation for 600 vessels and was policed by an armed watch of 100 men with muskets. The northern dock was the import dock, and the southern was the export dock.

In 1932 the original gateway to the West India Import Dock was removed to make way for more modern means of transport. Its fine pediment was surmounted by a clipper ship, which was inscribed with the names of some of its cargo, such as rum, sugar and molasses.

The West India Docks, 1802

Bells have played an important part in the history of the region. Its inhabitants are known as "Cockneys," if they were born within the sound of Bow Bells.

The bell recovered from the sunken "Lutine" is traditionally rung at Lloyds of London, to announce the loss of a vessel. The nearby bell foundry at Whitechapel, where the famous American Liberty bell was cast, is still in operation today.

The "Liberty Bell"

POPLAR

The borough of Poplar derives its name from the abundance of Poplar trees that once grew in this area. It is a curious connection that the Lombardy Poplar tree takes its name from the northern Italian region and family of moneylenders, who came to England in the wake of the Norman conquest—hence the name Lombard Street, the Wall Street of London!

THE WEST INDIA DOCKS

The West India Docks were founded to ensure that "West India produce might be effectually secure from loss by theft or other causes and the public revenue greatly benefited." The foundation stone was laid in 1800 by the Prime Minister, William Pitt, and opened by his

Parallelling today's undertaking at Canary Wharf was the opening of the West India Docks in 1802 on the very same site. Designed and built broad stone quays, 3000 feet length of warehouses, a series of progressive locks opening onto spacious basins of water, and a mechanical system that enabled the great clipper ships of the world to transact business safely and more efficiently than before.

At the centre of Canary Wharf stood Rum Quay. The Quay was enclosed by an immense, 25 foot wide glass roof, which is believed to have originally formed a covered walkway into the Crystal Palace when it was first erected in Hyde Park in 1851 to house the Great Exhibition.

Inside the structure were stored enormous puncheons of rum, each holding 103 gallons of spirit. On Rum Quay, curfew bells were mounted on a 45 ft. high iron ship's mast, which traditionally were rung for ten minutes every night and morning, marking the time period when no fires or candles were permitted to be burnt on the ships. This was to protect the highly flammable rum spirit. As late as 1928 the Rum Quay bells were still in use for time-keeping purposes, being rung at midday, and again an hour later.

Parish boundery mark, 1886. Canary Wharf is within the Parish Of All Saint's Poplar.

The parish of Poplar used the gateway in its common seal, as did the West and East India Companies. A replica of the ship forms part of Poplar's mayoral mace.

Trinity House high water mark

Symbol of the East and West India Dock Company

The borough of Poplar has now been absorbed into the district of Tower Hamlets.

A ship canal was cut, connecting Limehouse and Blackwall Reaches to obviate the circuitous route around the Isle of Dogs, however, it proved a failure and was later turned into a timber dock, now known as "South Dock."

Cutty Sark

The original house flags of the ancient trading companies and many shipping lines were once kept in the Poplar Public Library, and are now housed in the National Maritime Museum, Greenwich.

House flag of Devitt & Moore, London

Greenwich 0° Meridian

In 1884, at an international conference in Washington D.C., it was decided that Greenwich be chosen as the demarcator of the prime meridian, and arbiter of world mean time.

0°

"Flowers, a guinea each."

In the 19th century, an inquisitive nursery man noticed in a window on the Isle of Dogs some West India fuchsias growing. The following year, he sold 300 cuttings at 1 guinea each.

The latitude of the West Indies was such, that outward shipping went down to the latitude of the trade winds for crossing the Atlantic, returning on the anti-trades. Thus, West India vessels frequently called at the Canary Islands.

In the 1930's, Canary Wharf was the major receiving point for fruit from the Canary Islands.

THE GREAT EASTERN 1858

In 1858, Isambard Kingdom Brunel launched his iron ship, the "Leviathan," later named the "Great Eastern," close by West Ferry Road, Millwall. With a length of 692 feet, it was twice as long as any ship built to date. In 1865, the "Great Eastern" was used to lay the Atlantic telegraph cable.

The following verse is from a poem published in "Punch" on 10 June, 1858, on the occasion of Queen Victoria's visit to the ship:

"The River's perfume was so vile,
    The Sovereign, as she neared Dogs' Isle,
    Was fain to hold—nay do not smile—
    A bouquet to her nose."

Isambard Kingdom Brunel

The Plimsoll Mark

Samuel Plimsoll M.P. 1824-1898 was known as the "Sailors' Friend," by proposing a bill that all merchant ships over 80 tons register carry this legal loading line.

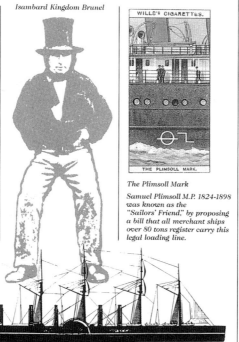

The "Great Eastern"

CANARY WHARF 1995

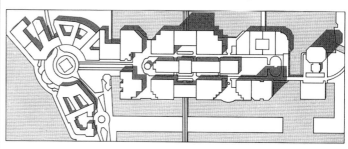

London's reputation as a leading international financial centre has been built over the centuries on the expertise of the City to adapt to change.

Today, change in the financial world is gathering pace as deregulation, coupled with new technology, is creating global capital markets and financial services.

As the home of more than 400 financial institutions and being situated in a critical time zone between Tokyo and New York, London is well placed to take advantage of new developments and to consolidate and expand its worldwide role.

The development proposed for Canary Wharf will revitalise 71 acres of the former West India Docks by providing some ten million square feet of accommodation, designed specifically for the expansion of the financial services sector.

Linked to the City by road, rail and river, it will become an eastward extension of London's existing financial centre.

THE WEST INDIA AND MILLWALL (1802-1980)

The Great Birthplace of Canary Wharf

City Trade and Commerce

The City of London waterfront was for centuries the centre of port activity and the focus of the city from Roman times to the end of the medieval period. By Elizabethan times the City quaysides were alive with activities, enjoying the benefits of Britain's links with many newly discovered parts of the world and its growing maritime power. In 1558 when London monopolised half of the nation's trade, 20 legal quays were established between London Bridge and the Tower of London for the handling of cargoes and collection of custom duties. During the 18th century, trade quadrupled as London became the world's financial centre and busiest port. Supported by financial institutions, commodity exchanges and insurance brokers, the quayside and warehouses were full with commodities brought from overseas. Imports provided the needs of Londoners and the rest of the UK, and were re-exported to Europe and the large number of Colonies of the growing British Empire. The City levied rates on shipping and received valuable duties on wine, oil, coal, grain, salt, fish and fruit. The forests of masts in the Upper Pool extended downstream. However so did the problems of pilfering and river piracy. By the end of the 18th century, chronic overcrowding and expensive delays, together with an alarming level of theft and dishonesty, had combined to threaten the future growth of the trade in the City.

Great Era of Dock Building

The great age of dock building in London started at the beginning of the 19th century when groups of traders obtained Parliamentary permission to promote schemes serving their own needs. In 1799 the West India Merchants in conjunction with the City Corporation of London, obtained the passage of a Bill through Parliament, giving them authority to construct docks on the marshy area of the Isle of Dogs. The Bill, while conceding the "free water clause" for free movements of lighters in the docks, gave the company a monopoly to handle all cargoes to and from the Caribbean for a period of 21 years. This trade was, of course, both important and valuable to the City of London. When the Import Dock was opened in 1802, emphasis on security made it a real fortress, with high walls and a moat and its own dock police. Earlier, the first river police in the world was formed with its headquarters in Wapping in the same place as it is today.

Availability of Land and Transport

The West India Docks were built on the Isle of Dogs, on the site of the present day Canary Wharf development, which was a marshland grazed by cattle belonging to the Abbey of Westminster. The river location was suitable because Blackwall, Greenwich and Limehouse had been used for anchorage of large ships since the beginning of the 17th century. More importantly, the land required for the 30 acre (12ha) Import Dock, the 24 acre (10ha) Export Dock, the two entrance basins and the large number of warehouses and sheds could not be accommodated in a built-up area. Distance from the City and its warehouses and wharves was not a problem partly because of the substantial storage facilities of bonded warehouses on the quays of the West India Docks and partly because of improved road links such as Commercial Road, constructed as a private joint venture between the two dock companies. This act was recently copied by the developers of Canary Wharf in providing rail and tube transport links with the City.

The design engineer for the docks was William Jessop, builder of the Grand Junction Canal; the resident engineer was Ralph Walker, while Rennie acted as consultant. The scale of the works with eight miles of quays was impressive, not only as regards the docks but also the warehouses and walls. It is mentioned that twenty four million bricks were used during one year of building. The Export Dock parallel and immediately south of the Import Dock, was opened in 1806.

Millwall Speculative Venture

Meanwhile the City of London Corporation built a canal across the northern end of the Isle of Dogs, south of the West India Docks, intending to save the ships the problems of navigation around the sweeping bend of the Isle. It was ill conceived as going through the locks of the canal took longer time, and shortly afterwards it became a regular haven for ships awaiting discharge in the Pool of London. In 1829, it was sold to the West India Dock Company which widened it under the name of South West India Dock. Much later in 1870, it was linked with the Import and Export Docks to make an integrated system. The Millwall Docks Company was another speculative venture, started in 1864, at a time when competition was already driving some of the older companies into amalgamation. The 'L' shaped dock went ahead and opened in 1868. In the 1920s the PLA made a cut between the northern end of the Inner Millwall Dock and the South West India, thus making all the docks on the Isle of Dogs into one group. Later the entrance was closed.

Shipping and Final Closure

As can be imagined, with docks that started with a monopoly of the West India trade, sugar was one of the main imports. It remained a leading commodity right through the 1970s, using the original method of handling in hogsheads, replaced first by jute bags and eventually by bulk shipment. Fruit, both dried and fresh was another important cargo, along with hardwood and canned goods. From the start, the Millwall Docks specialised in grain and the area was dominated by McDougall's Mills and the PLA Western Granary, a ten-storey warehouse with a capacity of 24,000 tonnes of grain. Both structures were demolished in the 1980s. Post war, new sheds were built along Canary Wharf and Millwall Docks to handle the Fred Olsen trade with the Canary Islands, for over thirty years many other lines used these docks as their base. These included the Strick/Ellerman joint service to the Persian Gulf, Ben Line to the Far East, Hellenic, Prince Line, the Burma Star, Lamport and Holt, and Nord-Deutscher Lloyd to name only a few. Early in 1980 the PLA decided to concentrate its activities at Tilbury and the docks were closed. In 1981, the newly formed LDDC tried hard to entice industry to move into the area and succeeded in attracting the giant Canary Wharf venture.

The Victorian West Indian Produce's building on the east side of the City, with a shop on the ground floor, office on the first and a Warehouse above. The building still survives with its cranes, little altered.

Top: This 1935 photograph shows dockers loading bananas into a train on the south side of Canary Wharf. About one ship a week arrived at the West India Import Dock, each carrying millions of bananas to keep people in fruit for months!! Middle: A force to be reckoned with - The Port of London had its own police force to patrol the docks. This picture shows a group snapshot of them on duty on the North Quay of the West India Dock during the Dock strike of 1912. The Chinese ship "Pinc Suey" is possibly discharging tea and other cargo onto the quayside. Bottom: Dockside activities at old Canary Wharf in the 1950s. New shipment of fruit is being loaded into lorries for Covent Garden Market and other parts of the country.

THE EAST INDIA COMPANY (1600-1874)

The Company that Ruled the Indian Subcontinent

British Crown's Interests

A stone's throw from Canary Wharf is Blackwall, which was for centuries the terminus of the exotic trade from the East Indies. The very mention of the East India Company is enough to conjure up images of empire of gun-boat diplomacy and everything, in fact, that put the 'Great' in Great Britain. The reputation is quite justified because the company in one of its later guises more or less ruled the Indian subcontinent for over two centuries and brought prosperity to London and Britain.

At the end of the fifteenth century the Portuguese had discovered the direct route from Europe to India. For the next hundred years they enjoyed alone the spices of their discovery and developed trade with the Indian merchants. But towards the end of the sixteenth century, the Dutch began to be interested in this trade. The successful mercantile Dutch, through the Dutch East India Company, had captured ultimately the lucrative spice trade. Eyeing the huge profits flowing into their coffers, a group of British merchants set up their own East India Company with their ships based at Blackwall on the north eastern end of the Isle of Dogs. The business was granted a Royal Charter in 1600, which gave it a trading monopoly among British firms between the Straits of Magellan and the Cape of Good Hope. The main condition was that it furthered the British Crown's interests. The first few years of trading were very promising and such was the demand for the spices in which it dealt that spectacular profits were pouring in.

Favour by Indian Emperor

Such a golden opportunity seemed too good to last and the Dutch company declared war through their fleet. Over the course of 1618/19 the Dutch pushed the British out of the Far East. Desperately the East India Company then turned its attention to the vast Indian sub-continent, where the Portuguese were trading along the coastal areas. Here the British were lucky as the Indian Emperor was weary of the Portuguese way of trading and at the same time British ships had sent the local Portuguese navy packing. The new English modus operandi was to the Emperor's liking and he and the East India Company were co-operating well. Fine Indian fabrics quickly replaced most of the spices as the Company's main import to London and within fifty years it had built up a respectable trade with good dividends.

About the same time, the Company constructed a small wet dock at Blackwall for specially fitting out their vessels after launching from the adjacent shipbuilding yards. The "Blackwallers" were, as the name implies, built at the Blackwall Yard for the Company. This dock was not used for the handling of goods and Pepys visited it on 15th January 1661. The dock was later incorporated as part of Perry's shipbuilding yard, which in turn was absorbed by the East India Docks. East India House, the headquarters of the East India Company, was built in Leadenhall Street in the City of London in the seventeenth century (page 25).

Exotic Imports

During the English Civil War there was a short hiccup, but Cromwell knew that economic and political strength went hand-in-hand, and he merely converted the organisation into a joint stock company. After the Restoration, King Charles II favoured the Company and from 1660 until his death it flourished, its ships bringing to Britain exotic prints, chintzes and silks. When William III came to the throne, the monopoly ended and a second company was set up, though, after a period of intense rivalry, which benefited neither, they were united under the Act of Parliament of 1708.

Virtual Indian Government

The beginning of the 18th century saw the company's position change from a normal business into a sort of virtual Indian government, and it was increasingly in collision with Whitehall in London, which saw its trading posts, growing into large commercial centres. By the middle of century much of India was being governed by a private company, whose board operated from a distant location in London. To curb the company's powers, the British Government introduced first the Regulatory Act of 1773, then more forcefully in 1784 the India Act of William Pitt. In 1813 the company's monopoly ended and India was opened to competition.

The East India Company's ships had anchored since 1600 at Blackwall and their docks were opened there in 1806 exclusively for the company's vessels. The location was that of the shipbuilder John Perry of 1790 at Brunswick Dock. Unlike the West India and London Docks, these docks had no warehouses; the company's valuable imports, such as silk, were carried by road under escort to the City's old warehouses in Cutler Street.

British Nabobs

During the 18th century, the wealthy British officials of the East India Company acquired the title of Nabobs to establish their authority as parallel to the Nawabs, the local Indian rulers and governors. Both the Indians and British chose the title carefully as they are derived from the author's name of Naib, which as described in the Concise Oxford Dictionary, means a Deputy. The practice continued even after the demise of the East India Company in the 1870s until India became independent in 1945.

British Empire including India

In 1834 the Company's charter came up for renewal. This was granted, allowing a 'strange' government in a young empire to continue for another 40 years provided it ceased trading subsequently. At this point, the shareholders' interests were effectively divorced from the rest of the company and were guaranteed a decent rate of interest. The British Government used the company as a front for its activities in India and expanded its acts of imperialism in the reign of Queen Victoria who became the sovereign of the British Empire, including India. In 1857 the Company's troops rebelled; the British Government stepped in and thereafter India was governed from Whitehall. The year 1861 saw the imposing East India House in the City of London demolished and only few of the Company's staff continued until 1874, when its charter expired. On 6th June of that year the Company finally ceased after nearly 300 years of operation. One of the world's most ingenious and particularly British institutions passed into history.

Howland Great Dock

The main reasons why docks were needed and why they were built in East London explain the early history of Canary Wharf and Docklands. The first proper wet dock built in Britain was the 4 hectare Howland Great Dock on the site of present day Greenland Dock in the Surrey Quays. It was completed in 1700 as a safe place for ships to lie up and with dry docks for repair.

Surrey Commercial Docks

In the 1760s, the old Howland Dock changed hands, becoming a base for the large whaling ships then working from London. This new use was marked by a change of name to Greenland Dock. There was no development until 1801, when an engineer named Ralph Dodd promoted the Grand Surrey Canal Company. The Grand Surrey Basin was opened but the canal did not go further than Camberwell. However, it became an important part of the dock system, being lined with timber yards served by lighters

In 1807 the Commercial Dock Company was formed and acquired the Greenland Dock and the smaller Norway Dock adjoining it, with the aim of catering for the growing timber trade. The Baltic Dock Company entered the same trade two years later. The result, as may be imagined, was a series of unrelated developments of docks and shallower ponds, where timber was rafted and stored afloat. These were given attractive names Canada Dock, Quebec Pond, Russia Dock, Acorn Pond, etc. There was no doubt that the Surreys had made the timber trade into Britain their own.

UK's Timber Trade Centre

These efforts continued under the Port of London Authority and achieved some success. They attracted a quarter of the whole UK's timber trade, and also handled a substantial volume of grain and general cargo, having a particularly strong connection with the Canadian trade. During the 1930s not only the Canadian Pacific were seen here, but also the Cunard White Star cabin class liners, the largest ships to sail regularly so far upriver. By 1939 there were undercover storage for about 200,000 tonnes of softwood in 324 sheds, nearly 200 of which were destroyed in the colossal bomb fires of the 1941 London Blitz. Later in the war the South Dock was drained temporarily and used as a building site for sections of the concrete Mulberry Harbours. They were then floated out in the river and transported for the D-Day landings by the Allied Forces (see page 20).

Recent House Building

After World War II, major expenditure was undertaken to improve the system but decline was setting in, resulting in some dock filling and the closure of the Surrey Lock, which gave access from the river for barges and small vessels. When unitisation came in the 1960s, it did not just bring containers but it also plywood stacked on pallets and pre-packed timber in two tonne bundles. The specialised deal porter and docker gave way to the forklift truck of Tilbury. Operations in the docks ceased in 1970 and water started to give way to in-filling rubble, including stones from the old London Bridge when, it was demolished and sold at that time. Under the LDDC house builders moved in and the wild flowers and birds began to move back among the huge estates, in what had been for about 170 years a scene of thriving commercial success.

The Surrey Docks in September 1964 They handled a quarter of the whole UK's timber trade and dealt with substantial volume of grain and general cargoes.

THE MIGHTY ROYALS (1855-1981)

The Largest Impounded Water in the World

Prized Possession

The Port of London Authority considered the Royal Docks as its prized possession, for these were the only docks selected to be visited by the tourist cruises which the Authority ran downriver from Tower Pier during the summer months. These excursions were started in 1934 and resumed after the war in 1948 and continued into the 1960s, where the Royals were still a subject of great wonder to the public. Obviously these magnificent docks had not grown overnight. The Victoria Dock Company, which was granted an Act of Parliament in 1850, had been another speculative venture, in this case promoted by those with no connection with shipping, rather, they would today be seen as 'developers'. They had big ideas; their dock being larger than any of those existing at the time and with an option to extend the system eastwards. The ground being so marshy as to be largely below high river water level, the spoil excavated from the dock did not have to be removed elsewhere but was used to raise the level of the quays and surrounding areas.

The Royal Victoria, Albert and George

The Victoria Dock was opened in 1855 and was an immediate success, outstripping the tonnage handled in the dock groups further upriver. As the promoters were involved with the railways, the dock was the first on the Thames to be connected to the national railway network. In fact the extensive rail coverage of the group remained an outstanding feature, almost to the end of their working life. After only nine years, the dock was sold to the newly amalgamated London and St Katharine Company, which exercised its option to extend eastward as the Albert Dock. Opening the new dock in 1880, the Duke of Connaught announced that Queen Victoria had given permission for it to be called the Royal Albert Dock and that "Royal" is to be added to the Victoria Dock.

A third dock in the Royals, south of the Albert, was planned before World War I, but work was stopped only by the outbreak of hostilities. Just before then, the successful tender surprisingly came from the Germans and it was 25% under the lowest British tender! The scheme went ahead after the war and King George V opened the dock that was to bear his name. It was the first major dock work undertaken by the PLA; thus the 'Mighty Royals' reached their final shape. The dock had the largest entrance lock and was large enough to accommodate the largest vessel in the world the "Mauritania" of 36,000 tonnes gross, when she visited London on her maiden voyage in 1939. Similar vessels used to berth regularly in the Royals, including the Shaw Savill and St Albion's "Dominion Monarch" and the 'A' Class - Amazon, Arlanza and Aragon of Royal Mail Lines. These used to berth at the western end of the Royal Victoria. At the south-east corner of the same dock, was the terminal of the United States Lines. The south side was also dominated by the mills and silos of Spillers, Ranks and the CWS, while the north quay specialised in South American chilled meat. The dock also became the port's principal entry and storage point for tobacco in the 'W' warehouse.

Meat from Australia and New Zealand

Apart from the import of foodstuff and export of manufactured goods, the Royal Albert was well known for handling frozen meat from Australia and New Zealand and for its specialised banana terminal. Here, the Jamaica trade vessel berthed every week. The King George handled enormous quantities of frozen meat, butter, cheese and fruit. The berthing arrangement was different and unusual. The vessels lay not alongside the quayside, but at 500 foot long dolphins which had between them and the quay a 32 foot wide barge way. As the shore cranes were mounted on the dolphin, they could be used to discharge to either quay or lighter. During the 1926 General Strike, the threat was posed of some three-quarter of a million carcasses were at risk of rotting when the electrical power was cut off. Two Royal Navy submarines sailed into the docks to save the Royal's bacon by connecting up their generators to keep the freezers going!

Passenger travel also became big business starting in the 1920s. King George V Dock could berth the largest liners for many decades. Passengers normally travelled from one of London's main railway stations, some staying overnight in the Galleons Hotel on the north side of the Albert Dock. The building is now Grade II listed and renovated.

The City of Ships

In its heyday in the 1950s and 1960s, it was a rare day on which one did not see there the funnels and houseflags of the Port Line, Blue Star, Federal, NZSCo, Shaw Savil (all engaged in the Australian and New Zealand trades), as well as the Royal Mail, the United States Lines, attractive vessels of the Jamaica Banana Producers, British India and Union Castle ships loaded for East and South Africa. Services to India and Far East brought the Ben Line, Blue Funnel, Brocklebanks and the P&O, as well as the vessels of India Steamship Co and the Shipping Corporation of India. The Bank Line, Glen, Shire, Lloyd and Cunard all came to the Royals. Often every berth would be occupied and it was not unusual to see vessels double or treble banked in the docks waiting their turn.

London City Airport

But change came, nevertheless. Shipowners were concerned by what they considered high costs, long journey along the river and by repeated strikes. The banana traffic and the New Zealand trade were moved to Sheerness. Even more important patterns of shipment and distribution changed. The riverside warehouses closed, as firms moved out of London, with the result that much of the transhipment business into lighters disappeared. At the same time road transport was putting the railways into eclipse. And of course the age of containerisation began. More and more such services were moved to Tilbury or other ports. In the event the formal closure of the whole system arrived in 1981. The LDDC was formed by the Government who took over from the PLA and there was talk of constructing a short take-off airport on the ground between Albert and King George V, which was completed in 1987 as the London City Airport.

Dockers operate a conveyor belt distributing tea chests to lighters on the north quay of the Royal Albert Dock, circa 1914.

The pride of the old Royals is the classic aerial shot of the 35,655 tonnes Mauretania when in 1939 in the lock entrance of the King George V Dock. Crowding the pierhead, spectators look like ants compared with the bulk of the vessel.

Dockers unload cartons of tinned milk from America at the Royal Victoria Dock, 1930s.

Aerial view of the Royal Albert and King George Docks full of ships looking east towards Gallion Reach of the Thames, 1960s.

17

LONDON AND ST KATHARINE (1805-1968)

Exotic Stores of the City of London

London Docks At Wapping

During the first thirty years of the 19th century, enterprises by the London merchants and business men to increase the Port's facilities for world trade followed one another in quick succession. The London Docks at Wapping were under construction before the West India Docks were ready to be opened. The London Dock Bill received the Royal Assent on 20 June 1800 and the dock itself opened in 1805. It was named the London Docks to emphasise its proximity to the City. Its future was assured by a 21-year monopoly on all ships coming to London with tobacco, rice, wine and brandy except those from the West and East Indies. The London Docks were unrivalled as the centre of wool trade as well as wines and spirits, the great warehouses above ground being matched by more than 22 acres of vaults. They also took a substantial share of the tea and spice businesses. In 1959, the PLA installed a special bulk wine facility at a berth in the Eastern Dock, with an 800,000-gallon capacity.

Towards the last decades of their life, the docks were mainly concerned with the short-sea trades, being used by Ellerman's Portuguese services, MacAndrew's vessels to Spain and North Africa, General Steam Navigation and Currie's lines with the Mediterranean ports, and so on. This trade also began to change pattern, with the emergence of the cross channel ro-ro vessels. So in 1968, the London Docks received their closure sentence, and in their case, unfortunately, there was no alternative maritime solution.

Now most of the handsome dockside warehouses have gone, the basins filled and only the lift bridge at Shadwell Basin entrance spans a lock, which no longer opens for ships. The whole area is now covered with new houses and blocks of flats. As an echo of past glory, there remains a group of riverside houses, Wapping Pierhead, once the homes of dock officials, marking the site of the old Wapping Entrance.

St Katharine 12th Century Origin

The Georgian dock construction in the Port of London culminated in the opening in 1828 of St Katharine Docks in a restricted location next to the Tower of London. Some 1100 houses and the St Katharine medieval church and hospital were demolished. The development was promoted by greedy City merchants who formed the company to take advantage of the free trade movement which began in 1813 when Parliament did not renew the East India Company's monopoly on trade with the Indian sub-continent. While the docks were being built, the first steam trains were running and the massive warehouses which surrounded the new basins became unsuitable for steamships. Later the warehouses became bonded places for storage of goods from the larger docks further downstream. Although the grandiose of St Katharine Docks were outmoded from the start, today they provide the Capital with the greatest boat haven and tourist attractions in the heart of London.

Last glimpse of London and St Katharine Docks, looking north east, St Katharine was sold in January 1969 by the Port of London Authority to the Greater London Council for £1.5million, which was £0.5 million less than the original cost in 1828!

Famous East Enders in New World

London Docklands has had strong connections with North America. The first colonists to settle in the New World came from the East End of London and began their voyage at Blackwall on the Isle of Dogs. The mother of Thomas Jefferson, one of America's greatest Presidents was born at Shadwell. John Quincy Adams the sixth President was an East Ender and the first Liberty Bell was cast in Whitechapel. The first settlers began their journey from Blackwall Stairs on the River Thames on the 19 December 1606. In total about 105 people sailed in the convoy of Discovery, Godspeed and Susan Constant, which was led by the legendary Captain John Smith. The three ships landed on 26 April 1607, near the site of what is now known as Jamestown in Virginia. A monument commemorating the founding of Virginia has been built on the Meridian line and can be seen from the Docklands Light Railway at East India station. Standing at Brunswick Wharf, the red brick building and looking towards the Thames, one is roughly opposite the first settlers point of departure.

Pilgrim Fathers

More than 200 passenger ships crossed the Atlantic during the 17th century, the most famous being the Mayflower. The journey began in London where some 65 Pilgrim Fathers, mostly East Enders boarded. Among later settlers was William Penn, founder of Pennsylvania. Penn was born on Tower Hill and christened in All Hallows by the Tower in 1644. He became a Quaker in 1667 and obtained land in America in settlement of a debt owed to his father by the King. The land became the State of Pennsylvania and was intended as a refuge for persecuted Quakers.

Thomas Jefferson Shadwell Roots

Voyagers prayed at All Hallows by the Tower Church before setting sail, and there are still models of boats hanging from its ceiling. John Quincy Adams, the sixth American President married there in 1797. Thomas Jefferson's family started life in London and some lived in Shakespeare's Walk, Shadwell early in the 18th century. Thomas Jefferson went on to become one of the greatest Presidents in American History and was largely responsible for drafting the Declaration of Independence. Today, Shadwell USA is partly owned by the Thomas Jefferson Memorial Foundation. St Paul's Church was rebuilt in 1817 with a Baroque tower. It stands just off The Highway in Wapping, a short walk from Shadwell Underground and DLR stations. Walk through a gate in the wall surrounding a graveyard and you are in Shadwell Basin, part of the 1805 London Docks, which were built over Shakespeare's Walk.

Whitechapel Liberty Bell

The Liberty Bell with its inscriptions "proclaimed liberty throughout all the land unto all the inhabitants thereof" is a symbol of independence known to every child in America. Thomas Leicester originally cast the £2000 bell in the Whitechapel Bell Foundry in 1751. Built in 1720, the foundry has a history to 1420 and is still in operation today. There are stories of other great men and a generous benefactor who linked London's East End with America. During the 19th century the City expanded due to growing trade in the Docklands area. Banks, factories, hotels and offices took over the land and displaced residents who migrated to the East End of London. The resulting demand for housing kept rents high, and it was common for whole families to live in a single room and even take in lodgers.

George Peabody's Donations and Trust

Surprisingly the man who made the biggest contribution towards solving this housing crisis was an American. George Peabody knew what it was like to be poor. One of 8 children growing up in Massachusetts, he left school at the age of 11 to go to work and help support his family. He made his money raising capital for large American building projects on both sides of the Atlantic. Arriving in London in 1837 he was shocked by the extent of the poverty in Docklands. Peabody asked friends and colleagues how he could best help the working poor of London. Lord Shaftesbury suggested low rent housing, so Peabody appointed trustees to administer his initial donation of US$750,000 to be used for the benefit of Londoners, who had to be poor, of good moral character and be a good member of society.

UEL Docklands Campus

Of the US$10million that Peabody gave to charity in his lifetime, the biggest single donation of US$2.5million went to house the poor of London. On his death in 1869 Queen Victoria granted him a burial place in Westminster Abbey and vast crowds lined the streets for his funeral procession. After temporary burial in the Abbey his body was returned to Salem, Massachusetts. The first Peabody houses to be built for the accommodation of 40 low income families, with the provision of shops, laundries and baths, still stands at 135-153 Commercial Street, London E1, although they are now privately owned. The Peabody Trust continues to provide affordable housing for 26,000 Londoners and more recently, contributed substantially to the building of the first University of East London, Docklands Campus, which opened in 1999. There is a statue of Peabody in Threadneedle Street, London EC2.

Discovery of Docklands by Americans

In the mid-1980s, the process of discovery was reversed when the Americans and subsequently the Canadian Company, Olympia & York, discovered London Canary Wharf and built one of the greatest 20th century developments in the world. Their dream proposal in 1985(see pages 4 & 5) for a major financial centre of 12 million square feet on Canary Wharf changed most significantly the scale and direction of development in Docklands, determined by the degree of imagination and ambition which was applied to this unique scheme. It provided a window of opportunity used by the London Docklands Development Corporation (LDDC), for promoting an eastward extension of London's existing financial market. London Docklands at the end of the 20th century became an international opportunity for developers from all corners of the world.

London Blitz

On Saturday 7 September 1940, there was a horrific site over London and Docklands. The sky was full of hundreds of German bombers dropping high explosive bombs on the docks and wharves of the Port of London. This was called Black Saturday, the first day of the London Blitz. There was an inferno of smoke and fume as hundreds of incendiary bombs hit the warehouses below, or landed on the closely packed terraced houses that surrounded the docks. The warehouses were packed with food supplies, ammunition and raw materials. Hays Wharf on the South Bank near London Bridge was known as the Larder of London. It contained enough food to feed 8 million Londoners for 12 months. Docklands was also a vital rail centre and there were oil refineries all along the river at Canvey, Thames Haven and Purfleet. In addition there were 8 power stations and the biggest gasworks in the world was at East Ham in the Royal Docks. The German planes used the river as a flight path, following it straight into the heart of London. The first group of 625 German bombers and their 650 strong fighter escort came in over the Kent coast between Deal and Margate, reached the Thames and simply turned towards London. The first targets were the oil refineries at Thames Haven, the Beckton Gasworks and Woolwich Arsenal.

Docklands Fires

At Canary Wharf the sugar warehouses on the North Quay were burned fiercely and the smell of burning sugar, choked fire fighters. At Surrey Docks the biggest fire in London since 1666 erupted as 250 acres of stacked timber went up in smoke and flame. A fire that burned for days. At Winkleys Wharf near Millwall, huge piles of nut kernels caught fire, blazing right next to barrels of paraffin. Cold stores of the Canadian producers at Surrey Docks, packed with butter, cheese and dairy produce also went up in flames. The fire brigade worked heroically to contain the fire. The men wore breathing apparatus against the poisonous fumes given out by the blazing cargoes of sugar, rum, pepper, wood, wax, paint, spirit and rubber. 16 firemen were killed that night, including the driver of a fire brigade lorry blown by a bomb onto the roof of a house in Peckham. As one can imagine the men, women and children in the streets and houses surrounding the docks lived through a nightmare. This continued for 57 days and Docklands suffered enormously because of this War experience.

Mulberry Harbours

Using civil engineering for military purpose stretches back to the beginning of recorded history. Seldom has the profession been so fundamental to the success of a major operation as it was in World War 2 when the Allied Armies crossed to Normandy beaches in France on 6 June 1944, in one of the most decisive battles for victory. Their ability to hold early guns to push forward depended entirely on sufficient army material put ashore fast enough. This depended entirely on artificial harbours, code-named Mulberry, being designed and built in Docklands and other sites in conditions of great secrecy. They were transported across the English Channel, sunk and positioned and then used as a safe harbourage for unloading soldiers, arms and ammunitions. Without the success of the top secret of construction operation carried out by a small group of engineers and many site workers under daily threat from the Luftwaffe bombing planes, the invasion would possibly not have happened at all.

The project involved prefabricating two harbours, the Mulberrys, comprised of 10 miles of floating roadways supported by hundreds of concrete and steel pontoons, and twenty three special pierheads, protected by six miles of reinforced concrete breakwaters known as Phoenix units. These formed temporary shelters, one each for the American and British landings. Each phoenix unit was fitted with anti-aircraft guns and crews. Inside each breakwater, which contained an area the size of Dover Harbour, the floating roadways and pierheads allowed fast unloading of soldiers, machines, heavy weapons and supplies, some 12,000 tonnes of stores and 2,500 vehicles a day.

Construction of Caissons in Docklands

Ten Phoenix caissons were built under the direction of Sir Robert McAlpine the well-known contractor, eight of these in the East India Dock and two downstream in an improvised dry dock at Erith, Kent. The East India Dock basin was dammed and dewatered to permit construction on a bed of bomb damage rubble. Work continued with site visits and pep talks; including one by Sir Winston Churchill.

In probably the biggest battle of its type, a fleet of tugs towed the concrete harbour structures. Given the scale of the project, it was surprising that the Germans apparently never had inkling about what was going on under construction. The labour force contained a large number of men from the Irish Republic, which was neutral during the war. They returned quite frequently to Ireland but not a word was overheard by the German Embassy in Dublin! German aircrafts of course spotted that work was underway and from some of their reports, it was deduced that a Cross Channel bridge was being built. The War Office no doubt encouraged another rumour that they were blocks for new housing!

D-Day Landings

A valuable role was played by London's lightermen in the D-Day landings. Among the 100,000 men who landed in Normandy on 6 June 1944 were hundreds of lightermen from the Port of London. They were there to ferry large numbers of tanks, vehicles and artillery from the landing ships which could not reach to the 15 miles of hostile shore which lay between Ouistreham and Arromanches. Shallow draughted ramped crafts acting as ferries provided the answer.

D'Day's Docklands Solution - "They must float up and down with the tide.. The anchor problem must be mastered. Let me have the best solution worked out. Don't argue the matter. The difficulties will argue for themselves." Sir Winston Churchill, 30 May 1942 Top left - The picture shows Mulberry Harbours under construction in the docks, c 1944. Top and middle right - The structure in place off the coast of France. Bottom right - the "still water" effect of the structures on the beach clearly demonstrated.

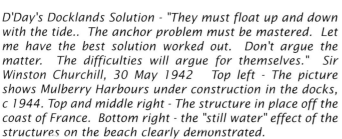

Right:
Sir Winston Churchill on a morale-lifting visit to East London, circa 9 September 1940.

Left:
Firemen fight the blazing warehouses in the Surrey Docks, circa 7 September 1940.

London and Blackwall Railway

Britain's first modern light railway system (DLR) was opened in July 1987 to serve Docklands regeneration sites, 147 years to the month when its predecessor the London and Blackwall commenced passenger operations. The DLR runs virtually on the same alignment using the same embankments and viaducts as the old railway for practically the whole of the western section of the route from Tower Hill to the Isle of Dogs as far as Island Gardens.

The pioneering days of the old railway started from 1825. The idea was that an iron railway be laid along Commercial Road for wagons hauled either by horse or a cable system to get goods to and from the docks faster than using the horse and cart. The major obstacle to this was that Commercial Road was a toll road. Its trustees were naturally concerned about the loss of revenue. With a weak support the Bill laid in dust at Parliament's stage in 1828. However, with the increase in freight and passenger traffic between the City and the East and West India Docks and Brunswick Wharf at Blackwall, the promoters of the railway combined forces for a second attempt.

Action by Toll Trustees

The toll trustees fought back and laid down a stone tramway. This consisted of a double line of smooth granite slabs that formed a friction-reduced track, making it easier for the horses to pull the loaded wagons. The wheels were set to the gauge of the tramway and the vehicles were known as caravans. The trustees charged four shillings (20p) per tonne of cargo for the service and stated that there was no need for a railway. But the railway promoters continued their fight with the trustees.

In March 1836 a Parliamentary Committee investigated the position. Shipping congestion in the Pool of London was a strong factor. Over 25,000 ships arrived in the Pool during 1835 and the Thames was a forest of ships coupled with steamers, lighters and rowing boats causing traffic jams in the river worse than road traffic today. During the same year road transport carried 180,000 tonnes of freight and 1.4 million passengers, while river travellers amounted to 2 million. The busy Brunswick Wharf was the departure point for emigrants, it handled pleasure boat traffic and was a port of call for European services.

Two Railway Schemes

Two railway schemes were proposed, supported by the railway engineers of the day George and Robert Stephenson and the Royal Assent was passed in July 1836 in favour of the Commercial Railway group. Mr William Cubitt was asked to undertake the engineering design and he suggested that 5ft wide gauge for the track to be laid for greater stability for higher speeds. Then another engineer George Parker Bidder (later he promoted the Royal Victoria Dock), a friend of the Stephensons, appeared on the scene. He recommended that to cut out fire hazards and other problems, it would be better to haul the trains by steel cables attached at either end of the railway line to permanent winding engines at the stations. The system was in use in other parts of the country for coal and other freight haulage, but it was not used for passenger service. When George Stephenson explained it to Members of Parliament, he was labelled as "visionary". George Parker Bidder and George Stephenson were appointed as the Company's engineers in January 1838 and Parliament agreed to extend it into Fenchurch Street, despite opposition by the City of London Corporation. The Commercial Railway became the London & Blackwall Railway and was constructed with nine stations. The line was formally opened on 4th July 1840 with a vast Victorian Royal gathering. A banquet was held in the East India Company's warehouse at Brunswick Wharf, especially carpeted for the day.

Extension to Millwall

Each morning a train of seven coaches would be ready at each terminus with a single carriage at each of the intermediate stations. With all of these gripped to the rope - each carriage had its own brakeman - the engines at both termini would start drawing the trains towards them. The coaches at the intermediate stations would travel singly to their respective termini followed by the main trains, quite a complicated operational procedure with drawbacks for travellers between intermediate stations. By 1849 the line was converted to steam locomotive engines and in 1870 the railway was extended to Millwall. Its brick viaduct is perfectly preserved and is used by the Docklands Light Railway (DLR) today.

Top - The single tank locomotive on the extension of Blackwall Railway at Millwall Station, late 19th century.
Bottom - View of Blackwall Station overlooking the Thames during the second half of the 19th century.

The modern DLR train passing over the entrance to Regents Canal at Limehouse today. Limehouse Basin Marina is in the background.

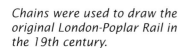

Chains were used to draw the original London-Poplar Rail in the 19th century.

The Blackwall Railway bridge for the extension of the line to Millwall, late 19th century.

Christopher Columbus' New World

The age of discovery by Europeans and adventurers from the Port of London started during the 15th century. While the Portuguese mariners were sailing round Africa to the East, others were planning to reach the same place setting out in the westerly direction across the Atlantic. The great explorer, Christopher Columbus, an Italian born in Genoa, backed by the King and Queen of Spain, sailed in 1492 westward into the unknown sea. His flagship, the Santa Maria and two other ships with a hundred and twenty men could not imagine the perils of the voyage. After many weeks of hardship they reached the islands of the Bahamas, then Cuba and Haiti. On later voyages Columbus explored the Americas, but he still thought it was Asia. He returned to Spain and died without knowing he had discovered the New World of America, 10,000 miles away from Asia!

New Routes to the East

The object of the later seafarers and the merchants who backed them during the 16th century, was to find new routes to the East. At first only those sailing round the continent of Africa succeeded to reaching India and the Far East Islands. In 1519 a fleet of five Spanish ships led by a Portuguese adventurer Ferdinand Magellan and his 250 men sailed south west across the Atlantic. He then passed through a narrow sea, named after him, the Strait of Magellan, dividing the southern point of South America from the Island of Tierra del Fuego (Land of Fire). He came out into the Pacific Ocean, meaning peaceful because it seemed so quiet after the Atlantic. They sailed across the Pacific until they reached the Philippine Islands, north of the East Indies. Unfortunately Magellan was killed in a battle with the natives. His companions continued the westward journey across the Indian Ocean, round the Cape of Good Hope and northward along the west coast of Africa and arrived in Spain in 1522. These pioneers completed the first voyage around the world.

Drake's Expedition

About 60 years after Magellan's expedition, the feat of sailing around the world was repeated by the famous English seaman, Sir Francis Drake, backed by Queen Elizabeth I. Five ships, including his own the Golden Hind, set out for the Atlantic in 1577, followed Magellan's route, crossed the Strait of Magellan and sailed along the west coast of the Americas until he reached California, where he hoisted the English flag at a place which he named New Albion. On this part of the voyage he attacked several Spanish ships and captured their treasures. By this time, four of his ships had been lost, but despite this loss he continued westward in his Golden Hind and made for home along the West African coast reaching Plymouth in 1580. For this great feat he was knighted by Elizabeth I on board his ship at Greenwich.

Adventurers Backed by London Merchants

During this period of discovery, several other English explorers, backed by the City of London merchants, attempted to find routes from England to Asia by way of northern America and northern Europe. In 1553 two navigators, Hugh Willoughby and Richard Chancellor, sailed in different ships in a north eastern direction, hoping to follow the northern shores of Scandinavia and Russia and so reach China. However, the Arctic waters were frozen and Willoughby and his men died. Chancellor abandoned his ship and travelled overland to Moscow where he made a treaty with the Tsar, Ivan the Terrible, giving freedom of trade to English ships. This led the London Merchants to the establishment of the company for trade between the two countries.

Equally bold efforts were made by English explorers to find the North West Passage following the north coast of Canada. Backed by Queen Elizabeth I, Martin Frobisher and John Davis made a number of voyages and left their names on the map of North America as Frobisher Bay and Davis Strait. Each made three expeditions and more or less reached the same bay but could not navigate further due to ice. So both the North West Passage and North East Passage routes had to be given up.

Fleet of East India Company

On 13 February 1601 there was a despatch from Woolwich of the first trading fleet of the East India Company, chartered on the last day of 1600 after a meeting of London traders under the chairmanship of the Lord Mayor to challenge the Dutch and Portuguese monopoly of trade to the Far East. From this Docklands venture sprang in due course the British Empire in India for over three centuries. The Company soon needed to set up a permanent warehouse and to do this they developed friendly relations with the Indian Government. At that time the larger part of northern India was part of the Moghul Empire. In 1663 the Emperor allowed the Company to establish a warehouse at Surat on the west coast. Shortly afterwards other centres were established and forts were built to defend them, around which the modern cities of Calcutta, Bombay and Madras grew.

Hudson Bay Company

Shortly after the death of Elizabeth I in 1603, another navigator, Henry Hudson, explored another part of Canada, named after him, Hudson Bay. Later, in 1670, the London merchants formed the Hudson Bay Company, which developed trade, especially in fur, with many trading posts in the area. The company still exists and has offices in the City of London and in Winnipeg in Canada.

New Age of Discovery by Developers

Docklands played an important international role, from the old Age of Discovery in the 16th century, reaching its peak as the hub of the world's greatest Empire in the late 19th century and later during the 20th century. Sadly, it could not adapt to new trading practices during the 1960s and went into major decline. In 1981 the government formed the London Docklands Development Corporation (LDDC) to regenerate the largest redevelopment project in the world. Over the last few decades the area has been transformed into a showcase for the new Age of Discovery for visitors from all corners of the world and flies the colours of international opportunity for the 21st century.

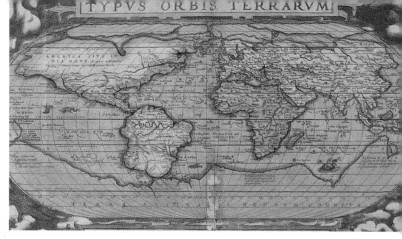

A replica of 15th century wooden sailing ship "Matthew" in which Cabot discovered Newfoundland in 1497 arrived in the Thames in 1996 visiting Canary Wharf on the way.

Typus orbis Terrarum published by Abraham Ortelius of Antwerp in Belgium, circa 1570, and considered to be the first atlas of the world, most probably used by the Dutch and English East India Companies.

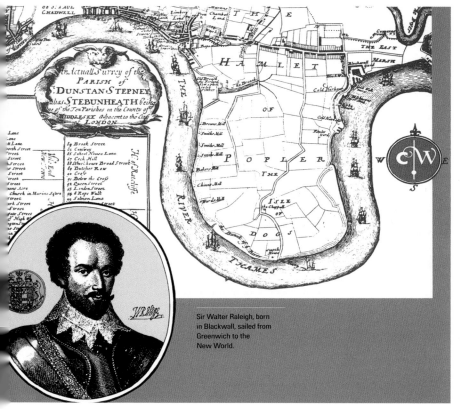

Sir Walter Raleigh, born in Blackwall, sailed from Greenwich to the New World.

Map of the Isle of Dogs, circa 1755, shows the seven windmills at Millwall on the west side, few tracks and grazing fields for fattening cattle and sheep. Blackwall Yard on the north east side was the destination of the East India Company ships. The Thames was the scene of ships passing continuously round the loop of the Island.

Top: A replica of the Golden Hind visiting London, the type of ship used by explorers and merchants for trading around the world during the 16th and 17th centuries.
Bottom: An 18th century engraving of the East India Company House in the City of London, demolished when the Company ceased trading in 1874.

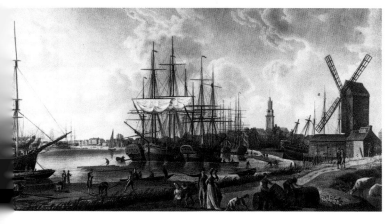

The Isle of Dogs in the 18th century. The view shows shipping at Limehouse Reach, circa 1793, looking north west from the top of the Isle. St Anne's Church can be seen in the background. Timber rafters are busy at work on the river.

A similar view of the Isle at the beginning of the 21st century, showing the three towers of Canary Wharf, developed by the Americans and Canadians after they discovered Docklands in 1985!

Wind of Change of 1966

The emergence of the Greater London Council (GLC) and the new London Boroughs in 1966 initiated the regeneration process of London Docklands on the East side of the City. For nearly 15 years there were a series of planning exercises reviewing the future of the Upper Docks in London against the background of progressive closure of these docks. These regeneration's Committees and Plans were tried culminating finally in the formation of the London Docklands Development Corporation (LDDC) as a Government regeneration agency in 1981.

Redevelopment Plans

In April 1971 the Government announced, with the GLC, to commission jointly an urgent and comprehensive study of the potential of London Docklands, which was so, named and defined for the first time. By the end of 1972, an inter-disciplinary team under the guidance of the consultants, Travis Morgan & Partners was set up. Their study was to report on the possibilities for comprehensive redevelopment of an area of 5,000 acres stretching from London and Surrey Docks in the west to Beckton in the east and prepare the cost of the various possible options.

Consultants' Proposals

The proposals were put in terms of their financial feasibility and social worth by any valuation, which made explicit the value judgements adopted for each problem in the area. The five options were as follows:-

1 New Town which had the highest population with about half the new housing for sale, a major new shopping and office centre was shown on the Isle of Dogs.

2 East End Consolidated emphasised public rented housing with some low priced private housing and industrial jobs.

3 Europa emphasised the private housing and office and service industry employment with commercial centres, all linked by a mini-tram rapid transit system.

4 Thames Park provided over 700 acres of wooded parks with relatively small increase in population and a mixture of office and industrial jobs.

5 Waterside option arranged housing around water parks based on reshaping the existing docks linked to the River Thames.

Docklands Joint Committee

During the year 1973 it became clear that the GLC and the Dockland Boroughs were looking at other ways to examine the options for the future of Docklands. Following extensive discussions with Government, agreement was reached on the setting up of a statutory joint committee for Docklands ensuring that the future was firmly placed in their control. The Dockland Joint Committee was established by the Secretary of State for the Environment in January 1974 under Section 102 of the Local Government Act 1972 with a remit to prepare a strategic plan for the redevelopment of Docklands and to co-ordinate the implementation of that plan. The Committee consisted of elected members of the GLC, the five Dockland Boroughs and co-opted members from the world of business and finance who were proposed by the Secretary of State.

Local Consultation and Strategic Plan

Of the 55,000 living in the borough, some 40,000 were employed there. Both residents and employers were to be fully consulted at every step of the regeneration process. Work on a plan was started in September 1974 and a draft of the plan was produced by publication consultation by the Committee in April 1976 with a request for comments to be submitted by 30 June 1976. The plan was subsequently adopted by the Joint Committee and published as The London Docklands Strategic Plan - July 1976. The overall objective of the proposed strategy was to use the opportunity provided by large areas of London Docklands. These areas would become available for development and this would redress the housing, social, environmental, employment and communication deficiencies of the area and parent boroughs and thereby provide the freedom for similar improvements through East London and Inner London. The plan primarily proposed a number of new major industrial zones, which were to be linked to road, rail and river interchanges providing opportunities for manufacturing sectors with new accommodation to rent and centralise facilities.

Formation of LDDC

Much of the new development was to be attracted through policies of public rent guarantees and subsidies. A number of assumptions had to be made in regard to the timing of release of redevelopment land from the landowners. The strategic plan published in 1976 envisaged public expenditure of around £1.7billion. Unfortunately development in docklands was ineligible for normal forms of Government financial support to transport, housing and other purposes. The Government had no plans for special forms of support over and beyond these. The Government response to provide any finance was not stimulated. Because of financial stringency at the time the Government more or less shelved the plan.

It was apparent with the approach of the Election Year 1979 that the strategic plan had not picked up momentum and that it required reviewing and the structure of the Committee to be changed. This finally led to the formation of the London Docklands Development Corporation (LDDC) in 1981. There was serious local opposition to the establishment of such a quango and a Select Committee of the House of Lords was appointed to consider the complaints. The Committee finally recommended that the principle of a UDA and a UDC (i.e. LDDC) should be accepted for London Docklands.

LONDON DOCKLANDS DEVELOPMENT CORPORATION

The British Development Idea for New Towns

Lord Reith's Inquiry

London's post war decentralisation plans of the 1950s included seven satellite towns for the capital's overspill and decongestion. A Committee of Inquiry chaired by Lord Reith considered a number of different kinds of authority to carry through the new town building programmes and choose a government-sponsored public corporation. The recommendation was for a development corporation selected by Government, which served the national interest with major political direction and long time scale. Such a body would have freedom of action comparable to that of an ordinary commercial undertaking. These recommendations were enshrined in the New Towns Act 1964.

With this in mind, the Conservative Government, which came into power in 1979, set up the London Docklands Development Corporation (LDDC) in July 1981. Its objectives were to use the opportunity provided by large areas of London Docklands becoming available to redress the housing, social, environmental, employment, economic and communication deficiencies of the area and the parent Boroughs; thereby providing the stimulus for similar improvement throughout East London.

LDDC Functions

The LDDC Board consisted of the Chairman, Deputy, Chief Executive, two Local Authorities and twelve other selected members. The Board had several committees, including the executive who prepared matters for the Board and had delegated decision-making powers, the planning of which was responsible for development control open to the public and the audit, which reviewed management procedures and cost effectiveness. The Corporation had a nucleus of central staff and four area teams including external consultants. Initially, the cost was about £60 million a year.

The functions of the LDDC were also clearly defined:

- Land assembly by Vesting and Compulsory Purchase followed by sale of 200 year leases.
- Development control but not the making of Statutory Plans
- Promotional investment in roads, public transport and services infrastructure
- Generating ideas for development and marketing them to the private sector, this being the predominant investor in development
- Implementation of administrative incentives including the benefits of Docklands Enterprise Zone
- Encouraging the Docklands Boroughs to provide rented housing by combined development schemes
- Improving the image of the place and the expectations of its people; education and training; employment generation contributing to community facilities; environmental improvement; highest possible quality of design by private sector
- Promoting interactive positive planning to encourage development.

The irony at the time was the creation of a public body when a number of similar quangos operating in the country were falling all round!

LDDC Formidable Powers

In 1980 Parliament passed the Local Government Planning and Land Act which established the development corporations in London Docklands and Merseyside. They were based on the model of the new town corporations of the 1960s. The LDDC were given three key and formidable powers. The first was the power of land assembly including compulsory purchase powers. Access to special vesting powers enabled it acquire quickly, without a public enquiry, land from other public bodies, such as the former Greater London Council and the Docklands Boroughs. The most important body was the Port of London Authority (PLA) which had closed the Upper Docks, but much land was acquired at Beckton from British Gas. Between its formation on 2nd July 1981 and the end of December in the same year, it used vesting orders to acquire 514 acres, about half the land in public ownership.

Secondly the LDDC was given the development control powers within its area of eight and a half square miles from the three Docklands Boroughs involved, namely Tower Hamlets, Southwark and Newham. Thirdly it had the sole powers to spend money which it received in Government grants to prepare land for regeneration and to bring about improvements in physical, economic and social aspects of the area. Direct Government grants funded the administration and staffing for the Corporation and the provision of environmental improvements and landscaping. Considerable improvements were made to transport and services, such as gas, water, drainage and electricity of the area. They also planted 160,000 trees!

Government money also funded activities expected to produce a direct financial return, particularly the preparation of land for sale. Once the land was sold, the Corporation was initially required to repay the proceeds back to Government, or, if it could not sell the land, borrow the cost from the Public Works Loan fund. In 1983, the rules were changed to enable the LDDC to keep and use the money. However, the LDDC was not given the powers for strategic planning; that was the responsibility of the former GLC and the local boroughs. The Corporation built the new roads in Docklands but the existing highways remained under the local authorities. It had reserve development powers but it did not use it; it never had to design and build.

Transformation and Demise of LDDC

In the mid 1980s, when Canary Wharf giant office proposals were presented, there was some antagonism between the LDDC and City of London Corporation. Suddenly the City saw its commercial power base shifted to East London. During the 1990s, however, the attitude was changed when it was realised generally that the only way forward was through partnership and not through confrontation. Two decades later with the LDDC demised in 1998; it is hard to believe that it is the same place. Canary Wharf with its smart shops and elegant bars and restaurants is there for the thousands of office workers; far removed from the original desolate place Docklands used to be for the LDDC staff. The change in a short span of time is incredible.

Sir Geoffrey Howe announcing at a press conference the establishment of the Enterprise Zone on the Isle of Dogs, Sir Nigel Broakes and the Mayor of Tower Hamlets are standing on the left.

Members of the first LDDC Board, c1982. From left to right: Mr John O'Grady, Mr Dennis Stevenson, Sir Hugh Wilson, Mr Jack Hart, Mr Robert Mellish (Deputy Chairman), Mr Nigel Broakes (Chairman), Mr Reg Ward (Chief Executive), Mr Paul Beasley, Mr Wyndham Thomas, Mr Lewis Moss and Sir John Garlick.

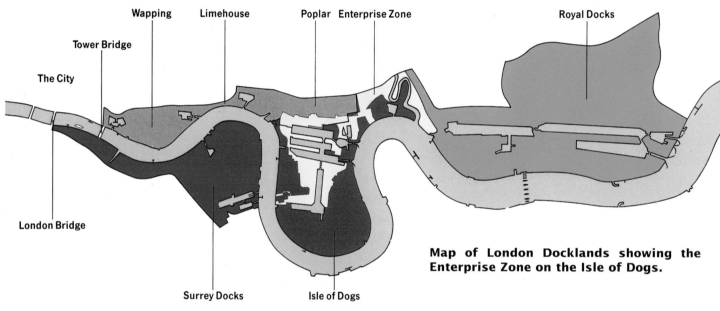

Map of London Docklands showing the Enterprise Zone on the Isle of Dogs.

Mr Michael Heseltine, Secretary of State for the Environment in 1982 at the official opening of the Savage Gardens private housing in Beckton.

Housing in Beckton - at the beginning of 1982 House builders were persuaded to build some low-cost housing for sale in Beckton. The result and success of these schemes developed into a major programme of house building throughout Docklands.

Dockland's new computer-controlled light railway system is the cornerstone of the former LDDC's commitment to increasing and improving public transport in East London.

Substantial expenditure was incurred by the LDDC in creating new waterside walkways in Wapping.

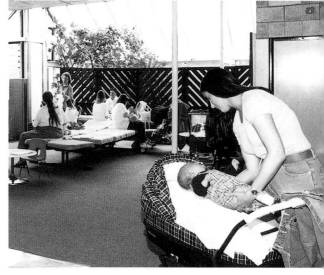

Diana, late Princess of Wales, on her visit to London City Airport in the Royal Docks in March 1992, where she was greeted by hundreds of Newham residents.

The LDDC invested in improving health care by funding the establishment of health centres in the Docklands Boroughs, including the above Kennard Health Centre at North Woolwich.

CURRENT LAND USE

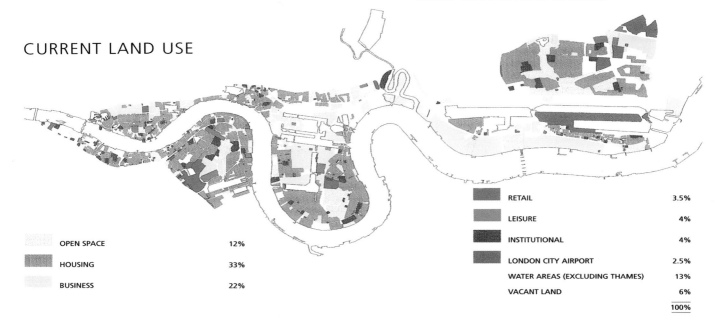

OPEN SPACE	12%
HOUSING	33%
BUSINESS	22%
RETAIL	3.5%
LEISURE	4%
INSTITUTIONAL	4%
LONDON CITY AIRPORT	2.5%
WATER AREAS (EXCLUDING THAMES)	13%
VACANT LAND	6%
	100%

Map of Docklands showing current land use following 17 years of regeneration by the LDDC which was formed by Central Government in 1981.

It all started on the back of an envelope --

Creation of Urban Development Corporation

Mr Michael Heseltine, Conservative MP and ex-deputy Prime Minister, sketched the future of Docklands on the back of an envelope soon after the Tories won the General Election in 1979. The rest, as everybody knows, is recent history. It was his idea, as part of the new policy issues he wanted to implement at the Department of the Environment (DOE). These issues covered inner cities and the creation of new urban development corporations. That was what he wrote on the back of his envelope - along with many other policies that have not only re-shaped the DOE, but also large chunks of the country.

Although the former London Docklands Development Corporation (LDDC) was easily the most successful offspring of Heseltine's scribbling of 1979, he is probably a hero of what has been achieved in Liverpool's regeneration of Albert Dock, which was one of his special projects. Nevertheless it was an air trip over Docklands on the way to look at Maplin as a possible airport site in the early 1970s as a Minister for Aerospace that sparked his interest in bringing back to life the inner cities. The flight took him across the East End of London by light aircraft and he could see the appalling dereliction that existed following the closure of the Upper Docks in London. Before he left the DOE in 1972, he had been working on schemes to try and bring what is effectively a kind of new town Corporation into the redevelopment of urban areas.

Legislation leading to LDDC

It was not until he came back to the DOE as Secretary of State for the Environment in 1979 that he had the chance to bring that new concept to apply to the East End through the formation of the LDDC. It took 18 months to prepare the legislation and to take it through Parliamentary procedure. Mr Heseltine also managed to appoint Mr Nigel Broakes (now Sir) and Mr Bob Mellish as Chairman and deputy Chairman of the LDDC. He was determined to bring opportunity and a new sense of hope to the East End and he believed strongly that was the way to do it.

In 1987 Mr Heseltine became again the Minister for the Department of the Environment (DOE) and visited Docklands and commented that the success of the LDDC was beyond the wildest dreams of those who were responsible for setting it up - the biggest building site in the world once Canary Wharf's construction started. He did not envisage a particular lifespan for the LDDC; instead to see it relinquish its control when its work was done and saw the Corporation as a "roving vehicle".

Local Pressure Groups

Over a number of years the local pressure group, the Docklands Forum, fought hard on behalf of the local community and their needs and criticised the LDDC's housing policies for not helping the local people. Mr Heseltine did not share their views. He stated that the Local Authority accounted for over 90% (pre LDDC) of housing in the area. It seemed to him that what was needed was a balance to correct the unbalanced situation created by the Opposition Party. He believed that the local Dockland Boroughs had a blinkered political approach by not experimenting with the new ways of helping their local communities with private sector investment and house building.

Setting Up the LDDC

It took some time to set up the LDDC Board and Committee Structure. To coincide with the Parliamentary approval of the orders setting up the LDDC, the Government first announced four names for the Board, all on three year part-time appointments, in July 1981, including Sir Hugh Wilson, the former Chairman of the Docklands Joint Committee. A phased build-up took place in respect of staff, including eleven who had been employed by the Docklands Development Organisation and a number of secondments from the Department of the Environment. Initially, the LDDC drew on the skills of consultants specialising, for example in economic research, business finance, law, property, engineering, architecture, housing, transport and public relations.

Man of Ideas

Mr Heseltine had a lot to offer to his country and he could not stop his unbridled enthusiasm for new ideas and subsequent action. He steamed into his work like an unstoppable train. He could not stop coming up with ideas. But quite a few of his pet theories were ideologically antagonistic to both the Tory and Labour groups. In his book "Where There's a Will" published in the late 1980s, he suggested the creation of many more interventionist arms of the DOE, and "English Development Agency", along the lines of those already existed in Scotland and Wales. He also would have liked to see the Department of Trade and Industry elevated from its status as the poor cousin of the Treasury. He believed that it was time for the Government to thrust aside the nation that Government and Industry can live at arms length. It was Industry's job to make itself competitive.

With his entrepreneurial skills as publisher and property developer Mr Heseltine is a highly intelligent visionary. In 1987 he predicted that in a decade from that time, Docklands would be a showcase. He was proved to be perfectly right.

LONDON'S ENTERPRISE ZONE

Investment Life, Exemptions and Planning

Reason for Creation

Enterprise Zones were set up by Government in a number of British cities as an urban experiment designed to attract new investment and property to run-down areas. In the case of London's zone on the Isle of Dogs, it was the closure of the docks which created the space and the need for new activity and regeneration. This zone was centrally placed within Docklands and came within the area controlled by the London Docklands Development Corporation. The Corporation, with its headquarters located in the middle of the zone, and with its extensive planning, development and acquisition powers, was in a unique position to assist investors wishing to develop in the zone.

Opportunities on Land and Water

There were 482 acres in the Enterprise Zone including 120 acres of water, which were mostly owned by the LDDC. The area had been fallow and the intention was to encourage new life and prosperity as fast as possible with the creation of various sorts of activities. In broad terms, the Corporation expected waterfront developments along the former docks, with office blocks, studios, shops, pubs and restaurants on the quayside. Elsewhere there was the opportunity for the introduction of modern factories, warehousing and sports facilities.

While the Corporation marketed specific sites to prepared briefs, it certainly welcomed approaches from developers with their own ideas but financially viable proposals. In all cases the following points were looked for:

a) The quantity and quality of the proposals in terms of job opportunities.
b) The quality of architectural design and planning including the choice of building materials and landscaping.
c) The financial bid for the site.

Sites were generally disposed of on a ground lease basis for 200 years for a capital premium for a peppercorn rent and no rent reviews. Initially, 16 sites were identified and prospective developers were invited to submit proposals, including the 15 acres of Canary Wharf lying between the West India Import and Export Docks.

Exemption from Rates

The central Government took over the burden of industrial and commercial rates within the zone for 10 years from its formal designation on 26 April 1982. This meant that individuals and firms operating factories, workshops, offices, shops, warehousing and hotels were only responsible for water rates. Properties were assessed by valuation officers of the Inland Revenue in the normal way and then Whitehall paid over to the London Boroughs of Tower Hamlets and Newham from central tax funds the money which was otherwise due. The exemption from payment of rates was automatic and no special application was required from tenants or owners. Domestic rates on housing however, had to be paid by the owner or occupier. If a property was mixed, for example partly housing partly shop, then the bill was split. The Government only picked up the share due from the commercial or industrial element of the building.

Capital Allowances

Within the zone, developers took advantage of special larger and speedier tax allowances to help offset the initial capital costs of new buildings, extensions and conversions to be used for industrial and commercial purposes. The same principle applied to factories, etc. Basically the owner qualified for an initial allowance of up to 100% of capital expenditure, which companies and individuals could then use to offset against corporation of income tax. This exact percentage taken in this initial allowance remained the choice of the tax payer. If the building came into operation in the same year as the money had been spent, then the owner received both the initial allowance at the chosen rate and the first 25% of writing-down allowance. Owners were eligible for the allowances on capital expenditure regardless whether or not they occupied the buildings themselves or let them to other people or firms. The allowances applied not only to spending during the ten year period from 1982 but also to outgoings incurred afterwards if they related to contracts signed before the period came to an end in 1992. If a building is sold within 25 years of first coming into use, a balancing charge is made, as is usual practice under the industrial building allowance rules, on which the Enterprise Zone scheme had been modelled. In other words, the investor may find that the money or allowances have to be returned.

Exemption from Development Land Tax

No development land tax was paid on projects started within 10 years of the formal designation of the Enterprise Zone. Normally the owner of a site paid the tax at a rate of 60% on the increase value which resulted from it being put to a more valuable use than formerly. Developers within the Enterprise Zone could for 10 years forget their worries about charging points and arguments about actual valuations since the development tax quite simply did not apply.

Faster Planning

One reason for the creation of enterprise zones in Britain was the belief that planning restrictions and delays caused by prolonged procedures might be damaging to the British economy. In enterprise zones, therefore, the process was greatly streamlined. While this did not mean a free for all, it did mean a new emphasis on getting schemes onto the ground as quickly as possibly rather than allowing projects to get bogged down in a mass of detail and seemingly endless discussions.

In the Enterprise Zone on the Isle of Dogs, many projects could go ahead without planning permission and although others still had to be considered and approved, the LDDC tried to give some indication of its views within a period of 14 days.

This composite picture highlights the LDDC's progress in transforming Docklands into a vibrant and dynamic part of London, as the curtain descended on the Corporation in 1998.

Contributions to:
5 New Health Centres
6 Centres Redeveloped

25.1 million sq.ft of Commercial/Industrial Floorspace Built

2,106 acres of Derelict Land Reclaimed in London Docklands

24,042 New Homes Built

85,000 People now Work in London Docklands

2,600 Businesses Trading

145 km of New and Improved Roads and DLR Constructed

£7.2 billion Private Sector Investment

2.1 million Visitors

£1,859 million Public Sector Investment

1,061 acres of Land Sold for Redevelopment

94 Awards for Architecture, Conservat and Landscaping

Funding For:
11 New Primary Schools
2 Secondary Schools
3 Post-16 Colleges
9 Vocational Training Centres

83,000 People now Live in London Docklands

The end of the beginning: The regeneration agency London Docklands Development Corporation closes on 31st March 1998. Since 1981 the Corporation, together with its private sector partners, has laid the foundations for a successful future. Once again this part of East London has thriving business and residential communities - and is a magnet for visitors.
There's A Great Future Ahead

The Best End of London
London Docklands

THE ENTERPRISE BUSINESS SECTOR

Tax Haven Near Bank of England

Package of Inducements

By the middle of the 1980s decade, it was clear that the seeds of an exciting new city of Docklands was growing and, at its heart, was the London Enterprise Zone on the Isle of Dogs. Occupying 215 acres within a total Docklands area of 5000 acres, the enterprise zone was the most significant business sector of the whole Docklands regeneration. With the announcement of Canary Wharf project, a staggering 20 million square feet of commercial, high-tech and leisure complexes were being developed here, making it the world's largest commercial development.

An enterprise zone was, by Government decree and blessing, a very special prized location indeed. In order to attract the scale of private investment needed to persuade companies of all sizes into Docklands, a package of inducements was made available, including a rate-free facility until 1992, a simplified customs facilities and very relaxed planning procedures through the London Docklands Development Corporation. But even beyond these perks, one allowance outshined all the others: 100% investment allowances were granted by the Inland Revenue on the cost of a property purchased to offset against corporation tax or income tax. This provided a perfect tax shelter for both individuals and companies seeking to reduce their tax liabilities.

Allowances for Private Investors

To qualify for the enterprise zone allowances, buildings had to be designed for use as offices or for the purpose of any trade, profession or vocation. Residential properties were excluded although if the cost of the residential part was less than 25% of the whole building, all the expenditure qualified.

If the allowance were passed on before the building was occupied, the purchase would be entitled to the capital allowance of 100%. The total effect on the purchase price was obviously very significant. If a company was purchasing either for its own occupation or investment the initial allowance could be fully offset against corporation tax in the year of assessment and unused allowances could even be carried back to the previous year or forward if appropriate.

For the private investor on non-corporate owner-occupier in the higher tax brackets, the advantages were even more drastic. A top scale 60% taxpayer at the time could shelter against the property bringing the true cost to just 40% of the purchase price. Nor did the purchaser need to claim all the allowances at once. A purchaser could take what he needed in the first year and the allowances in the second and subsequent years was 25% of the original purchase price relative to his tax rate until the whole of the 100% allowance was taken up. In addition to capital allowances, the investor enjoyed retail income and growth from the property. This was substantial as in less than two years office rents doubled in Docklands and property values escalated.

Legal Scheme

The legal scheme set out the broad planning policy and the manner in which it hoped to deal with planning applications. Basically, the requirements were to ensure that land is not developed badly, dangerously or wastefully. In addition, adequate space for access and parking had to be provided, so that individual schemes would not put off investment by other people; that pollution was kept to a minimum and that projects were compatible. Apart from specific exclusions which were likely to cause a nuisance of some danger, the guidelines specified that height of buildings and structures should be not more than 120 feet and the size of food shops not to be more than 500 square metres. The height restriction appears to have been waived for Canary Wharf!

The LDDC set up a small unit to co-ordinate, process and determine all development within the Enterprise Zone for final approval by the LDDC Board. The zone benefits expired in 1992.

Early Days of LDDC

When it was formed in 1981, the LDDC had a small group of staff, some in temporary positions, in the middle of the Enterprise Zone. They had to be flexible in those early days. No two days were alike and Docklands was not in any way a glamourous place as it is today. The area was derelict with run-down sheds. The enclosed docks were suddenly upgraded with considerable publicity and opened to the public who could gain access to the water edge. There had been plans to re-develop the docklands since the early 1970s. However nothing appreciable happened until the Conservative Government was elected in 1979 and Mr Michael Heseltine, the Minister for the Environment, transferred land from the Port of London Authority (PLA) to the LDDC and introduced legislations. Suddenly there were funds and the legal powers to regenerate this historic area of East London.

Getting to work in the early days, according to the staff, was not an easy matter. There was a mini-bus service from Mile End underground station to the office, in the middle of nowhere, which was located in the old Fred Olsen shipping shed on the east side of Millwall Inner Dock. However, the bus ran for only two hours in the morning and if staff missed it, they were authorised to hire a minicab. Also, because of the level of development and construction of new infrastructure, the offices quite frequently had no water or electricity. But the administrative staff were all young and there was a real pioneering spirit about the place. Staff were also expected to attract people and investors to visit Docklands. To do this they had to arrange a whole series of events. These included helicopter trips, boat races and in 1986 they held the Formula One Power Boat races.

Despite the optimism and activity of the LDDC staff, there was inevitable friction between the local residents and the newcomers. On one occasion people protesting against the LDDC's proposal to remove the Surrey Docks Farm led a horse to the LDDC building and threatened to slaughter the animal on the steps unless the proposal was cancelled. Happily, the residents won on this occasion.

LDDC DEVELOPMENT PLANNING AND POLICIES

Market Led by Private Enterprise

Attracting Private Investors for Development

The Government's instructions to the LDDC were to attract and retain private investors. There was a belief that the "market" would provide the solution to the problems, which had eluded the public sector. There was, however, no 'market' in Dockland as the private sector had shunned investment in the area. This meant that the LDDC's first task was to change the image of the area and create an environment to encourage and welcome new developments.

Docklands is not a small easily identified area but it is large and complex. The development contents and policies vary substantially across the 22 sq. km urban zone. The fine historic districts of Bermondsey, Wapping and Limehouse contrast dramatically with the vast stretches of industrial land and water of the Royal Docks. The concept of various city districts was therefore used to divide Docklands into four areas of Wapping & Limehouse, Isle of Dogs, Bermondsey and Surrey Docks and the Royal Docks. Four area groups were set up which recognised the concerns and interests of each particular locality. It was felt that the regeneration of such a large urban area would take a number of decades during which many changes - political, social and economic - would occur.

Unique Environment and Conservation

The development and planning process was also seen as flexible accepting and welcoming changes as a positive contribution to viable development. In this respect the LDDC was the luckiest of all UDCs in attracting the biggest and most prestigious development of Canary Wharf to change the course of Docklands history and to establish Great Britain as a powerful financial centre in the world. The LDDC was also lucky in recruiting architects and planners who were interested in conservation of Docklands heritage. One of their first actions was to formally invite the Department of the Environment to inspect the historic buildings of Docklands. This was completed in 1982 and 116 buildings were added to the statutory list of Buildings of Architectural and Historic interest. Eight new conservations were designated in addition to the five already existing.

The docks and the River Thames are most powerful features of the environment with unique visual and recreational amenities. These features distinguish Docklands from any other part of London and are therefore most important assets to be saved and promoted. A policy was established that no in-filling of the docks would take place and the water areas would be retained as an integral part of Docklands regeneration. The in-fill of some docks did take place by local authorities in Wapping and the Surrey Docks to create more land for housing. Riverside access along the north and south banks were also established to form part of the national Thames path.

Priority for Housing

With the encouragement of Government, early in the 1980s, house builders commenced building residential estates for sale in Docklands, starting with the huge area of Beckton and the houses proved instant success. The These builders in fact maintained initial momentum of regeneration and some priority for housing was given to local residents. Between 1981 and 1998 when the LDDC was demised 24,000 homes were built, the biggest house development event in London and the whole of the UK. There was a commitment to improving the environment and public open spaces including a comprehensive network of cycle tracks and walkways providing a 24km (15 miles) of waterside access. More than 150,000 trees were planted as part of a programme of landscaping works. Two urban farms on the Isle of Dogs and in the Surrey Docks were supported with annual grants.

In the regeneration of Docklands, the historic imbalance between east and west London has been reversed. A huge investment by the public sector has generated an even larger investment of private capital. The substantial number of new homes has relieved the pressure for residential development in London's Green Belt and has encouraged house builders into the inner city. Furthermore, the success of Docklands has provided the springboard for the regeneration of Thames Gateway, which will maximise the region's opportunities for benefiting from its proximity to Continental Europe.

Planning Consultation

With the exception of the Enterprise Zone on the Isle of Dogs, which affected about 11% of Docklands area between 1982 and 1992, the Town & Country Planning Acts applied to the development which took place as they did to the rest of the country. The Corporation agreed a code of consultation with the three Dockland Boroughs, originally allowing two weeks to comment on Planning Applications which was totally inadequate. In 1989 this was increased to three weeks for Tower Hamlets and extended to Southwark and Newham in 1991 when most of the sites in Docklands were at an advanced stage in developments. In addition public notices in Docklands News, which was run by the LDDC, were used to publicise planning applications and meetings with local residents.

It is not clear how much public opinion was taken into account and what changes were made to the submitted schemes. Much criticism has been made about the extent of regeneration in Docklands and the level of consultation with the local residents. It is impossible to compare the benefit to the local people with the benefits which have resulted through the LDDC, and whether if carried out differently the result would have been better. There has been a considerable improvement in the physical and social infrastructure of Docklands which now matches anywhere in the London area. The LDDC had its own local areas for consultation with local residents. How much the LDDC was prepared to accept local criticism and amend their plans is very difficult to establish.

London City Airport in the Royal Docks is now the country's fastest growing airport.

Canary Wharf has been the single most influential development in the regeneration of London Docklands and has acted as the barometer of the area's economy.

Horse riding at Newham City Farm with limited disabled access.

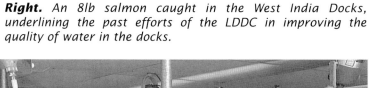

Right. An 8lb salmon caught in the West India Docks, underlining the past efforts of the LDDC in improving the quality of water in the docks.

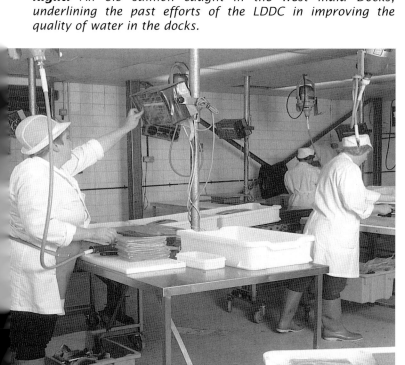

Smoked Salmon Curer on the Isle of Dogs. By providing grants, the LDDC encouraged new businesses in various parts of Docklands.

New storm water pumping station on the Isle of Dogs was built by the LDDC to improve drainage.

LDDC LAND POLICY AND FINANCE

Reclaim Land and Exercise Control Over Development

Land Policy and Reclamation

The LDDC placed a high priority on land acquisition partly to enable it to reclaim land and put in infrastructure, and partly to exercise control over the development that took place in Docklands. Their successful policy on land was to acquire as much as resources permit of the development land in Docklands where sites are not the subject of suitable active redevelopment plans by their respective owners. The reasons for this policy were to ensure development momentum and to enable the Corporation to obtain the benefit of increasing land values. Moreover, they wanted to own land so that they can reclaim it and provide essential services. In essence, land ownership was a pre-condition to attract private investment in Docklands.

By early 1985, the LDDC owned over a thousand acres of land after disposals largely in London Docks, Surrey Docks, Isle of Dogs, Royal Docks and Beckton. About two-thirds of this land was transferred to the Corporation by means of Vesting Orders in 1981. Later they acquired the huge area of the Royal Albert and King George V Docks under compulsory purchase. The LDDC aimed at comprehensive clearance, thus requiring existing users to relocate on compensation. Huge sums of money were set aside for such purposes.

Increased Land Values

Over the first four years of its existence land values increased sharply largely as a result of land reclamation, the proposals for major construction of road and rail links and the demand for high-priced housing, warehouse conversions and commercial development in the Enterprise Zone. The rise was 6 to 7 times over the period, from £160,000 per hectare to £1 million in 1985.

The LDDC regarded this as a mark of their success and described the changes as perhaps the most accurate barometer of physical and economic regeneration. An additional reason for seeking high land values was to please the Treasury Department, since increasing values reduced the public expenditure costs of the LDDC, or to put it another way improved the rate of return on public investment. The local boroughs were unhappy about this because they regarded the benefits of increase had been recycled back into the LDDC development process and to developers, rather than being used to benefit the local community.

Substantial Budget and Expenditure

The Corporation had a substantial budget each year but was not accountable to Docklands people and boroughs for the way the money was spent. Its function was defined clearly by central government to bring the barren areas back into more valuable use. The grants came from the Department of Environment and it was left to the Corporation how to spend it. The first ten years of its operation, the spending patterns were uniform with certain priorities.

The Corporation's Annual Report for 1984/85 showed an expenditure of £206 million in the four years since its creation. The biggest single category of expenditure was land acquisition of 26 per cent of the total, followed by transport of 40 per cent including expenditure on the Docklands Light Railway, which was under construction. Administration costs were approximately 10 per cent. The breakdown of expenditure reflected the LDDC's role which was limited to preparation and marketing of land for development and to helping to create the physical, social and economic environment to encourage investment in housing, industry and commerce, as specified by central government.

Land was bought, reclaimed, serviced for infrastructure and in some cases landscaped at public expenditure. This resulted in an increase in land values, which later went as a parcel package for investors. The justification for this was, without it, there would have been little incentive for private development. The relatively high cost of land preparation may not have produced sufficient or no profit for the private investors, which in many instances later was transferred to the occupiers.

Market Led Policy

The policy was market-led and was not orientated for the local people who were primarily of ex-Dockers families. The Corporation initially targeted specific prestige areas and created a glossy image. The opportunities were publicised and the land and new infrastructure were sold at subsidised rates. The Corporation appointed their own auditors. The performance indicator was by means of the amount of private investment in Docklands compared to the net public expenditure, i.e. by the 'leverage ratio'. In the Isle of Dogs business sector, this ratio was as high as 1:7 and similarly for housing in Beckton.

Docklands Light Railway: Bank to Canary Wharf: 12 Minutes

Taxi: Trafalgar Square to central Docklands: 25 minutes

"The Docker knows the future is only minutes away". Advertisement by LDDC, c 1995. Time travel is no longer science fiction. Dockland's hi-tech offices of tomorrow can now be reached in a matter of minutes!

Does your present office overlook bricks and mortar? Or water?

Does it have a lunch queue? Or a lunch view?

"Life is more beautiful in Docklands" - part of the LDDC's advertising campaign in the 1990s to attract more companies to move their offices to Docklands. The budget was over £1 million a year.

New business unit at Indescon Court, one of the first low rise buildings completed in the Isle of Dogs Enterprise Zone. The development housed Skillnet Training Centre for local people.

ASDA opened two superstores in Docklands - one on the Isle of Dogs in 1983 and the other in Beckton in 1986.

The new Connaught Crossing swing bridge in the Royal Docks is a Dutch design built by the LDDC.

The Millwall Sports Centre on the Isle of Dogs is one of a number in Docklands funded by the LDDC.

Docklands boasts the finest water sports centre in the South East. Many people, young and old, learn sailing.

Docklands Dream Comes True

The period 1985-86 could be acknowledged as one of the most significant years in the life of the LDDC. It could be considered as a landmark of change, not only with the news of the giant Canary Wharf development proposals, but also by the extent of demonstrable physical change. Where previously there were plans, or discussions or artists impressions, there were buildings taking shape, many of them were unfinished but already committed. The Docklands Dream was beginning to come true. It was also clear that the proposed Canary Wharf project would carry Docklands into the next important phase of regeneration.

In the Surrey Docks and Wapping for example, there was an impressive track record. The rapid transformation of these Docklands meant that it was no longer necessary for the LDDC to present ideas to developers in the district. They invited business people to come and look at what had been achieved and to see how they could go about their own schemes and what sort of finance they required. Docklands was chosen as the site for London Earth Satellite teleport because it was discovered to have the least interference area in the capital.

Freedom of Choice and Evolution

Developers also discovered a refreshing freedom of interference in the area, once principles had been established. The completion of basic transport infrastructure was seen as developing rapidly. Both of these factors created an important stimulus to progress. There was evolution in the way business people and the City perceived Docklands. As recently as 1984, there were those in the "Square Mile" who regarded Docklands and the endeavours of the LDDC as a brave but over-adventurous project. Certainly nobody realised how soon the tempo of commitment and enterprise would quicken with the arrival of Canary Wharf on the scene.

Eyebrows raised previously in scepticism were now raised in impressed surprise. The number of firms and financial institutions who had switched from saying "maybe" to a firm "interested" was extraordinary. It all became part of the growing momentum and the desire to be part of the success of Docklands for the future.of London in the 21st century.

Rising Employment

With unemployment still unacceptably high in East London, many of the local people had hoped for improvement to be realised. Yet during 1985 for the first time the number of people employed in Docklands was rising. Until that time people were leaving Docklands or travelling out to find work but the tide had turned. More were staying and more were coming to live in Docklands. The psychological barriers of East London were beginning to be demolished and there was a feeling of enterprise about the Docklands place.

Measures of Success

The economic performance and impact of the Corporation was analysed by leading management consultants, Peat Marwick during 1985/86.

In the three prime areas - jobs, private sector investment and land values - the Corporation had successfully stimulated a stronger employment base: a 6.4 to 1 ratio of private to Corporation funding; and a fivefold increase in land values.

The Peat Marwick analysis also included the Employment Survey of 1985, which showed a marked switch from manufacturing to service sector jobs and a reversal to the 27% decline in Docklands employment between 1978 and 1981. At least 8,000 new jobs have been generated during the first four years of the life of the Corporation, a figure that represented nearly one in three of all Docklands current employment. New firms had provided more jobs than those lost by industrial closures. 70% of all jobs in the area were in the service sector, with more than 2,000 new jobs in financial and business services alone. The research analysis showed clearly that more people have jobs in Docklands than in 1981, the last year of docks-related losses. Most of the new jobs - 61% - were in Tower Hamlets, which included the Isle of Dogs Enterprise Zone. The borough's share of the total Docklands employment rose from 33% in 1981 to nearly 50% in 1985.

Land values within Docklands had risen rapidly since the formation of the Corporation - especially during 1985-86. Across the range of land usages values had increased approximately fivefold since 1981, with many sites showing considerably greater increases. The cumulative net economic benefit attributable to the Corporation was £304.5m spread over the whole area, with the Enterprise Zone accounting for £62m.

For every £1 invested by the Corporation the private sector had invested an average of £6.40 in all land in the Docklands area. In total, private sector investment had exceeded £1.1 billion. This success in attracting private sector investment had been critical in the regeneration of the Docklands economy. On average the leverage ratio on Corporation-owned land was slightly lower, at 5.3 to 1 up to 1985086. In the Isle of Dogs there had been the greatest impact of all, every LDDC £1 produced £9.70 from private investors.

Environmental Services for Docklands

Isolated from other parts of London for over 180 years, Docklands in 1981 required the provision of extensive public services on a massive scale. These included the expansion of vital utilities such as gas, water and electricity, provision of new drainage both surface and foul, as well as the construction of new roads, rail and other transport networks. Much of the engineering works had to be made in advance of known development requirements of private sector responses to investment in the area. Such circumstances posed many challenges particularly in the early years of the regeneration game.

Apart from above provisions, the restoration and maintenance of existing structures above ground and below water level had to be assessed particularly the conditions of marine structures such as dock and river walls, bridges, lock gates and relevant infrastructure. All of these structures had to be surveyed by consultants and then decisions were made on what to renovate, repair or replace when the regeneration had just started and during the transformation of the whole area.

Windsor Park Contaminated Land

One of the first cases of dealing with contaminated land in Docklands was at the site of the former Beckton Gas Works. Treatment of the material was largely impractical because of the variability of material present and timescales requires for the completion of the process. It was concluded that the only viable approach for the reclamation of the area was by containment system. This has the advantage that no material needed to be removed from the site and the system was instantly available once the engineering works were completed. The capping works consisted of constructing clean imported sub-soil material 1.2metre depth directly above the contaminated material which is graded to pre-formed shape. This layer is vented to ground level. Gas stand pipes were installed at different heights to monitor methane produced by breakdown of organic material in the natural alluvial soils below the site. The foundations of new houses were built on piles penetrating below the perimeter collecting rain which allowed for ground water discharge. Shallow rooted trees were planted in the top soil for a depth of 300mm.

Giant Drainage Scheme for the Royals

By the middle of September 1986, two different tunnel boring machines were in operation as part of the first major tunnelling contract on the huge drainage scheme for the Royal Docks at the far eastern limits of Docklands. The £30million project included construction of two foul and surface water sewers each one over 17km with diameters of up to 2.1m, plus two pumping stations up to 28m deep. Like most docklands infrastructure works, speed was paramount. London Docklands Development Corporation, which was paying for most of the scheme, wanted the new system in place as soon as possible, to permit redevelopment of the area. The actual design started in 1984 and the LDDC expected the network to be completed by 1989.

The sewers discharge into a new surface water pumping station, at the north western corner of the ` Royal Victoria Dock. This new 28 m deep tidal basin pumping station brings the effluent up to a high level, twin rising mains between 6m and 3m below ground level. The mains run into a new outfall which empties into the Thames. Foul water sewers followed the same line as surface water to a new pumping station in the south east of the Royal Docks area at North Woolwich.

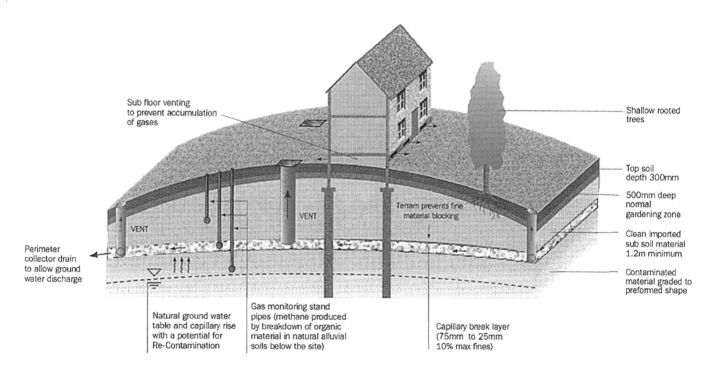

Schematic diagram of dealing with contaminated land at Windsor Park social housing at the site of the former Beckton Gas Works, north of the Royal Docks.

THE FUTURE OF ROYAL DOCKS

The Largest Urban Regeneration in Europe

Slow Regeneration

There are reasons why the Royal Docks have taken longer to regenerate. The dock estate is vast and there was no enterprise zone. The area is Europe's largest redevelopment site, comprising about a quarter of the whole of Docklands. With the housing development in Beckton to the north, the district is the furthest away from the City and West End. The docks themselves cover some 230 acres (94 ha) of water, surrounded by 540 acres (220 ha) of land, an area equivalent in size to Central London and the City. The scale of the derelict land and disused buildings in 1981 was greater than anywhere else.

During the LDDC's reign, transport and infrastructure were substantially transformed. London City Airport, built on a quay between the Royal Albert and King George V Docks, is Europe's fast growing airport, serving more than one million passengers a year. The housing picture has been further expanded with the completion of the UK's first new urban village at West Silvertown and a complex of luxury apartments at Barrier Point to the south. In 2000 the Royals became the homes of the University of East London Docklands Campus and ExCel International Exhibition Centre which London needs.

LDDC Strategy and Agreement

The first development framework for the Royals was published in 1985. The framework, and its revision published in 1992, sought to encourage business building of a similar scale to the position the dock had held in the British economy, and also to find employment generating uses that could benefit the local people, as well as Londoners as a whole. As elsewhere in Docklands, regeneration was to be achieved by a combination of public and private sector. The public funding would be used on infrastructure by environmental improvements, new roads and public transport and services including drainage. The private sector would build, making use of the dock landscape and providing developments of international quality. With adequate funding, by Government, a network of new and improved roads, a footbridge, a comprehensive drainage system and the DLR Extension to Beckton were all completed.

The private developers responded positively with various schemes totalling some 12 million sq. ft (1.1million sqm. The principal land uses were residential, retail, leisure, exhibition and community space. Planning permission was granted by the LDDC, but the property recession at the end of 1980s and early 1990s meant that none of them proceeded and only few other schemes were completed since 1998.

In 1987, the LDDC signed a social and community contract, the Memorandum of Agreement, with the London Borough of Newham. This sought to achieve a package of housing, employment, training and community benefits for the people of Newham and a range of new facilities for the area from schools to health care centres.

Regional Water Sports Centre

The Royal Docks Water-ski Club was established in 1985. A commercial operation since 1986, it has used approximately two-thirds of King George V Dock. This and the Royal Victoria Dock Watersports Centre, focusing on sailing and windsurfing, are of regional significance.

The Future International Opportunity

The LDDC has laid the foundations for the future development of the Royals. Most of the infrastructure schemes have been completed but only a few private developments have taken place. Designated as a showcase area, the Royals will play a crucial role in the ongoing regeneration of Newham. Along with Stratford, Canning Town and Beckton make Newham Council a major player in achieving balanced regeneration, including: establishing a strong and diversified community, providing an environment that supports a high quality of life for residents, expanding business and improving greater employment opportunities. The Council is already promoting a plan of regional and European significance that builds on the Borough's strategic location for Channel Rail Link.

From the 1st of April 1998, English Partnerships - the Government Regeneration Agency - formally assumed responsibility for completing the regeneration and development in the Royals, in partnership with Newham Council. The Agency has inherited the freehold of the water areas of about 240 acres (97ha). Newham has assumed responsibility for all the local authority functions in relation to planning and infrastructure. Strategically located, it is hoped the Royals is destined to become a future leading business and residential district within London.

Jobs for Locals

Newham Council's regeneration team are keen to see acceleration of development in the Royals in order to secure thousands of jobs for its unemployed. A major break came with the completions of ExCel Exhibition Centre and UEL Docklands Campus (see pages 156 & 157). The ExCel developers claim that fourteen thousand new jobs will flow to make it one of the most important job creation projects in the UK in terms of jobs for local people. There are opportunities for trades men and women to get the skills needed to build up and take down a huge exhibition every week. Thousands more are needed to keep things running smoothly and preference has been given to East Enders. Hundreds of local firms are supplying the 85 acre giant complex and the exhibitors. People are given the chance to operate their own cafes and wine bars. Hundreds of jobs are created with the establishment of three hotels on the site. ExCel is seen as a mix of Covent Garden and St Katharine Docks where restaurants, bars and nightclubs provide activities for thousands of people after the exhibitions are closed.

West Silvertown Urban Village, located on the south side of the Victoria Dock, illustrates the changing face of housing in the locality. The development is designed to include 864 homes, a local shopping centre, a pub and a multi-purpose community building which includes health facilities and a nursery.

The Royal Docks - Site Opportunities

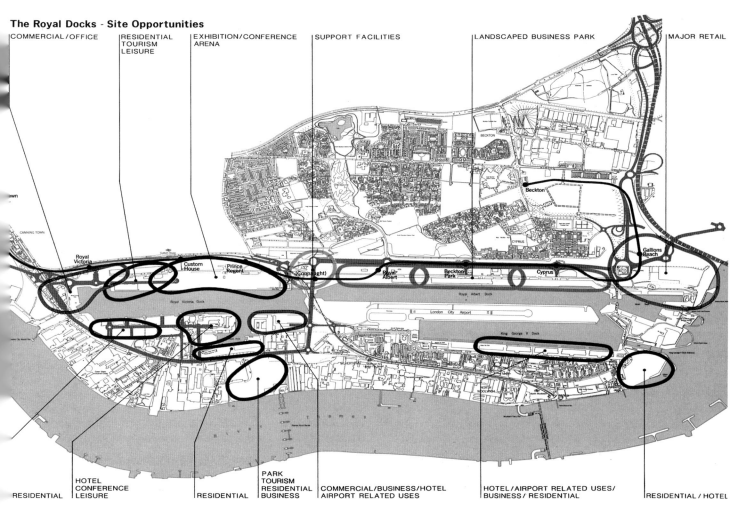

The Royals are an area of national and international opportunity for business development. With serviced sites from 5 acres (2ha) to 90 acres (36 ha), schemes can be tailored to the needs of developers, secure in the knowledge there is a high standard of infrastructure already in place. This map shows the proposals previously prepared in the 1990s. The Royals is a special place which will require a great deal of vision to fulfil its regeneration potential. But then the spirit of London Docklands has always been one of vision and opportunity.

Area and Investment

The London Docklands Development Corporation was set up on 2 July 1981 under the Local Government, Planning and Land Act 1980. Size of the Urban Development Area (UDA):

8.5 sq miles	22.0 sq kilometres
5,500 acres	2,226 hectares

Up to 31 March 1991, an estimated £8,420bn had been committed by the private sector in the UDA. The cumulative Government Grant receivable for this period was £1,119m. This generated an estimated private to public investment ratio of 7.5:1

Jobs and Businesses

Employees working in Docklands: Potential end-state employment for over 200,000 people. This was equivalent to two thirds of the current estimate for the number of jobs in the City of London.

Employment Estimates for the London Docklands Area
Total UDA Area

1981	1987	1990	1996(+)	2001(+)
27,2000;	42,000	53,084	149,774	228,511

End (+)/State(*)
255,644

Notes: 1(+) these figures did not include jobs on temporary sites eg. Construction workers.
2(*) when all sites were fully developed and occupied

Unemployment Trends: The unemployment rate for the London Docklands area had fallen from 18% in 1981 to 12% in 1991. This was based on the economically active resident population.

New Businesses and Jobs in the UDA

New	873	16,862
Relocated	802	24,559
Total	1,675	41,421

The total number of local businesses has more than doubled from 1014 in 1981 to 2174 firms in 1990.

Population

Resident Population: A potential residential population (115,000 by 2001) comparable in size to the City of Oxford.

Population Estimates and Forecasts:

Year	1981	1986	1990	1996	2001
Total	39,429	45,700	61,500	98,000	115,000

The local population had increased by 56% from 39,429 people in 1981 to 61,582 in 1990. The total number of households had increased even more by 74% from 14,743 households in 1981 to 25,577 in 1990.

There was a high distribution of people of a working age compared with national figures. Almost 50% of local people were aged between 20 and 44 which compared with 37% for Great Britain.

Housing

Cumulative figures to 31 March 1991

Number of housing units under construction	1,600
Number of housing units completed	15,220
Number of housing units started	16,820

There was scope for a further 20,000 housing units to be built on the remaining sites in London Docklands.

Up to the 31 March 1991, an average of over 1500 homes had been completed each year since 1981. This represented four new homes being completed every day. The London Docklands area alone accounted for over 10% of the total number of new dwellings built in London over the last ten years (1981-1991).

Capital Employed

Cash expenditure of the LDDC from designation in 1981 until the 31 March 1991 is detailed below:

Areas of Expenditure	
Services	£142m
Land Reclamation	£113m
Roads and Transport	£344m
Land Acquisition	£155m
Community	£65m
Social Housing	£147m
DLR	£158m
Environment	£72m
Total	£1.2billion

Estimated Dwelling Stock

	1981		June 1990	
	No.of		No. of	
Tenure	Units	%	Units	%
Owner Occupied	700	5	12,550	44
Rented	13,300	95	15,360	53
Shared Ownership	0	0	390	1
Other	0	0	580	2
Total	14,000	100	28,880	100

In 1981, the rate of owner occupation in the LDDC area was 5%. This rate in 1991 stood at 44% which compared with national figures showed a 66% rate of owner occupation in the UK.

Commercial Development

Floor space: The total potential for commercial development (65.8 million sq.ft in 1991 was more than the current estimates for the total stock of offices in the City of London.

Enterprise Zone: 191 hectares including water. Designated April 1982 with a ten year life for capital allowances and rates concessions.

There was a total of 27.5m sq ft of business floorspace under construction or completed up to the end of March 1991.

Waterside Access: 21km of waterside access had already been provided in 1991 and this increased to 52km (75% of the Docklands water edge).

LONDON DOCKLANDS REGENERATION ASSESSMENT

LDDC Organisation Structure

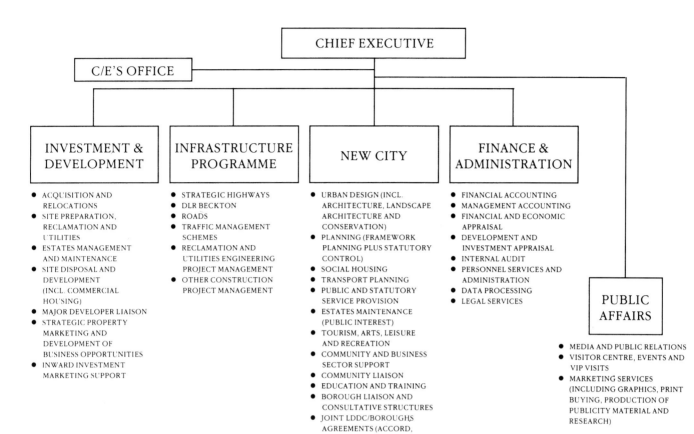

CHIEF EXECUTIVE

C/E'S OFFICE

INVESTMENT & DEVELOPMENT

- ACQUISITION AND RELOCATIONS
- SITE PREPARATION, RECLAMATION AND UTILITIES
- ESTATES MANAGEMENT AND MAINTENANCE
- SITE DISPOSAL AND DEVELOPMENT (INCL. COMMERCIAL HOUSING)
- MAJOR DEVELOPER LIAISON
- STRATEGIC PROPERTY MARKETING AND DEVELOPMENT OF BUSINESS OPPORTUNITIES
- INWARD INVESTMENT MARKETING SUPPORT

INFRASTRUCTURE PROGRAMME

- STRATEGIC HIGHWAYS
- DLR BECKTON
- ROADS
- TRAFFIC MANAGEMENT SCHEMES
- RECLAMATION AND UTILITIES ENGINEERING PROJECT MANAGEMENT
- OTHER CONSTRUCTION PROJECT MANAGEMENT

NEW CITY

- URBAN DESIGN (INCL. ARCHITECTURE, LANDSCAPE ARCHITECTURE AND CONSERVATION)
- PLANNING (FRAMEWORK PLANNING PLUS STATUTORY CONTROL)
- SOCIAL HOUSING
- TRANSPORT PLANNING
- PUBLIC AND STATUTORY SERVICE PROVISION
- ESTATES MAINTENANCE (PUBLIC INTEREST)
- TOURISM, ARTS, LEISURE AND RECREATION
- COMMUNITY AND BUSINESS SECTOR SUPPORT
- COMMUNITY LIAISON
- EDUCATION AND TRAINING
- BOROUGH LIAISON AND CONSULTATIVE STRUCTURES
- JOINT LDDC/BOROUGHS AGREEMENTS (ACCORD, COMPACT)

FINANCE & ADMINISTRATION

- FINANCIAL ACCOUNTING
- MANAGEMENT ACCOUNTING
- FINANCIAL AND ECONOMIC APPRAISAL
- DEVELOPMENT AND INVESTMENT APPRAISAL
- INTERNAL AUDIT
- PERSONNEL SERVICES AND ADMINISTRATION
- DATA PROCESSING
- LEGAL SERVICES

PUBLIC AFFAIRS

- MEDIA AND PUBLIC RELATIONS
- VISITOR CENTRE, EVENTS AND VIP VISITS
- MARKETING SERVICES (INCLUDING GRAPHICS, PRINT BUYING, PRODUCTION OF PUBLICITY MATERIAL AND RESEARCH)

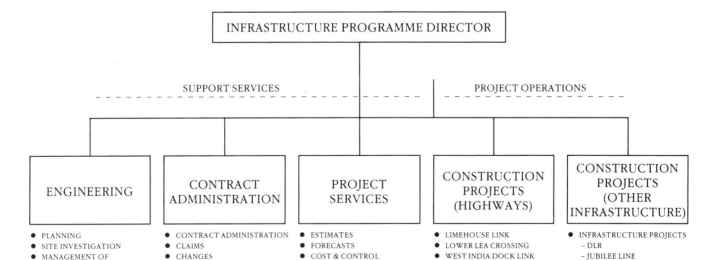

INFRASTRUCTURE PROGRAMME DIRECTOR

SUPPORT SERVICES — — — — PROJECT OPERATIONS

ENGINEERING

- PLANNING
- SITE INVESTIGATION
- MANAGEMENT OF ENGINEERING CONTRACTS
- "NEW ENGINEERING"
- SUPPORT CONSTRUCTION
- OPERATIONS MAINTENANCE PLANNING

CONTRACT ADMINISTRATION

- CONTRACT ADMINISTRATION
- CLAIMS
- CHANGES
- NEW CONTRACT FORMATION

PROJECT SERVICES

- ESTIMATES
- FORECASTS
- COST & CONTROL
- PLANNING & SCHEDULING
- REPORTING
- ANALYSIS
- PRESENTATIONS (MI)
- MEETINGS CO-ORDINATION
- SYSTEMS CO-ORDINATION
- SPECIAL STUDIES
- ASSISTANCE TO PROGRAMME DIRECTOR
- CO-ORDINATION WITH ASSISTANT CHIEF EXECUTIVE – FINANCE & ADMINISTRATION

CONSTRUCTION PROJECTS (HIGHWAYS)

- LIMEHOUSE LINK
- LOWER LEA CROSSING
- WEST INDIA DOCK LINK
- POPLAR LINK

CONSTRUCTION PROJECTS (OTHER INFRASTRUCTURE)

- INFRASTRUCTURE PROJECTS
  - DLR
  - JUBILEE LINE
  - ROYAL DOCKS
  - PRESTONS ROAD IMPS
  - E.Z. ROAD IMPS
  - CANARY WHARF ACCESS ROADS
  - OTHER
- TRAFFIC MANAGEMENT
- COMMUNITY INFORMATION
- STATS CO-ORDINATION
- CO-ORDINATION WITH OTHER LDDC BODIES

WATER, WATER ALL AROUND

Docklands Water City of the 21st Century

Docklands Water City

East of Tower Bridge in London, is a magnificent resource which has over 400 acres of compounded water. With a powered history dating back to the middle of the 18th century, the dock basins offered fresh opportunity for regeneration and revitalising the depressed urban area in the early 1980s. Mention London Docklands these days and you will most likely be told the Water City of the 21st century. Water is a catalyst for harmony by offering unrivalled watersport opportunities for all. In what can be described as the greatest open space London has seen developed in the United Kingdom in the last century.

During 1985 the East London Marine Venture at Shadwell Basin, a community water sports centre for young people, was locked in struggle with the London Docklands Development Corporation concerning the height of the proposed private housing being built around the water, which would affect the wind for board and dinghy sailing. The LDDC at the same time was preparing a report funded by the GLC, Sport Councils and Local Boroughs whose recommendations did not exactly conform with what the LDDC had in mind. In January 1987 the Corporation produced a strategy and gave responsibility for developing the use of water towards the realisation of recreational aspects towards the Water City of the 21st century concept. This became a controversial issue within the Corporation, for constructing high value buildings which retained their attractiveness while making the water around which they were built, available to all for water sports have not been universally considered to be totally compatible.

Regional, National and International Importance

The enclosed waters of Docklands represented an unparalleled opportunity for the development of water-based recreations for a number of reasons. This included their location close to the centre of the largest city in Europe; the fact that they were available for redevelopment; their proximity to the River Thames, and perhaps most significantly their scale and diversity. They had the ability to satisfy many of the recreational and leisure needs of the community living around the Docks, other Londoners and people from further afield, whether they required the opportunities and facilities for water enjoyment, or training for competition up to international standards in many sports. Whilst the first priority was to accommodate local requirements, their potential as a recreational and tourist resort of regional, national and international significance was not be under-estimated. Rarely before had such an exciting opportunity arisen to create a major water facility in the heart of the city to the benefit of all.

Testing of Building Designs

Gradually the attitude to making the Water City dream a reality became widely accepted. Fortunately at that time the Chief Executive of the LDDC was also a keen wind surfer! The size of dock water - almost one and a half times the size of Hyde Park had 55 miles of waterfront. The docks were split into four main areas - the London Docks, the West India and Millwall Docks, the Royal Docks and the Surrey Docks. Some stretches of water were more suitable for certain activities than others.

Wind tunnel testing of proposed building designs to gauge the effect of construction would have on local wind patterns became a policy. Wisely it was decided to concentrate powered sports in one area, the 230 acre Royals which also had room for an international rowing and canoe course. The West India Docks were particularly suited to canoeing; Millwall Docks is a favourite for wind surfing and the Surrey Docks were utilised for board sailing, sub-aqua, fishing, rowing and dinghy sailing, while a section of the South Docks housed London's largest marina. Shadwell Basin has long been recognised as providing the facilities for skill training for young people. St Katharine's Docks is a long established marina and the new Limehouse Basin has become a haven for canal boats visiting Docklands through the inland waterway system.

Voluntary and Private Clubs

The Docks also house many individual voluntary and private operations like the Docklands Scout Project and various water-ski, wet bike and wind surfing clubs, as well as water sports. The new approach was beast typified by the opening of Dockland Sailing Centre in the Millwall Docks, built at a cost of £1_ million jointly by the Corporation and the Sport Councils, it is now run as a registered charity on a commercial basis by a management team drawn from the local community, government and business with funding drawn partly from these sources mixed with its own ability to generate income. This mixed economy approach was considered as a way to go for the future.

Commitment and Organisation

Evidence of the growing corporation of the various sectors was exemplified by the formation of the London Dockland Water Sports, a joint venture backed by the Corporation in 1989 which aimed to publicise the 22 facilities offered by its members. This was done by the publication of overall and individual brochures, supported by exhibition stands available to any of the participants and advice and information on obtaining sponsorship. It was considered essential and the organisation looked forward to a time when Docklands Water was not only enjoyed by the locals, but also increasingly used for national and international sporting events, as well as being available to the many visitors expected to fill the hotels built in the area. Youth games, regattas, fun-days and other events took advantage of the calm, sheltered waters with local organisations like Shadwell Basin being in the forefront by encouraging competitions for colourful and spectacular dragon and peacock boats. Barriers were also broken when many more London women and a significant proportion of black people were trained as canoe instructors. Sports for all was considered as the goal in Docklands. Whatever the faults of the past, there was an enlightened organisation believing in a spectacular way forward. About £100 million was devoted to every aspect of water development in London Docklands, which has been an obvious contribution to the success of the sports clubs in the area.

Above - Wet biking in the Royal Docks

Left - A Dragon Boat crew sweats it out during a charity final while the Cox, suitably dressed, urges for greater effort!

Above left- Thousands of young people have been introduced to the pleasures of water sports in Docklands, including canoe and sailing training - thanks to the Docklands Scout Project which is based at Dollar Bay, West India Docks.

View of Greenland Dock in the Surrey Quays with sailing and other sport activities overlooked by new residential estates.

Wind surfing is widely enjoyed in the Royal Docks.

Dockland Water Sports

For the more intrepid water baby, the London Wetbike Club will see you skimming across the water at speeds in excess of 30 miles per hour. Docklands provide an opportunity for major water sports facilities such as sailing, canoeing, rowing and dragon boat racing in the Royal Docks, Millwall Dock and Greenland Dock. The UK International Power Boat Grand Prix in the Royal Victoria Dock attracted many thousands of spectators. Wet biking is a regular sporting activity in the Royal Docks.

Prior to 1985

The period between July 1981 and March 1985 saw the development of some commercial premises and the building of over two thousand homes. Early commercial activity was concentrated in the Enterprise Zone with the provision of low-density business and warehouse units. The first residential schemes were typically low cost family homes at low densities with gardens in Beckton and Surrey Docks. Emerging confidence in the housing market accelerated the conversion of redundant riverside warehouses to stylish and loft type apartments, exploiting riverside views in Wapping, Limehouse and Bermondsey. The first phase of development was made possible with the promise of the initial Docklands Light Railway (DLR), which was under construction high above the docks and the expectation of an eastern extension to Beckton.

Canary Wharf Scheme

At the same time rising office rentals and the shortage of suitable buildings and sites in the City led three American banks to propose the Canary Wharf scheme in 1985 through their architect and advisor G. Ware Travelstead. He proposed the building of a massive 10 million square feet (0.9million sq.m) office complex on Canary Wharf on the Isle of Dogs Enterprise Zone. This was envisaged as London's third business and financial centre, alongside the City and West End. Canary Wharf at that time was housing Limehouse Studios in one of the old dockside sheds. This was a successful Independent TV studio in association with Channel 4. The news of Canary Wharf and modest public investment in transport and infrastructure services began to stimulate private sector interest and to attract redevelopment proposals particularly from international organisations.

Availability of Cheap Land

Land ownership was crucial to the development process. Prior to the setting up of the LDDC in July 1981, 80% of land in Docklands was already in the ownership of various public agencies, but not necessarily available for development. They included nationalised agencies such as British Rail and statutory bodies such as British Gas, and the Port of London Authority. Also included were local authorities, the GLC, and London Boroughs of Southwark, Tower Hamlets and Newham. Virtually the whole of the Enterprise Zone consisted prior to 1981 of Port of London Authority owned land and water. The Docklands Joint Committee, a strategic body set up by the GLC and the Docklands Boroughs and superseded by the LDDC envisaged using the West India and Millwall Docks systems for light industrial development and public housing.

All land in the West India Dock system where Canary Wharf was built was vested by the LDDC from the Port of London Authority in 1981-82 between £20--30,000 per acre. The ability of the LDDC to acquire this land was crucial to the development of Canary Wharf. Equally important were the LDDC's powers of compulsory purchase, for it had to instigate this team's compulsory purchases in order to acquire land necessary for the construction of the Docklands highway. This would be a network of new roads passing through Docklands, providing a link at one end to the City and at the other to the Outer London motor network such as the A406 and M11. This Docklands highway was a crucial element in the Master Building Agreement for Canary Wharf. The LDDC was directly accountable only to the Secretary of State for the Environment and had no local political accountability.

View of the Isle of Dogs looking west towards the City, where the Canary Wharf development was proposed in 1986. On the right were the old sheds approached by the red brick road of the enterprise zone. The end shed was converted into Limehouse studios.

CANARY WHARF TRAVELSTEAD SCHEME

First Master Plan Submitted to LDDC in 1985

East End Boosted by Canary Wharf

London's East End would share in the prosperity of the City through the development of a major financial centre in Docklands. New jobs, new amenities and much improved transport would benefit the whole community. This became clear when details of the Master Plan for the development of a 10 million sq ft financial centre at Canary Wharf in the West India Docks were revealed on 2nd October 1985. The plan, prepared by leading architects Skidmore, Owings and Merrill, was submitted to the London Docklands Development Corporation by the international consortium, which had an option on the site. The development was designed to meet the specific needs of London's growing financial community, which could not be met in the City of London without destroying its historic character. Some 40,000 people could work in the new complex which included 8.8 million sq ft of offices and large, modern financial trading floors, two hotels with some 800 rooms and 500,000 sq ft of shops, pubs, restaurants and other amenities (see pages 4/5).

Overview

London's reputation as a leading international financial centre was built over the centuries on the expertise and adaptability of the City. Change in the financial world was gathering pace as de-regulation, coupled with new technology, was creating global capital markets and financial services. Situated in a critical time zone between Tokyo and New York, London is well placed to take advantage of these developments.

But the City must grow to meet the requirements of brokers, traders and bankers - requirements such as open-plan trading floors of 40,000 sq ft or more, the most advanced, secure, on-line communications and computer facilities and up-to-date, purpose-built offices to house them. Within the Square Mile, these demands were difficult to meet without large-scale upheaval and the destruction of the City's historic character. A new location was therefore required within easy reach of the City, with plenty of space at reasonable cost, and excellent transport facilities.

Canary Wharf, some 2 miles from the City and linked to it by road, rail and river is an eastward extension of London's existing financial centre. Its development revitalises 71 acres of the former West India Docks by providing some 10 million sq ft of accommodation, designed specifically for the expansion of the financial services sector. The development provides buildings to meet the highest international standards whilst maintaining an urban and landscape tradition that is distinctly British. Canary Wharf makes a substantial contribution to the overall regeneration of Docklands. Apart from the direct employment generated, a large number of jobs are created indirectly. Furthermore, the new hotels, restaurants, shopping and commercial facilities and improvements in transport would benefit East End as a whole.

Development Team

A development the scale of Canary Wharf required a team of experienced professionals to assure its success. The sponsoring consortium consisted of Affiliates of Financiere Credit Suisse-First Boston, Morgan Stanley International Inc and First Boston Docklands Associates. Affiliates of First Boston Inc. and G Ware Travelstead who acted as developers for the consortium, assembled a highly qualified team for this effort. The Chicago office of Skidmore, Owings & Merrill led the design effort for the architecture, planning and engineering. In the master planning process, they collaborated closely with I M Pei & Partners and a group of local and international consultants.

Site Description

Canary Wharf is in the Isle of Dogs in the London Borough of Tower Hamlets. The 71-acre site is within the West India Docks formerly part of the Port of London. It is now under the aegis of the London Docklands Development Committee (LDDC), set up by Government to promote the regeneration of the area. Most of the site is within the London Docklands Enterprise Zone. Benefits available until April 1992 included exemption from rates, 100% capital allowances on new construction work and a greatly simplified planning approval process.

The development site extends over half a mile west from the Thames to Blackwall Basin. The wharf itself is some 380 feet wide and 2,500 feet long or some 21 acres. The impounded dock water within the site covers some 25 acres. The river frontage is some 1,650 ft long with some 25 acres of developable land between it and the wharf. Buildings on the site included Limehouse television studios, empty warehouses and two small sales centres.

The Narrow Street and West India conservation areas are to the immediate north west of the site. To the north, across the water, is North Quay, a development that includes a "festival market" shops, restaurants and offices, together with a new hotel and housing. The Heron Quay development on the south provided new offices and housing. The residential district of Cubitt Town and Millwall lie a short distance to the south. In Wapping, to the west, many vacant warehouses and industrial buildings are converted for residential and other uses. The Surrey Docks redevelopment area is across the river to the west and the Royal Docks redevelopment area is to the east of the site. A short take-off and landing airport (STOLPORT) in the Royal Docks provides scheduled air services to other British and North European cities. The Docklands Light Railway (DLR) crosses Canary Wharf from north to south, providing direct communication to the City. The initial occupancy of the development in early 1988 was planned to coincide with the opening of the DLR line. London Regional Transport announced plans to extend the DLR from Minories to Bank with financial support from the consortium. Road access to the City was via the Highway and Commercial Road. A new road, the Docklands Northern Relief Road, was built to the north of the site to relieve congestion on the strategic road network.

Design Programme

The development comprised some 10 million sq ft of space in all, including hotels, shops, restaurants and other support amenities as well as offices and financial trading floors. It included at least 8.8. million sq ft of offices and state-of-the-art financial trading floors; two hotels, with some 800 rooms and associated conference and banqueting facilities; and at least 0.5 million sq ft of shops, pubs, restaurants and other support amenities. There is also 100,000 sq ft of facilities for services such as transport, maintenance and utilities and parking for at least 8,300 cars.

Building Density

The overall density is similar to that found in the City of London with individual building plots substantially larger than those typically found in the City to meet the special needs for space for the financial services sector. Furthermore the Master Plan provided for more than one third of the site to be devoted to public open space. To achieve these ends, the Master Plan included three high-rise landmark buildings to contain about a third of the total office accommodation. The remaining two thirds would be in buildings of limited height.

The full development of the site and provision for open space called for buildings to be constructed over the water at some points, thus the impounded water has been transformed from long linear passages into a sequence of water and pedestrian courts. Development of the wharf itself was organised along a central linear open space, intersected by public amenities, such as the DLR station, a hotel and shops, to create three distinct areas, each with its own identity, referred to as Founders' Court, Docklands Square and Blackwall Landing. The latter is similar in area to Bedford Square. The planning of the western end of the site, between the river and the wharf, was based on buildings surrounding a public open space, Westferry Circus, which is as large as the Place de l'Etoile in Paris. Most of the parking is in multi-level car parks beneath the open spaces which are raised up to provide views down to the water throughout the site.

Circulation

Cars using the main car parks approach via an underground service road entered at Westferry Circus. This road forms a loop around the site and also carries service vehicles to the loading bays beneath each building. A two-lane boulevard above ground is used by taxis, visitors' cars and shuttle buses that circulate throughout the site. This road is in the form of a loop but intersects the wharf at various points. It is entered from Westferry Circus and two new bridges. One, to the north connects with North Quay and Docklands North Relief Road. The other, to the east provides access from Prestons Road.

Slip roads at various points enable cars to transfer between the two levels, enabling entry to the car parks after dropping off passengers. There are drop-off points at each building, which have their own VIP parking within its site, in addition to the public car parks. Footpaths give pedestrians access to all parts of the site, including the river frontage and the dock waters. Access for the disabled is provided throughout the site.

Illustrative Plan

The illustrative Master Plan is inspired by the variety of open spaces and detail which gives London its distinctive character. Development around each of the three major open spaces on the wharf included a landmark building. This pair of elements -open space and tower- forms the core of a district with its own identity and texture. A central feature of the development is the glass-roofed concourse, on a similar scale to the train shed at Paddington Station, constructed around the DLR station. Shops, restaurants and other services enliven the concourse.

Public Open Space

The public open spaces include planted and paved areas, vehicular and pedestrian circulation paths, and areas of open water and waterside walks. Westferry Circus establishes an initial identity for Canary Wharf and is the starting point of a sequence that continues east onto the wharf itself. It links the development with the river, where a riverbus landing stage is sited.

The organisational concept for the rest of the site defines the linear open space running the length of the wharf by buildings constructed along its northern and southern sides. The intersection of this space by the DLR station concourse, shops and other commercial facilities and a hotel creates three principal open spaces. Founders' Court is a paved area featuring an oval basin with a fountain. A terraced pathway beside a cascading waterfall leads pedestrians up to the DLR station concourse. Docklands Square, at the intersection of the wharf and the north road bridge, is a classic English landscape with a waterside esplanade. Blackwall Landing, a formal garden square at the eastern end of the wharf serves as a forecourt for vehicular traffic arriving by the east bridge. Thus, pedestrians can walk from Westferry Circus through to Blackwall Landing experiencing a sequence of open and enclosed spaces, long vistas to the City and views to the water, busy squares and quiet courtyards. This east-west sequence is further enlivened by changes in level. Additional open spaces include waterside paths with private developments, creating a continuous pedestrian circulation route along the waters edge.

CANARY WHARF DEVELOPMENT CONCEPT

A Kind of Analogue to the Site's Former Life

First Principles

In a fundamental way the functional, circulatory and spatial organisation of the Canary Wharf Master Plan are governed by the austere geometry of the wharf itself. Indeed, the development has been conceived as a kind of analogue to the site's former life: office buildings arrayed at dockside where great ships once berthed; cars parked at the centre where goods for export once were stored; and access provided on a loop road following the same route that once served both ships and warehouses. All this bespeaks the first principle of the Master Plan: respect for an ordering discipline that is specifically related to this unique site and that should prove as serviceable to the present enterprise as to its predecessor.

But there is yet another analogue to the past that is immediately apparent in the Plan: just as the Limehouse Entrance Basin (long since filled in) once provided a necessary link between the impounded waters of the Docks and the upper reaches of the River Thames, so the new development will be given an essential window and gateway to the Thames by way of a great circus touching the western shore of the Isle of Dogs and offering a long view upriver to Tower Bridge, the City and St Paul's. As a corollary, this circus also opens the development to view from the river. And in both these aspects - looking out or looking in - it affirms the second principle of the Master Plan: acknowledgement of Canary Wharf's destined role, inescapably more than parochial, in contributing to the larger image of the City.

Mention of the circus hints also at the third principle of the Plan: pre-occupation with the making of spaces. Indeed, despite the inevitable prominence of the three office towers, the Master Plan is less concerned with the design of individual buildings - this came later - than with the shaping of spaces: the array of streets, squares, parks, terraces and waterside promenades that together constitute the public realm of Canary Wharf.

Use and Function

The great majority of the programmed floor space in the new development, was allocated to offices for the financial services sector. A special characteristic of this use is the requirement for extremely large open-plan trading floors - 40,000 sq ft or more - with direct connection to associated office floors in the range of 15-25,000 sq ft each. To meet these requirements, individual building sites must be substantially larger than those generally available in the City. The Canary Wharf Master Plan created a number of such sites, most of them placed around the perimeter of the wharf, with the remainder framing the boulevard and circus at the western end of the site.

As a corollary to placement of office space on the periphery, the programmed support amenities - hotels, pubs, restaurants and shops - are concentrated toward the centre of the wharf, where they can most conveniently serve both office workers and visitors. The greatest concentration of these facilities is found in the Canary Concourse, the great glass-roofed terrace flanking the Docklands Light Rail station, the principal point of arrival on the site. Two hotels are planned, one

on the wharf just east of the Concourse, and the other overlooking the Thames south of the circus.

Enclosed parking for 8,300 cars are provided for on site, with two or three levels below the street in most areas and two above the street beneath the raised terrace of Canary Concourse. Enclosed service decks as well as supplementary private parking for individual office buildings would be located below street level on the periphery of the wharf.

Efficient Transport

The provision of an efficient transport infrastructure is crucial to the success of a development of this magnitude. Of prime importance will be the extension of the western section of the Docklands Light Railway to Bank Underground stations. Technical studies demonstrated the practicality of this extension, which ties Canary Wharf to the City and integrates Docklands with the rest of London by providing a direct link with the underground system. A detailed analysis was undertaken to assess the developments transport requirements and to determine how these requirements could be accommodated by improvements to the surrounding road network and public transport. A workforce in excess of 40,000 was projected for the full 10 million sq ft development. The number of peak hour journeys that would be generated was estimated on the basis of the size of the workforce and characteristics of the working patterns of financial institutions.

Commemorating the Explorers

As with every other aspect of Canary Wharf, care has been taken over the naming of the roads and streets. Some commemorate the explorers of North America (page 24), including Cabot Square, Chancellor Passage, Columbus Courtyard and Cartier Circle. Cubitt, Nash, Adams and Wren four families of architects and builders, who changed the face of London in their time, are also commemorated in water courts and squares. Fisherman's Walk, Westferry Circus and West India Avenue, refer to the former commercial life of the Isle of Dogs. Canada Square is a reminder of the origin of the developer Olympia & York, Toronto, Canada. Their pride has been in the attention given to detail in every aspect of their development, from the colour of paving stones to the irrigation of plants (see map on page 123).

A VIEW OF CANARY WHARF

Elevation and Site Plan of Phases 1 and 2 of Canary Wharf, as released by developers Olympia & York, in November 1988. The most significant change by Olympia & York to the original master plan effectively brought the buildings closer to the dock water.

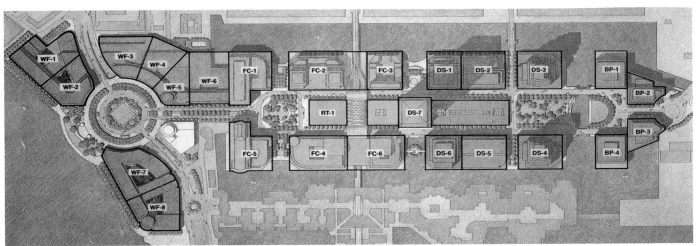

SITE PLAN

ARCHITECTS & ENGINEERS: Skidmore, Owings & Merrill
LANDSCAPE ARCHITECTS: Hanna/Olin, Ltd.

KEY: Phase 1 Buildings / Phase 2 Buildings

CONSULTING ENGINEERS: Ove Arup & Partners
TRANSPORT CONSULTANTS: Steer, Davies & Gleave, Ltd

SUBJECT TO CHANGE WITHOUT NOTICE   November 1987

West Ferry Circus

Parcel Designation	Parcel Size (s.f.)	Gross Floor Area (s.f.)
WF-1	79,400	361,000
WF-2	61,700	281,000
WF-3	61,300	163,000
WF-4	52,600	239,000
WF-5	47,000	234,000
WF-6	81,300	299,000
WF-7	91,200	369,000
WF-8	74,800	302,000
TOTAL	549,300	2,248,000

Founders Court

Parcel Designation	Parcel Size (s.f.)	Gross Floor Area (s.f.)
FC-1	75,200	722,000
FC-2	121,600	627,000
FC-3	45,900	278,000
FC-4	75,000	570,000
FC-5	75,700	638,000
FC-6	74,500	382,000
TOTAL	467,900	3,217,000

Retail

Parcel Designation	Parcel Size (s.f.)	Gross Floor Area (s.f.)
RT-1	32,600	90,000
TOTAL	32,600	90,000

Docklands Square

Parcel Designation	Parcel Size (s.f.)	Gross Floor Area (s.f.)
DS-1	51,400	365,000
DS-2	65,500	499,000
DS-3	65,500	1,150,000
DS-4	74,900	1,150,000
DS-5	58,500	462,000
DS-6	45,900	345,000
DS-7	138,000	1,700,000
TOTAL	499,700	5,671,000

Blackwall Place

Parcel Designation	Parcel Size (s.f.)	Gross Floor Area (s.f.)
BP-1	48,400	296,000
BP-2	36,300	291,000
BP-3	35,000	291,000
BP-4	43,200	296,000
TOTAL	162,900	1,174,000

GRAND TOTAL	1,712,400	12,400,00

50

Olmpia & York employed Britains's leading experts for the stunning design of shops and restaurants in Canary Wharf's retail locations. The basic principle was to make people feel at home here.

The spacious and modern Daily Mirror new offices at Canary Wharf Tower, One Canada Square. Inset: A docker in the old days.

A two-storey Classical loggia tops Phase I building FC5 that guards the western approach to the Wharf, c1992.

Stark and multifaceted FC1, one of the largest buildings on the Wharf, forms an impressive barbican gateway, c1992.

HENLEY'S FORECAST REPORT

Jobs for Docklands People

Announcement for Local Residents

Twenty one thousand Dockland residents will get jobs in the financial centre to be built at Canary Wharf was the news from the Canary Wharf Development Company in 1986. This was based on the conclusion of an independent survey into the development. Of the new jobs 15,000 will go to people currently registered as unemployed in the three Dockland boroughs. People, who do not appear on the Register such as married women, will take up the rest. These were the key findings of a study carried out by the Henley Centre, which was considered to be Europe's biggest and most respected forecasting agency. The centre also predicted that additional 7,000 jobs would be created during the construction stage of Canary Wharf. The team of building and civil engineering contractors, who will be doing the work, would be committed to making sure that a fair number of these jobs would go to local people. It was stated that Canary Wharf would be the biggest construction project in London since the city was rebuilt after the Great Fire of 1666.

The site, which runs from Blackwall in the east to Limehouse Reach of the river in the west, would be as long as the Mall in London's West End. It would contain office buildings, hotels and shops and restaurants needed to serve them. These would all be built around a series of public squares and courtyards, which could be enjoyed by residents, commuters and visitors who came to see what was the most exciting urban redevelopment in the world. The Henley Centre forecasted that 200,000 jobs would be created in the financial services in London over the next 10 years if the right sort of buildings were made available.

Modern Facilities for Finance Corporations

Canary Wharf would meet between a quarter and a third of that requirement for buildings, supplementing the facilities of the City of London itself. The resources the developers were prepared to put into the project were enormous. For example they were putting up £45million to extend the Docklands Light Railway into Bank station.

New technology has altered the financial services industry as much as other industries. Communication satellites and computers mean that it is possible to do business 24 hours a day with Tokyo in the East and New York in the West. But high technology has special requirements in office buildings. It needs to be housed in buildings that can cope with it. Modern day bank needs to have very high, large rooms that can house the huge amount of cabling needed both beneath the floor and above the ceiling for the equipment and ducts that allow this cabling to be served all over the world.

Canary Wharf was considered as one of the few sites near the city, which would allow these new developments to be constructed. At the time it was free of the difficulties that a medieval street plan imposes in this City itself.

Henley's Forecast for Jobs

The Henley report also forecasted that Canary Wharf development would create 57,000 new permanent jobs for Londoners in addition to those who would be employed in construction in the years to come. Of this total 49,000 would be created in the locality, while a further 8,000 would be generated elsewhere. Approximately 21,000 permanent new jobs would go to local people. Of these 13,500 would be office workers at professional level; secretarial and clerical levels. Another 4,200 would be the service jobs required for the running of offices, security and cleaning. 300 would be created in the two hotels planned for the site and a further 3,000 jobs would be generated as a result of the money spent by people working at Canary Wharf.

Additionally there would be 7,000 construction jobs and the developers would be committed in ensuring that a high proportion of these would go to local people, including some based on new training schemes. These statistics were taken from the Henley Centre Forecasting into the economic impact of Canary Wharf development in London. The Centre is an independent business-forecasting organisation. Despite these promises for jobs, the local people were not convinced. There were demonstrations and protests by the residents backed by unsuccessful challenges to the LDDC by the local Boroughs and the Greater London Council (GLC).

GLC's Challenge

The GLC's ground for the challenge that the LDDC failed to have regard to the Greater London Development plan, especially in regard to its high buildings policy, the impact on areas of special interest such as Greenwich and the LDDC had failed to consult the GLC and London Boroughs and to give proper opportunity for representations. In effect the GLC said that no reasonable enterprise authority would have given such approvals for Canary Wharf scheme. However, the GLC's challenge was not upheld and in any case they were demised by 31 March of that year.

Government also refused to hold the Public Inquiry. They considered that in their view having established through the Enterprise Zone system a particular means of providing planning permission in parts of the country that are in urgent need of regeneration, it would not be right for the Government to intervene. A local MP for Newham, described the whole event as possibly the largest commercial project in the world being subject to less review and scrutiny than a planning application for an illuminated sign on a fish and chip shop in the East India Dock Road!

OPPOSITION TO TRAVELSTEAD'S PROPOSALS

London's Wall Street on Water

Travelstead Proposals

The world's largest finance centre being built in the heart of historic Docklands initially evoked descriptions from a 'monster' to a 'dream'. The first proposals for the scheme in 1986 unveiled a £1.5 billion development of Canary Wharf on the northern fringes of the Isle of Dogs Enterprise Zone, which indicated three biggest skyscrapers in Europe. Two of the three towers would peak at 256 metres (840 feet), surpassing the Nat West Tower in the City of London, which is three-quarters the size. In addition to the giant towers, vast concourses, office blocks, shops and restaurants would also be built. At the time the Chinese Government was negotiating the creation of a 'Chinatown' at the nearby Poplar Dock. With this in mind, the area was said to become a 'Wall Street on Water'.

The Canary Wharf Development Company, led by the architect G Ware Travelstead, with tentative backing by an international banking consortium, was given planning permission by the London Docklands Development Corporation to build more than 12.5 million square feet offices across the 71 acres site. They were given a licence for preliminary work on the wharf including demolishing old warehouses, erecting fences and developing site security.

Giant Scale

The sheer size and scale of Canary Wharf commanded its own electricity, telephone, water and rail infrastructure. There was the promise of nearly 60,000 jobs and the rebirth of the decaying and deserted warehouses and docks into a 21st century model of bustling and expanding businesses. Changes in shares and bond trading in other countries forced the largest banks and brokers to search for more space, as the huge dealing rooms required vast floor areas of 2,000 to 4,000 square metres.

Coupled with the 'Big Bang' in the City on 27 October 1986, which had de-regulated the out-dated practices of the Stock Exchange, the stage was set for the old City Square Mile to be revolutionised and shifted downriver to East London. Despite hitches with computers on the first day of de-regulation, many brokers were working away from the 'sacred' floor of the Stock Exchange and operating from terminals in their offices.

Resentment and Opposition

With the 'Big Bang' and big plans came huge opposition to Canary Wharf. Jostling in the forefront of protestors were the environmental conservation people critical of the towers, claiming they were far too big and would spoil the view from Greenwich Royal Naval College built by Christopher Wren. The Borough Councils of Newham, Southwark, Lewisham and Tower Hamlets, parts of that were included in the Docklands area, were furious at the lack of public consultation and their inability on planning. These Borough Councils called for a public inquiry and considered High Court action. Local residents argued that majority of the new jobs would be given to outsiders. While many traders in the City were reluctant to leave the traditional stronghold of the Square Mile and raised objections to transport, particularly

doubt on the poor design of the Dockland Light Railway. The Government however poured scorn on the opponents and argued that ten years ago vast tracts of Docklands were inactive and decaying. Despite plans, committees, public consultations and strategies nothing was achieved until the LDDC was created in 1981.

Critics Off Target

At the time the Isle of Dogs was developing with new factories, offices and showrooms. Building sites were hammering the message that £1.2billion of private capital had followed the £270 million invested there by Government since 1980. While unemployment was rising in Britain by about 3%, in Docklands it had fallen by the same percentage and more people were finding new jobs, especially on construction sites. The Governor of the Bank of England stated his belief there was room for the old and new to exist side-by-side without fragmentation.

The LDDC were adamant the critics were wrong and emphasised that the Docklands success would have been impossible under statutory local authority planning control. They insisted the central issue was not height but architectural quality and a well-designed structure would be a great improvement. The LDDC, however, agreed to re-site the controversial skyscrapers in response to criticisms.

With unemployment a burning issue the LDDC forecast that some 11,000 of the newly created jobs would go to local people. They considered the number would increase significantly if they had the co-operation of Local Councils, by ensuring that young people were trained and received education to prepare them for jobs at Canary Wharf. Realising the future financial revenue from rates and employment benefits, Tower Hamlets Council dropped plans for a public enquiry, choosing instead to enter into discussions and co-operation.

Concerns and Final Commitment

But elsewhere, resentment and despair at the actions of the LDDC ran high. Greenwich Council accused the Government of creating a 'monster' in the LDDC, which had gone out of control. The Docklands Councils were concerned about the planning implications for the rest of the capital, especially on transport and the ability of the Docklands Light Railway and highways to cope with the considerable increase in traffic. Shifting the positions of the proposed towers did not ease their concerns over the looming skyline.

Despite the protests and frustrations at grass roots level, Canary Wharf construction was on target to become the centre of global banking and business with an ideal geographical position practically on the Greenwich Meridian line, with a foot between the time zones of the other major financial centres, namely New York and Tokyo. Due to the overwhelming international interest and investment to develop the areas, including the gradual development of the infrastructure, Docklands was considered a great success and the Government was not prepared to bow to any pressures since more than £100 million would have had to be paid in compensation.

LIFE AND WORK IN CANARY WHARF

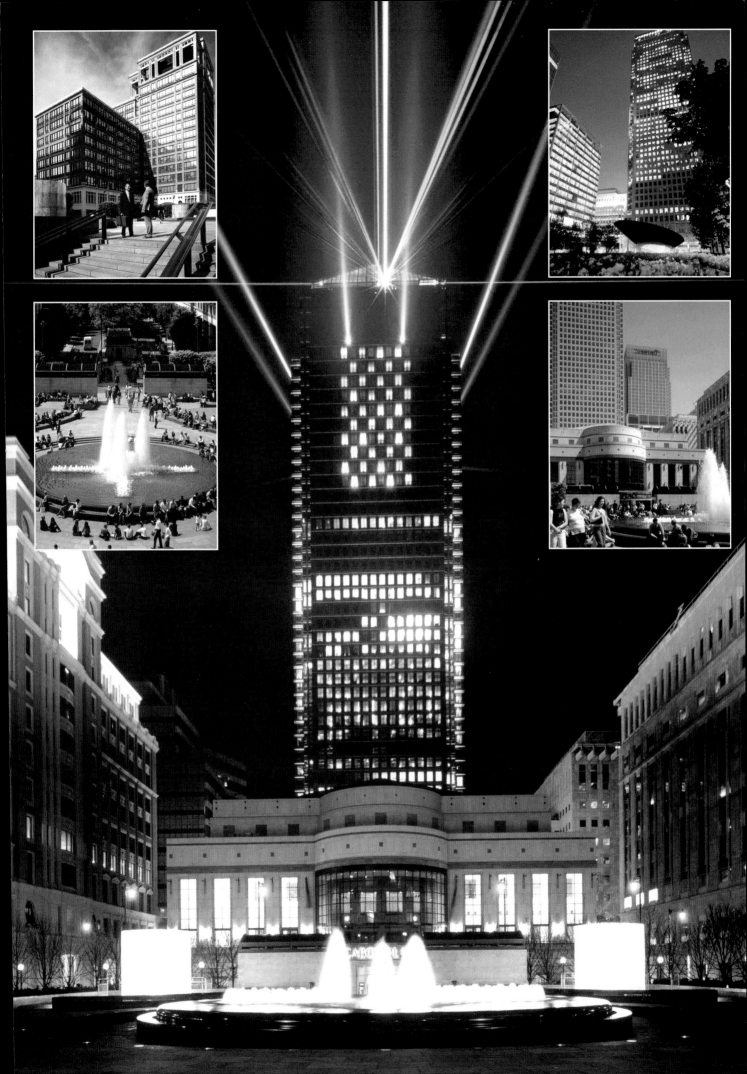

Project Developer
The Canary Wharf Development Co Ltd

A wholly-owned subsidiary of Olympia & York Developments Ltd.

Location
Canary Wharf is located on the Isle of Dogs, in the London Borough of Tower Hamlets, 2 miles east of the City in London's Docklands.

The Development Site
The site extends over half a mile eastward from the River Thames along Canary Wharf to Blackwall Basin.

Total size: 71 acres
The site is made up of three elements:

The Wharf	21 acres
	380' wide
	2,500' long
Building platforms above existing water	25 acres
Land between the Wharf and the River Thames	25 acres

Planning Authority: London Docklands Development Corporation (LDDC)

Enterprise Zone
All of the site, except the land west of the existing Westferry Road is located within the London Docklands Enterprise Zone.

Within the zone, the following benefits apply:
- No rates are payable by occupants until April 1992
- 100 per cent capital allowances can be claimed on buildings under construction by April 1992
- Greatly simplified planning approval process.

The Concept of Canary Wharf
Canary Wharf represents the creation of a major business centre on a green field site within ten minutes of the City. It will be tied into London's transportation infrastructure by a new high-capacity light rail system, £700 million of local and regional road improvements and a new airport serving the capital cities of Europe. The development is planned to provide buildings which meet the best international standards within a high quality urban environment. The Company has drawn on its prior European experience in Toronto, Ottawa, Calgary, New York, Boston, Chicago and Los Angeles among other major cities.

The Master Plan
Skidmore, Owings and Merrill, IM Pei, YRM Associates and a group of local and international consultants have created a Master Plan for the co-ordinated layout of the project and a set of Design Guidelines which will ensure a cohesive architectural expression and set a high quality standard throughout the entire development (see picture on page 50).

The Development Programme
The Canary Wharf Master Plan establishes 22 separate building sites, with the majority located along the perimeter of the Wharf and the remainder framing the boulevard and circus at the western end of the site.

Three sites have been identified as locations for high-rise office towers. The mid-rise sites are capable of accommodating buildings ranging between 300,000 and 700,000 square feet gross. The towers range from about 1.2 to 1.7 million square feet gross. The total project will comprise:

- Office space of 10m net sq.ft
- up to 400,000 net sq ft of retail, restaurant and leisure facilities
- 6,500 car parking spaces
- two 400 bedroom hotels and associated conference and banqueting facilities
- a series of interconnected, landscaped courtyards, parks and plazas. Waterside promenades will allow the public access to the water's edge along the entire perimeter of the Project

Project Description
The Project is conceived as four neighbourhoods or precincts, grouped around major public spaces. The first is the group of buildings, primarily low-rise, framing Westferry Circus. These buildings constitute the major formal entry to the Project. The second group of mid-rise buildings are grouped around a public plaza, called Founders Court. The third precinct, while continuing the mid-rise street wall of Founders Court, is the domain of the high-rise towers, which form the Centre piece and focus of the project. These buildings group themselves around a three acre square which bridges the water to tie into the fourth neighbourhood, of four primarily low-rise buildings which form the eastern gateway to the Project. These four precincts are tied together by the water that surrounds them, by the waterfront promenade that encircles the Project, by the line of central public spaces, and by the main loop road which runs from one end of the project to the other.

Project Amenities
There are up to 400,000 sq ft given over to retail, restaurants, leisure and other amenities. The majority of this space is located in the central concourse. There are however, shops and restaurants within the individual buildings. Throughout the Project a full complement of shops caters to the needs of executives, office staff and visitors alike. At the completion of the project there will be approximately 75 restaurants and two major hotels, providing over 800 rooms, conference and banqueting facilities. One third of the site is dedicated to open space made up of courtyards, parks, plazas and promenades.

Car Parking
Canary Wharf is designed to accommodate approximately 6,500 car parking spaces. This represents one space per 1,500 sq ft of office space. Approximately 3,500 of these are incorporated in Phase I. While most of the car parking is dedicated to tenants and employees adequate parking is available to accommodate visitors and shoppers.

The entire project will take an estimated 7-10 years to complete at a current cost of approximately £3-4 billion.

A principal objective of the design was to encourage pedestrian routes through the many buildings and allow views from the wharf to the water.   These corridors take the form of passages through buildings, arcades, colonnades or courtyards.

Another principle of the plan was the pre-occupation with the making of places, such as an array of streets, squares and small parks that together constitute the public realm of Canary Wharf.

OLYMPIA AND YORK OF CANARY WHARF

A property Company previously unknown in the UK

Largest Developer of Offices

A Company previously unknown in the United Kingdom, Olympia & York was a £20 billion dollars conglomerate with its roots firmly fixed in property assets. But the organisation spreads among a mass of strategic financial investments. It was also unusual given the scale of this operation that it remains a private family company, run primarily by the three Reichmann brothers. It had large energy interests including controlling 70% of Gulf Canada, one of Canada's largest producers of oil and natural gas and 83% of the Consumers Gas Company, one of Canada's largest gas distributors. Olympia & York's main interest however were in the property market, being the largest developers of office space in North America. By 1990 Olympia & York owned more than 50 million sq. ft. in North America and half of that was in New York.

Olympia & York was a partner in some of the biggest redevelopment schemes in North America, these included New York's World Financial Centre at Battery Park city, Toronto's First Canadian Place and Queens Quay Terminal. It was in 1975 that Olympia & York first completed First Canadian Place, a 5 million sq. ft. office development which is still one of Toronto's biggest commercial districts. Later Olympia & York bought 8 office blocks in Manhattan for US$50 million in cash plus the mortgages. From there they moved on to build the World Financial Centre, 8 million sq. ft of offices on a piece of landfill near Battery Park on the southern tip of Manhattan.

Agreement with LDDC

Olympia & York were persuaded by cheap land, Enterprise Zone and the contents of the Master Building Agreement to invest in London's Canary Wharf. The MBA development signed between the LDDC and Olympia & York, which sets out, amongst other matters, the legal issues, land acquisition, supporting infrastructure, phasing of the development and statutory requirements on both parties to the Agreement. Of most importance to Olympia & York was that built into the MBA is an upgraded and extended Docklands Light Railway and a major roads programme to be undertaken by the LDDC at public expenditure.

In an interview with International Business Week, Paul Reichmann, the senior partner of Olympia & York expressed confidence that Canary Wharf would be successful in 1990. He described the partnership they were involved in as putting up the finance and the Government providing cheap land. He was sure Canary Wharf would be a success. He stated that the service industry revolution just beginning in Europe and as banking, insurance and trading companies flourished, they would have to become competitive in the global market. Since office space in Europe's big cities was relatively inadequate next to that of most North American cities, Europe was still at a relatively stage of renewal and London would be the business capital of Europe, and possibly of the world. Once committed to the scheme, Olympia & York and the LDDC launched a major promotion of Canary Wharf as a financial centre to rival the City of London. Never before had London seen such a promotional campaign as that for Canary Wharf. The LDDC considered that Canary Wharf represented London's Eastern extension to the City of London. It would reinforce London's pre-eminence in the financial world.

Momentum for Docklands

The Canary Wharf project was the initiative that provided the springboard for the whole momentum that was at that time pulsing through Docklands. The dramatic scale had of course proved Docklands position as an essential part of Central London property scheme, doubling the size of the market. Government Ministers also supported and promoted Canary Wharf. It was stated that London is bursting at the seams and they had to find somewhere to accommodate that growth. The only way to go was east and that was the whole of Docklands and not just Canary Wharf was about. The whole balance of London would change with effect to maintain and will maintain London as the main financial centre in the world and to consolidate it as a financial centre of Europe.

Speedy Approval of Application

When Olympia & York took over the development of Canary Wharf in July 1987, they adopted, almost in its entirety the original developers master plan for Canary Wharf, which was submitted to the LDDC in October 1985 and which won the LDDC's approval 15 days later! It is claimed that the LDDC did not consult the GLC, which is now demised, or the local Boroughs until the week it had given its approval. This master plan set out a comprehensive blue print for the entire development including details on design, planning and access. Enterprise Zone approvals were granted for 79% of this 71-acre site, which lay inside the Enterprise Zone. A planning application for that part of the Canary Wharf scheme inside the Enterprise Zone - half of Westferry Circus roundabout and approximately 1 million sq. ft of office development was submitted to the LDDC on 11 August 1986 by the original development consortium G Ware Travelstead and including two of Canary Wharf's sponsored tenants, Credit Suisse First Boston and Morgan Stanley International.

Despite lobbying by a combination of local community groups and local authorities, such as Newham and Greenwich, the Secretary of State refused to call in the planning application on the grounds that neither the local Planning Authority, the LDDC nor the local council Tower Hamlets supported this course of action. Tower Hamlets did not oppose the development because of the benefit that it considered might be gained from the development. A judicial review on behalf of the GLC took place in the High Court on 18 March 1986, the month when Government was demising the GLC. The GLC case had sought to quash the decision of the LDDC to give approval to a building of more than 120 ft in height in the Enterprise Zone and the approval of development within the Sensitive Boundary Sub-zone.

Aerial view of Canary Wharf and the Isle of Dogs looking east towards the Dome c2002

CANARY WHARF MASTER DESIGN

Creating a New City Initially of 50,000 People

Master Plan

A project of such a huge scale posed several challenges for the developers. Their aim was to create an integrated support system for a city initially of 50,000 people, provided with the highest quality working environment. To achieve this they had to bring together the financial and physical resources that would make the project a reality. An international team of architects, urban planners, engineers, landscape architects, graphic designers and historical consultants were employed, headed by the American consultants Skidmore, Owings & Merrill (SOM). They are internationally known for the urban design plans of Constitution Gardens in Washington DC and the design of major buildings in New York and other parts of the world. Their expertise, along with that of IM Pei American Consultants, YRM Planners, Architects and Engineers and many other organisations created the first Canary Wharf Master Plan including three Gothic style towers.

Extending over three-quarters of a mile from the River Thames to Blackwall Basin, Canary Wharf is composed of five neighbourhoods - Westferry Circus, Founders Court, Canary Concourse, Docklands Square and Blackwall Landing, each with a distinctive layout and character. The wharf itself is bounded by dock water on three sides. Within the development there are twenty four building sites encompassing over ten million square feet of commercial space, including offices and business trading floors, half million square feet of shops and restaurants, two hotels and a covered car park for more than 8,000 cars. All the buildings tie into Canary Wharf infrastructure - a multi-level service platform located beneath the street level and extending the full length of the wharf.

The Canary Wharf designers looked carefully at the character of London, observing both its formality and informality. Their aim was to make the places both memorable and comfortable. They considered that when people went there, they would see at one end, near the Thames, a large tree-ringed square surrounded by buildings, with one segment open to the waterfront. This is something they are not likely to forget!

Tower Design

The design of the high tower was conceived for three reasons. Firstly, it makes a statement; it expresses confidence not just to London, but to the world, confidence that it is still one of the world's great financial centres and the financial capital of Europe. Secondly, it gives a sense of place and identity. It helps to make the whole of Canary Wharf a destination. It would remind Londoners that a whole new district exists in their capital. Thirdly, and perhaps this was considered to be more crucial, by building high into the sky they would release land at ground level, so much land that the open spaces, the squares and the courts - the public places - at Canary Wharf would spread over no fewer than 25 acres of the 71 acre site. They were attempting to graft into London a whole new piece of a city, in an area where they didn't have to destroy buildings to do it. A lot of effort was expended by the developer to design an environment such that when people come to visit they feel this is not an alien place, but that they are comfortable; that it is a total environment for them. The real raw materials for making the place were 20 to 30 buildings, with 12 million square feet of office space. A thoroughly modern district is born, supposedly echoing the capital's valued characteristics. It is considered that there is a sense of London as one walks, the sense that just around the corner is somewhere else. You look across one of the great London squares to a road leading off to the other side, or through an archway into a courtyard in the City, and you just know that if you go as far as your eye takes, there you will find a view or a little corner that will amply reward the journey. The whole development by 2010 will change the face of London.

Office Flexibility

Problems of cost control and expense management dominate today's business world. Canary Wharf provides organisations with an opportunity to consolidate their activities under one roof, thereby centralising operations and easing the financial management process. The new premises give companies an efficient and productive workplace with maximum flexibility to meet continuing changes in staff and technology. The floor plans, with virtually columnless clear spans, permit optimal office layouts. Increased floor to ceiling heights allow for raised floors and suspended ceilings, thus providing efficient and unobtrusive cable distribution and ventilation systems. They provide the largest and most sophisticated dealing rooms on earth.

THE MASTER BUILDING AGREEMENT (MBA)

Ensuring Canary Wharf's Viability

Government Support

Canary Wharf became synonymous with Docklands in the mind of the LDDC and the Government. The development was essential to them and they did much to ensure its viability through Government subsidies and the provision of new transport systems to connect the scheme to the City and other parts of London. Olympia &York's initial proposals included over 10-million sq. ft. of net lettable commercial space of which 95% was inside the Enterprise Zone on the Isle of Dogs. Of the floor space half a million sq. ft. was for the retail and shopping industry. They were all eligible for capital allowances. However, it was not just the construction of buildings that was eligible for these allowances. Much else was also eligible including roads within the development, as they were access roads and considered an integral part of the building. The rates exemption on Canary Wharf was relatively small because much of the space that has already been let would not have been occupied before 1993.

As at January 1992 only about half of Phase 1 had been let and 22% of Phase 2 totalled approximately 2¹/₂ million sq. ft. Of this only a third was occupied for up to six months during 1992 when the Enterprise Zone expired. The total exemption up to April 1992 was estimated several hundred millions of pounds. Substantial allowances were claimed on construction costs, which included the cost of site preparations, service roads and car parking. The cost of construction for Phase 1 was estimated at £4million. Since only nearly 80% of the construction lies within the Enterprise Zone, then 80% of £4billion is approximately £3.2 billion. With Corporation Tax payable at 33% capital allowances were potentially available at Canary Wharf were estimated at £1 billion. This amount was considered excessive by the London Boroughs who thought that it was one third of all expenditure by the Department of Employment during 1990/91.

Master Building Agreement

These allowances formed part of the Master Building Agreement (MBA) and was a development agreement signed between the LDDC and Olympia & York which sets out legal issues and matters of land acquisition, supporting infrastructure, and phasing of the development and statutory requirements on both parties to the Agreement. The MBA was signed on 17 July 1987. The press release stated that the price paid for the 20 acres of LDDC-owned land on Canary Wharf equated to £1 million per acre, of which 8 million was payable in cash and 12 million was represented by the developers commitments to various on-site works on public benefits. The land price taken with all other aspects of the agreement yielded a value at least equivalent to the market value of the LDDC land as at April 1987.

It was stated that Olympia & York had agreed to contribute £68 million towards the Docklands Light Railway to the City. The on-site works of public benefits referred to public spaces, internal roads and riverside walkways, all of which were also eligible for capital allowances. They were integral and necessary parts of the project. Some considered that Olympia & York was given £12 million towards the construction of necessary works and on which tax breaks were claimed. Under these conditions Olympia & York effectively was considered to be £400,000 per acre for LDDC-owned land. Some also considered that the price of land on the Isle of Dogs was higher, at least £3 million per acre. In November 1988 a site on North Quay just facing Canary Wharf was sold at £5 million per acre. The National audit office report of May 1988 on urban development corporations criticised the sale of land at Canary Wharf at £400,000 per acre. It stated that the selling price of the land was maintained at this figure throughout negotiations, although land prices in the Isle of Dogs was rising rapidly, admittedly as a result of this scheme.

Arrangements for Upgrading Transport

The financial arrangements for upgrading the Docklands Light Railway in capacity by tenfold and the extension of the railway to Bank station were part of the Canary Wharf MBA. Olympia & York contributed £68million for the Bank station and its extension. The total cost for the extension and upgrading at the time was estimated to be £282 million. The Docklands highway that runs from the East London River Crossing to the Highway in Wapping in the West was also a part of the MBA contract. The cost for the highway was estimated to be £651 million early in the 1990s. The Poplar Link Road formed part of the Docklands highway with the Limehouse Link at one end providing a link into the City and Central London and the lower Lea crossing at the other end providing a link to the Royal Docks, M11 and M25.

At around £250 million the Limehouse Link was the most expensive part of the Docklands highway. Under an accord agreed between the LDDC and Tower Hamlets Council in June 1998, tenants living in four estates affected by the Poplar were rehoused by the LDDC. The Limehouse Link is relatively the most expensive stretch of road ever to be built in the U.K. The 1.1mile road was built using a cut and cover technique. Cost related to construction and did not include the LDDC's expenditure in housing and rehousing displaced tenants of Tower Hamlets. The method of construction of the Link freed 14 acres of land above the tunnel, which the LDDC had intentions of using to develop private housing.

Jubilee Line Extension

Canary Wharf Company was adamant that long term future of the development couldn't be secured without linking it into the London Underground network. The Government also was determined to back Canary Wharf in its decision to favour the Jubilee Line extension, as part of the strategic transport planning for London as a whole. The initial cost of the scheme was estimated to be £1 billion. And the Government made it a condition for the go-ahead for Olympia & York to contribute 40%. This meant a contribution of £400 million. The contribution was for £100 million to be paid within three years. The remainder was to be paid at regular intervals once the service is running over a period of up to 20 years. The actual final cost when the line was opened at the end of 1999 was estimated to be well over £2billion.

Aerial View of Construction Site 1988

Start of Phase I at Canary Wharf - In the heart of London Docklands on the Isle of Dogs, the largest commercial development in the world started in May 1988. With the scale and scope of Canary Wharf undertaking, it was estimated that the entire project would take between 7-10 years to complete. As a consequence, it was divided into three phases.

From air or from the ground, even the initial view at the beginning of construction was impressive. The degree of activity was virtually unprecedented in London's commercial history. Well over 50 cranes marked the site of Phase I and over 1000 construction workers were busy everywhere. The project was served by a concrete batching plant at Limehouse Reach which

This aerial view was issued by Olympia & York in 1988 at the commencement of the construction. All writing text refer to that date.

Once Docklands Square and adjacent open spaces are completed, during the second phase of construction, they will provide a venue for live music which can be enjoyed from the pavement and waterside cafes all around the Square.

Once the whole development is completed, a total of 500,000 square feet of shops and restaurants housed in sky-lit arcades and walkways will provide an attractive and comprehensive shopping destination for both the work force at Canary Wharf and residents of surrounding areas.

The DLR runs right through the Canary Wharf site. A glass covered station is being designed and constructed by Olympia & York in cooperation with Docklands Light Railway Ltd.

Marine piling, currently underway, shows the acoustic shrouds, or mufflers, in action, helping to deaden the noise.

To ensure that mud does not create a hazard on the roads, every lorry leaving the site has its wheels washed by a special machine.

Canary Wharf has an up-to-date medical centre, staffed by qualified nurses who provide full-time first aid and nursing care for the workforce. Sister Elizabeth Henderson is in charge of the unit, and has her own radio frequency so that she can respond immediately to any calls for assistance on site.

Olympia & York has designed and constructed this relief road to enable traffic on the Redbrick Road to be diverted, avoiding the need for a traffic light controlled contra-flow system.

This relief road is intended to take Westferry Road traffic to enable construction of Westferry Circus to be completed.

CANARY WHARF

OFFICE HOURS

Community Relations

8:30 AM – 12:00 NOON   1:00 PM – 5:00 PM

Telephone: FREEPHONE 0800 289115

Recruitment Office

10:00 AM – 1:00 PM   2:00 PM – 4:00 PM

Telephone: FREEPHONE 0800 289114

produced up to 2000 cubic metres of concrete each day, and the work continued at an unflagging pace across the whole site. Naturally, a construction activity of this scale produced enormous volume of unwanted material which subsequently had to be removed. To achieve this, a fleet of river barges was employed to remove the waste every week , while in counterpoint, over 100 piles were hammered into the ground for foundation each month. The steel was also starting to rise for the tower and the other buildings situated around Cabot Square.

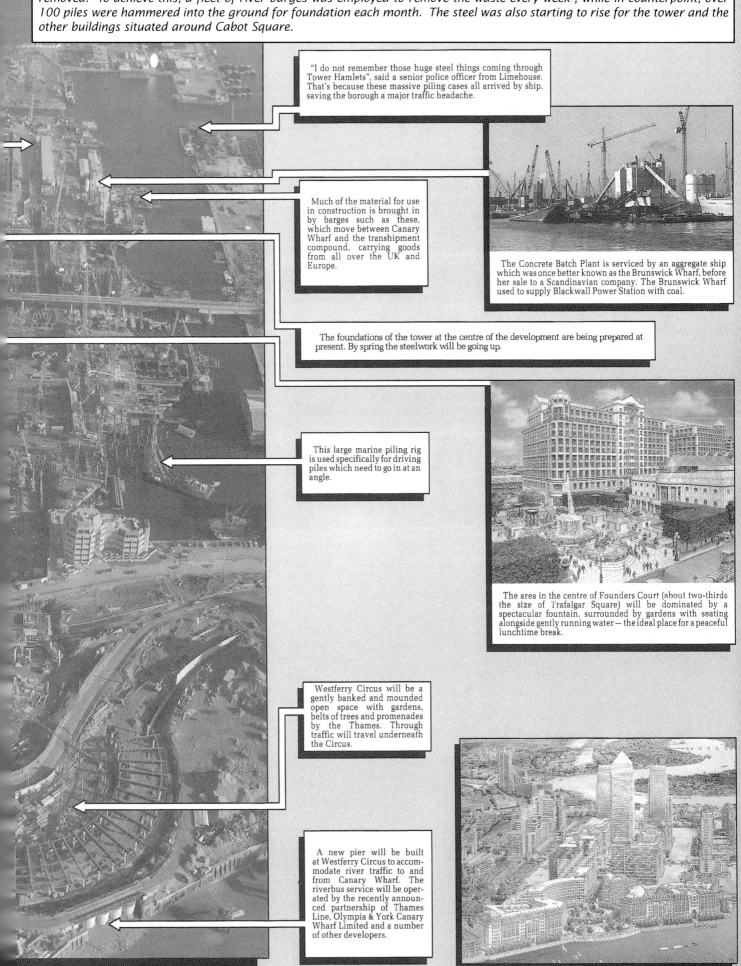

"I do not remember those huge steel things coming through Tower Hamlets", said a senior police officer from Limehouse. That's because these massive piling cases all arrived by ship, saving the borough a major traffic headache.

Much of the material for use in construction is brought in by barges such as these, which move between Canary Wharf and the transhipment compound, carrying goods from all over the UK and Europe.

The Concrete Batch Plant is serviced by an aggregate ship which was once better known as the Brunswick Wharf, before her sale to a Scandinavian company. The Brunswick Wharf used to supply Blackwall Power Station with coal.

The foundations of the tower at the centre of the development are being prepared at present. By spring the steelwork will be going up.

This large marine piling rig is used specifically for driving piles which need to go in at an angle.

The area in the centre of Founders Court (about two-thirds the size of Trafalgar Square) will be dominated by a spectacular fountain, surrounded by gardens with seating alongside gently running water — the ideal place for a peaceful lunchtime break.

Westferry Circus will be a gently banked and mounded open space with gardens, belts of trees and promenades by the Thames. Through traffic will travel underneath the Circus.

A new pier will be built at Westferry Circus to accommodate river traffic to and from Canary Wharf. The riverbus service will be operated by the recently announced partnership of Thames Line, Olympia & York Canary Wharf Limited and a number of other developers.

RELOCATION OF FIRMS TO CANARY WHARF

Commercial Development of Isle of Dogs

Canary Wharf First Tenant

Shortly after construction started, Merrill Lynch Company signed on to relocate its London headquarters to Canary Wharf. The US Investment Bank was the first new tenant to commit itself to the £4 billion scheme since its launch three years earlier, with pre-lets already agreed with Credit Suisse First Boston and Morgan Stanley. The deal provided a major boost for the Wharf and Docklands area as a whole as there was a fear that the office market was flagging. The rental was for a 25 year lease commencing 1991, when the building was due to be finished, on half of Founders Court 2, a ten-storey building, to accommodate the 1200 employees relocated from the City. The philosophy was for a financial services firm to compete in the market place to take an active role in controlling costs. The Canary Wharf development enabled the company to significantly reduce its infrastructure costs in London. They were aware that if they stayed in the City, a rent review in a few years could more than double their rental.

However, there was more to the deal than a straightforward letting. Olympia & York agreed to buy up Merrill Lynch's office lease in the City, which had twenty years to run. Olympia & York arranged similar transactions with its World Financial Centre in Battery Park, Manhattan, including a deal with Merrill Lynch that relocated its headquarters and 6000 staff to 3 million sq.ft. of the New York World Trade Centre. It was also thought that Merrill Lynch had taken on an equity stake in Canary Wharf as it did in the World Financial Centre.

Relocation of Texaco to Canary Wharf

Canary Wharf gained a high-profile tenant, Texaco, the giant multi-national oil company, when it decided in 1989 to move its UK headquarters from Knightsbridge to Docklands in three years time, mid 1992. Nearly 1000 staff had to move into a 20,000 sq.metre purpose-built office on eight floors at the western end of Canary Wharf.

Knowing that their lease in Knightsbridge would not be renewed, the company spent three years exploring a new location. The case for Canary Wharf became compelling because it was financially competitive and offered a superb working environment. While BP and Phillips Petroleum had moved out of London in recent years, Texaco reversed the trend with a brave decision to go against the herd. Overcoming the fears of their employees was, however, a significant task for the developers of Canary Wharf, Olympia & York. Once models and architects' drawings were used to show the inside of the building and shopping facilities, Texaco, like other clients, always asked about transportation and staff travel. It was probably the biggest single issue

Fortunately, Texaco were making their enquiries at a time when Docklands systems were beginning to take shape, though late. During the end of 1988, the transport jigsaw puzzle had come into place. Work to lengthen station platforms of the Docklands Light Railway (DLR) was in hand day and night to operate two-unit trains. The new DLR station at Canary Wharf, standing next to a four-storey shopping complex and food hall was well advanced.

Engineers were also digging tunnels to extend the DLR from its terminus at Tower Hill down to Bank station in the heart of the City, connecting it directly to London's underground network. Olympia & York was paying a considerable proportion of multi-million pound cost but it regarded it as the cornerstone of the Canary Wharf project. Geological problems and the complexity of tunnelling beneath the most crowded parts of the City caused problems and delays on the nine-month programme.

Another tunnel, this time carrying a road, had received Government authorisation. The Limehouse Link Road was planned to start just on the eastern side of News International Printing Works in Wapping and to surface within 200 metres of Canary Wharf. It would join a new road crossing the River Lea and out past London City Airport in the Royal Docks. Here, the owners, Mowlem, had lodged a second application to operate a BAe 146 jet aircraft. It was predicted that the Civil Aviation Authority would grant approval and the airport would be operating with jets by 1991. This would open virtually all the European cities to Docklands.

Best Headquarters

Realistically, most Texaco employees were more concerned about public transport than the executive jets. The biggest news for Canary Wharf was the expected announcement in November 1988 of a six-mile extension of the Jubilee Line tube trains east from Waterloo station to the Isle of Dogs with Canary Wharf Company footing part of the bill. By tunnelling beneath existing British Rail tracks, many planning and property complications could be avoided.

The Chairman of Texaco believed that Canary Wharf was the best that Europe had to offer. They thought that out of the contractor's mud and concrete would rise a complete landscaped environment, which would outclass anything else in Britain. Ironically, thus far it was the foreign businesses that felt this way and had the vision to plan moves to Canary Wharf. Olympia & York themselves placed their European Headquarters there, replacing rented offices scattered around Westminster. Morgan Stanley, Credit Suisse First Boston Bank, Merrill Lynch and Texaco had signed for 1.45 million sq. ft of space, out of the total to be completed in the first phase of the eight buildings which was 4 million sq. ft.

Were Londoners and the British business world being too conservative and thus missing the boat? Analysts thought it was probably easier for a North American executive who did not have any particular image of the East End of London to accept what was being created there. Also the British did not do a lot of pre-lets with projects as big as a corporate headquarters, but once one came, they all followed suit.

There is no doubt that the consequent development at Canary Wharf has been a significant factor in enhancing London as a financial services centre. It has also enhanced British influence in commerce and that means jobs, improvement and prosperity and all that flows from them, benefiting not only the local people but also everyone else in the UK.

The lobby of the Tower at One Cabot Square is three storeys high and contains 32 lifts in 4 banks providing access to the 48 storeys of offices. Clad in nearly 200 tonnes of marble, from Guatemala and Italy, it is the impressive entrance point for all companies having office space in the Tower.

Five lasers, 14 search lights and 800 floodlights ensured that Canary Wharf gave a unique and spectacular welcome on New Year's Eve of 1992. The light show was accompanied by foghorns and fireworks.

Canary Wharf Riverside, Isle of Dogs, overlooking Limehouse Reach of the Thames, is the only residential development at the Wharf. It comprises of 322 apartments, health club and spa and Four Seasons Hotel, a five star complex with restaurants, c 2000.

IN THE WAKE OF CANARY WHARF

The Year of Arrival for Docklands

Increased Investment

Further expenditure by Government and the promise of creating more enterprise zones around the country strengthened the commitment to Canary Wharf. This was a clear official indication to developers in Docklands that London's Wall Street on Water had become a reality! Travelstead was unable to fund his dramatic scheme, and it was taken over in July 1987 by one of the largest North American developers, Olympia scale of development York, based in Toronto, Canada.

Canary Wharf generated the case for a level of infrastructure which nobody in Docklands or the Government had ever contemplated nor did the Government had any intention of funding it fully. The giant plans for Canary Wharf were disclosed in 1985 and approximately 18 months later investment completed and committed in Docklands exceeded £1billion. The following year it had grown to over £2billion, bringing the cumulative total to £4.4billion since the Corporation started in 1981.

New Buildings

The 1987 Stock Market crash had little impact on the confidence of investors in Docklands. By the beginning of 1988, Canary Wharf construction had already started, and they were very few large undeveloped sites left in the Enterprise Zone. Outside of Canary Wharf a total of 2.7million sq ft (260,000m2) of development, mainly office space was either committed or under construction. The Charterhouse Group 1.7million sq ft (162 m2); impressive Harbour Exchange office development which involved the demolition of the West India House occupied at the time by the LDDC. Other developments included the second phase of South Quay Plaza, City Harbour, Glengall Bridge, Scandinavian Centre and Meridian Gate, all in the Enterprise Zone around the South Quay.

Although it was maintained that Canary Wharf and the Isle of Dogs development would be a compliment rather than a challenge to the Square Mile, the expansion on the Isle of Dogs alarmed the City of London. The Planning Committee lifted the restraints on office development in the City and research proved that the fears of the City of London were groundless, in fact in 1997, the best year for Docklands, lettings reached nearly 2million square feet, compared to over 4million in the City of London. But a far higher proportion of the Docklands property was modern and air conditioned.

Move of Journalists

Meanwhile, the Docklands boom continued in the late 1980s with construction of the East India office complex at Blackwall and in 1987 the first phase of South Quay Plaza was completed and journalists and other staff of the Daily Telegraph moved in. The magazine publishers "The Builder" group moved into Great Eastern enterprise, Barclays moved into Hertsmere House a year later. Betwen 1987 and 1990 it appeared that the second wave of regeneration was taking place, particularly the prospect of pulling down some of the shed like structures from the early days of the Enterprise Zone south of the West India Docks and replacing them with taller higher density buildings.

Year of Arrival

The year 1987 was the year of arrival for Docklands according to the London Docklands Development Corporation's land review at the time to coincide with the opening of the Docklands Light Railway. With the thrust of Docklands new public system finally in place and the opening of London City Airport on target for later that year, Dockland was now considered firmly on the map. The wave of demand which existed for site from major developers made land prices increase fivefold in the previous eighteen months and the new developments were responding to the quality and scope of the original Canary Wharf concept. Most dynamic of all Canary Wharf proposals had triggered second wave redevelopments of existing space almost before that space had been completed and occupied. The LDDC also reported the three major developments consortia who had come up with schemes for the Royal Docks.

Departure of Chief Executive

The publication of the LDDC annual report in 1987 was accompanied by the news that Reg Ward, LDDC Chief Executive, was definitely leaving Docklands, confirming reports that had been circulating the property world for sometime. He would retire on 1 Jan 1988. Mr Ward was the inspiration for what had happened in Docklands during the previous six years. His imagination and energy was very hard to match and it was particularly fitting that his decision to leave the LDDC was announced shortly following the signing of Canary Wharf Agreement a project which Mr Ward identified with from its conception.

Complementing the City

Although the City was slow to respond to the opportunity to occupy major buildings on the Isle of Dogs the intervention of Olympia & York with clear development timetables seemed sure to change this situation soon afterwards. Canary Wharf had exceptional competitive advantages over Central London, it was predicted it would succeed because it offers a unique combination of size, (units of 500,000 sq ft plus), cost (lower rents and lower prices for owner/occupied), specification (shell and core completions allowing occupiers to fit out to their own specifications), flexibility (sites not restricted by the proximity of other buildings or strict planning regulations) an environment not matched with many City buildings which have a high level of pollution due to traffic. Many saw Canary Wharf developing on an international basis complementing the City, rather than competing with it.

COMMENCEMENT OF CONSTRUCTION

The Caged Canary Set to Fly

Site Preparations

In September 1986, preliminary works were well under way for the largest and most difficult property development ever attempted in the United Kingdom, even though there was still no guarantee that the giant Canary Wharf scheme would go ahead. For the first time, five of the UK's major contractors formed a joint venture to cope with the project, a massive, but controversial Canary Wharf office, retail and hotel complex which was proposed for the Isle of Dogs. The US banking and finance organisations, behind the scheme would not commit themselves until the City extension for the Docklands Light Railway brought preliminary approval. Then construction started immediately, in line with the fast North American procedures to which the developer was accustomed. To this end, the UK contracting consortium, established a joint project office, site preparations were in progress and consulting engineers and architects were working out detailed designs. The effort was not one-sided. Apart from Consultants' fees, the American developer was meeting most of the cost of the 18 strong project office staff and all of the cost of site works which included demolition of existing sheds, service diversions and ground investigations.

Canary Wharf was considered a huge development, covering 28 hectares costing up to £4billion. It was a welcome sight for hungry building and civil engineering firms and it was considered that the effects on the surrounding area were likely to be immense. The sight was just a series of rundown, empty warehouses, except for the Limehouse Studio, at the western end of the wharf. Once the news of the development spread and the building work started, it was easier to get any development to happen. The whole of Dockland was driven by it. It was the point of no return. Once official approval was given, Canary Wharf Development company signed the London Dockland Development Corporation's Master Building Agreement, the contract binding the US group to develop in Canary Wharf.

No Public Enquiry

Local councils and community groups reckoned that the LDDC did not give enough consideration to visual environmental and social effects of Canary Wharf, which included three tall towers. The Greater London Council (GLC) started a separate legal action against the LDDC, before it was abolished on 1st April 1986. The GLC's case was dismissed but Greenwich, with support from Newham and Southwark Council appealed. There was little prospect of overturning the original verdict, as the purpose of development corporations such as LDDC is to encourage investment by removing as many planning obstacles as possible. In addition Canary Wharf was in an Enterprise Zone with even fewer restrictions. However the developer Olympia & York was watching the proceeding closely and had declared that the project would be cancelled if a public enquiry was called, as this could incur delays. The court case was just one of the aspects of the UK planning process which had amazed the developers. The group had even found the LDDC's slimmed down development regulations frustrating, compared to the high-speed US construction scene.

Alien Procedures to Americans

Alien procedures to the Americans had involved such oddities in their eyes as discussions with the Royal Fine Art Commission and English Heritage over the appearance of the scheme and its affect on existing buildings and structures around the site. Consultation with local community groups had also been a new experience with the developer, more accustomed to promoting the slick Manhattan Towers were speed of construction and upmarket image were paramount. Local groups such as Docklands Forum submitted a list of clauses they would like to see included in the Master Building Agreement. These included a requirement for construction firms and occupiers of the finished buildings to employ 40% of their staff from people living in the five Dockland boroughs, of Greenwich, Southwark, Newham, Tower Hamlets and Lewisham. They insisted that the developer, contractors and occupiers should contribute to the cost of training local people. The forum also wanted to restrict deliveries of materials and site activities to between the hours of 8am and 6pm weekdays only. It was understood that the developer was willing to employ local labour, although would have been probably unwilling to bind itself and future occupants of Canary Wharf to an exact proportion. Restrictions on construction times and movements of material could cause more problems and the timescale for completion was tight and contractors were planning on working 12 hours a day. The developers kept the scheme under way, despite all the difficulties, as they thought there was a prospect of substantial profits.

American Consultants

London is one of the most important markets in the world for financial services with its significance enhanced by location midway between the trading time zones of New York and Tokyo. English is also the language of the financial world. The high technology and advanced telecommunications needed for wheeling and dealing in today's money markets, demanded purpose-built structures with huge 4.3metre floor to ceiling height to accommodate raised floors concealing huge volumes of cables and other services. Floor areas needed to be very large to take the hundreds of visual display units which were used to buy and sell money, bonds, shares and a range of commodities. These parameters did not sit in the City's crammed and narrow streets which was the reason why the US group formulated plans for Canary Wharf.

The developer drew up proposals at the beginning of 1985 with the Chicago office of USA multi-disciplinary practice, Skidmore, Owings and Merrill. By May 1985 a UK transport consultant, had been appointed to provide assistance to the American consultants and give US architects an insight into British codes of practice, building regulations and other aspects of the UK construction industry.

Canary Wharf Phase I Construction
On London's Isle of Dogs, a spectacular construction project started in May 1988: the Canary Wharf new city on water. At its heart, the tallest tower in Britain (right) was rising rapidly storey by storey. This aerial view was taken on 24 February 1990.

THE BIGGEST BUILDING SITE IN EUROPE

80 Contractors and 1000 Workers

There is not a lot of height for the infrastructure works that formed the backbone of the Wharf even though it was one of the most expensive contracts of construction. Getting the work done also demanded the co-operation from a variety of contractors. Although the Tower had become the symbol of Canary Wharf, it was necessary to lay the infrastructure package of roads, car parks, retail space, running down the spine of the wharf from west to east. Estimates of the works amounted to approximately £200 million. Construction of the infrastructure started in May 1988. The original plan for the job was that the roads would take all construction traffic, but before those could be put in, all of the piling and concrete decks for the buildings where they stand over the water had to be completed and the floating, piling rigs moved out of the way.

Once the vast army of workers, plant and machinery was mobilised on the wharf, fortnightly meetings of the management contractors were held to discuss any problems. Until the roads eased congestion, the plot of land taken up by the infrastructure works was a three dimensional maze of access ramps and Bailey bridges. In the middle of it were piling rigs, bantonite, mixing plant, excavators, crawler cranes, dump trucks and thousands of workers. At its peak there were 80 contractor staff supervising about 1000 workers. The plan was to cater for the complex needs of all the contractors on site. What happened was to progress a north roadway as far as could be up to a level, put in the sewers, cover it with a temporary surface and then transfer all the traffic to this north road. This meant that the south road could be constructed to finish level and then swop the traffic over and get back to finish the top of the north side road. The finished level of the roadways is about 5m above the old level of Canary Wharf. Foamed concrete was used as fill material between the old and new levels.

Underground Car Park

Travelstead 's original idea in May 1985 was to get as many cars on to Canary Wharf as possible. So the notion grew of putting more and more car parks over the Docklands Light Railway. One of the problems was this that the buildings were stuck up in the air and did not relate to the major asset of Canary Wharf, mainly the water. When Olympia & Wharf took over the project in 1987 they simplified the design considerably by lowering the height of the road network to allow the buildings to relate to the water. Olympia & York created a two-level road system. The main spine road runs 5m above the old quay. Beneath it are the roads that give access to the subterranean five-storey car parking areas or for service vehicles calling at the eight Canary Wharf buildings.

The infrastructure included a 4 or 5 floor car park running along Canary Wharf, with a service road on top, plus an access road above that which would give visitors and the public, transport access to the office buildings. The roads were piled out onto the dock on either side. At their western end, the roads linked in with a two level roundabout at Westferry Circus on the Thames riverfront. Sewers, water, electricity, gas and communications were installed at this stage.

Foundation of Buildings

Another detailed design consideration related to the foundation of the building that straddles Canary Wharf grade 1 listed sugar warehouses and dock walls. Built in 1800 by the engineer William Jessop, the dock wall got its name because of its convex shape that allowed boats to snuggle up against the quay. Although virtually none of the wall is now visible, its listed status ensured that demolition was out of the question. First, the wall was stabilised by fill material being discharged into the dock to form an underwater embankment. Crushed demolition rubble from the old buildings that had stood on the wharf was used for the fill.

Then came the task of designing the piles to take the enormous loads of the 12-20 storey buildings that sit out over the docks. Virtually all of the footprints of the buildings are under water with just a strip a few metres wide over the ground on the quayside. Two types of piles were therefore used. Over the water, steel piles around 20 metre long and diameters of 1.25 and 1.5 metre capable of carrying loads up to 800 tonnes were driven to tow into the layer of Thanet sand. The upper 6-7 metres of silt, gravel and clay within the power castings were removed, steel reinforcement cages added and concrete poured into the shaft. Because the top 15 m of the piles are exposed to the dock water and silt and will corrode in time, 25mm sq. bars are welded to the inside of the casting lower down. These act as share quays to transfer the load onto the concrete to the lower section of steel casing when the steel higher up eventually corrodes.

Equally innovative is the design of the land piles. These are base grouted board piles, also founded in the Thanet sand. The piles were bored and concreted and grout pumped at the pressure of at least 30 bars down tubes fixed to the reinforcement cage. The pressurised grout discharged out around the base of the pile to fill any voids in the Thanet sand, preventing any settlement problems.

Enormous Project

One of the first jobs after site work started was the construction of a temporary Bailey bridge northward from Canary Wharf to the North Quay. The Fire Brigade insisted on the bridge, so that there were two points of access to the wharf. At the time Limehouse Film Studios, an existing tenant of the site would also use the bridge, until it moved into alternative accommodation, as well as construction traffic. In 1986, it was predicted that Phase 1 of the project of around 200,000m² of office space would be completed by early 1989. Actually the construction started in May 1988 and was completed in January 1992. The Americans had taken on a development, which was enormous. They had taken it by the scruff of the neck and had gone a long way down the road to getting it off the ground. Some engineers considered that UK developers would have taken much longer or else abandoned the project.

TRANSFORMING THE WHARF INTO A CITY

The Developers became the Project Managers

Design Changes

There were many changes when Olympia & York took from Grant Ware Travelstead as the developer of the £4billion Canary Wharf project in July 1987. For the initial infrastructure works, Travelstead had selected five of the UK's largest contractors who thought they would be doing the bulk of the building work at the Wharf. There was also many smaller British firms that wanted to cash in on the Canadian developer that had never worked in this country before. By the time the first pile was driven on the wharf in November 1987, Olympia & York had already made other plans and showed itself as no respecter of previous deals. The consortium of five big contractors, who thought they would be getting the lion's share were given the building of Westferry roundabout at approximately £70million. Olympia & York and the original consultants, Thomas Skidmore Owings and Merrill, set out redesigning Travelstead's ideas to make the 8 major buildings of phase 1 relate more closely to the water environment.

Project Management

Project managers were appointed who understood the attitudes and approaches taken by North American developers, while access was given to directory of sub-contractors as well as bringing on board the UK firm versed in construction management and management contracting. Orders were placed around the world for suppliers and subcontractors and even though Olympia & York decided that the way into the UK would be into management contracting, British management contractors did not have it all their own way. Canada's second largest contractor was invited over by Olympia & York to team up with other British contractors.

The bankers Morgan Stanley chose to stick with its own original intention to project management the construction of their own building. Adding to the difficulties were the steel work strikes, the sheer logistical problems created when constructing eight buildings totalling 600,000 sq metres in just over $3^1/2$ years and forming from scratch a construction company capable of turning around £300 million a year.

Olympia & York was not afraid to speak against what it saw against deficiency in British construction practices. Having brought successfully phase 1 in on time and on budget, the Company was unrepentant about the approach they adopted. Olympia & York was portrayed as a hands-on client and a very knowledgeable one.

Prompt Payments

They were prompt for measured work but those who had submitted claims or been issued with variation orders reported much longer payment periods. The Company employed a total staff of around 600 plus that would probably place them among the top ten construction firms in the world. Part of the success has been attributed to the breakdown of individual identities and the reference always to Canary Wharf culture. In the early days some organisations were treating this construction in the same way as they would be building separately somewhere else and were looking for claims opportunities. That attitude took a bit of time to shift.

Contractors that adapted easily in the early days of the project were rewarded with peak business. Good contractors with slightly higher prices kept jobs on the Wharf. Anyone coming onto the project had to go through a learning curve of getting used to the way the Company worked. Some where less successful than others. As they did in the past in the USA, the developer took over as construction managers for the five buildings on the second phase of the development along Westferry Circus roundabout. The Company considered construction as mostly human being related - there were good people, average people and not so good people in any organisation. Their theory was always to understand the strengths and weaknesses of organisations and individuals and support the weaknesses where needed and exploit the strengths. That was the art the developers practiced until the end.

Towering Achievements

In 1802 the West India Docks were opened with a flourish. The Docks and the magnificent warehouses were celebrated nationally and worldwide. In 1992 celebrations took place for the completion of the glittering group of buildings that made the first phase of Canary Wharf in London Docklands. Although separated by 190 years, both are pinnacles of their age. Building the first wet docks in London in two years was an unmatched triumph of 19th century engineering. The creation of a new city nucleus of eight large buildings in a fully landscaped setting in well under four years is without doubt the most heroic feat of engineering and building during the 20th century. And not only in terms of construction, the engineering services and infrastructure that fuel, warm, air conditioning, keep safe, move people and connect Canary Wharf to the outside world are also an unmatched triumph of latest technology.

Lessons for Construction

The British construction industry has more to learn from the experiences of this project and to reflect upon. None of the standards met the forms of contracts of methods of measurements were used, they were all imported and obviously not suitable for this giant task. But there is no doubt that the methods of Canary Wharf could, and should be, tailored to British tastes. British taste is also occasionally offended by the North American project managers. The recipe of potent mixture of loyalty to those who performed to exacting standards and butt kicking bluntness to those didn't. One day when the dust has settled, Canary Wharf will be recognised as one of the great adventures in design and construction internationally. It stands as a tribute to all the personnel involved. Everyone from the owners of Canary Wharf at the time down to the stone masons should be proud to say, they helped to build Canary Wharf - a monument to endeavour that will probably stand much longer than any other project of the 20th century.

No 10 Cabot Square (FC2) has an unusually large floor space and the first two floors have particularly high ceilings.   There is an elegant atrium in the centre to give a feeling of spaciousness and light to the offices which surround it. The atrium has reverbation frequencies on par with those of St Paul's Cathedral.

Prised in two halves by the Docklands Light Railway, the FC4 (20 Cabot Square) and FC6 (30 Cabot Square) buildings with their Vermont marble cladding, form a grand canyon entrance to Canary Wharf from the south.

Cabot Square

This complex forms the dramatic Barbican gateway into Canary Wharf on the north west side. The buildings have much in common and they both have an L-shaped footprint, the majority of which overhangs the former West India Import Dock. Both buildings which are of similar size were designed by USA architects. Like its neighbour across the road, the complex has a tenant the firm that backed Grant Ware Travelstead's original plan and stayed on after Olympia & York took over. The Suisse First Boston bank has taken about one third of the building. Basically the largest building is 18 storeys high, with plant at the top, but nothing is unique. Apart from fitting out the lobby and lift cars, it is normal shell and core building for trading. The 65 metre wide by 110 metre deep building, of which 3/4 rest on steel piles rising from the waters of the dock is second only to the Tower in height. The building is distinguished from the outside by the number of step-backs in the cladding.

Granite was shipped across the Atlantic from Georgia and Jura with limestone trucked from Germany to the Belgian home of the contractor. There workers fashioned the stone into pre-cast concrete panels before the last leg of the journey across the Channel. At the same time in Belgium the steel frame was fabricated. About 30 Portuguese workers were employed to cut and fix external and internal decorative stone on the building. Beautifully cut stone, sand blasted or honed features in the lift lobbies. The building has 16 passenger lifts.

10 Cabot Square

The visitors guide at Canary Wharf during construction had a novel way of impressing people when they were taken around this building. They took them first inside this spectacular atrium in the heart of the 83,000 sq metre building. They kept sharply on the exquisite inlaid marble floor and a few seconds later the sounds reverberated around the 9-storey high atrium. The sounds were similar to the reverberation frequency of St Paul's Cathedral. It was considered to be a marvellous place to hear a really good solo singer! The atrium is certainly the most stunning feature of this building interior and is a blend of marble, bronze grills and delicate gilt work. On the outside of the building the pre-cast cladding has to be seen in close up to appreciate the craftsmanship. Classical design has helped soften what is an enormous building. With a net office space of nearly 61,000 sq metres, it is second only to the Tower in net lettable terms, but it can boost a footprint nearly double the size.

25 The North Colonnade

British architects broke the North American stronghold on Canary Wharf architecture when their design for this building was unveiled in April 1989. The smooth building outline is achieved with a curtain wall that lets natural light into the 15 storey block on the Wharf. On two elevations of the building, the north and the south, glazing was originally specified was changed to plain glass. The structural silicone glazing system from Italy was designed around a frame within frame concept that allows the glass which extends from floor to ceiling to be replaced from inside the building. The grey Canadian granite spandrel panels that coated the floor slabs can also be changed at a later date without tipping the complete curtain wall. Again Portuguese and Brazilian workers were used on this building.

20 Cabot Square

This building has steel beams stub ends that stick out through the sheer walls of white Vermont marble cladding dressing both this building and its smaller adjacent building across the DLR tracks. This gives the impression that the two buildings have been set apart according to the architect. The white painted beam ends adds something to the rear elevation that face one another from either side of the railway. They contain two over height floors designed to serve as dealing rooms. The roof scape of the west building is designed to be looked down on. There is none of the usual clutter of window cleaning cradles, cooling towers or ugly plant rooms littering the roof. The air conditioning plant is hid behind louvred cladding.

25 Cabot Square

This building is the new European headquarters for US Bank Morgan Stanley International and was built by the bank itself. Work on piling the foundations for the 14 storey building started in November 1988. Architects and engineers, Skidmore Owings and Merrill's design for this building comes closest to the original design guidelines for an agreed in principle between the LDDC, Travelstead initially, but then Olympia & York, for the master plan on Canary Wharf. The guidelines specify that the buildings should have some form of horizontal expression at the point of about 11 metres above ground, the limit of peripheral vision for a pedestrian and then a major step-back of about 32 metres of street level. They also suggested colour graduation for the main elevations with lighter stones at the bottom and darker tones above.

Cabot Place and DLR station

In 1987 all that surrounded the Canary Wharf DLR station was waste land. The old station had two plain concrete platforms with bus shelter style canopies that only partially protected passengers from the weather, as they waited hopefully for a DLR train. In 1991 the old station had gone. Replacing it was a 22metre high parabolic arch of steel and glass covering the new station. Sculptured granite seats take the place of metal perches. The old bus shelters have been swept aside by buff coloured masonry that forms the walls of the retail areas that close in either side of the new station. The 9,5000 sq metres of retail space has two parts, Cabot Place east and west. Included in Cabot Place west is the Cabot Hall which is used for exhibitions, conferences and receptions. Either side of the main hall are smaller meeting rooms and they are wired up for the latest gadgetry such as video conferencing. Master craftsment had been at work creating the top hand curved hardwood doors that screen off one end of Cabot Square. A snub-nosed entrance greets visitors to the retail and conference hall areas.

CANARY WHARF TOWER

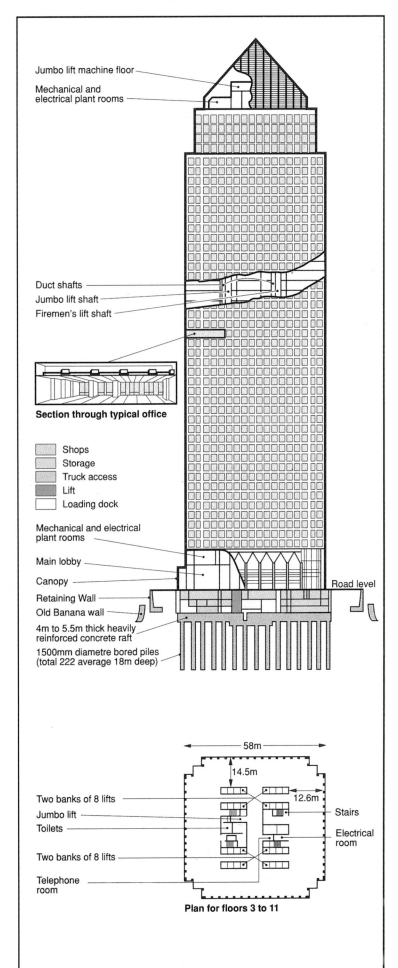

Jumbo lift machine floor

Mechanical and electrical plant rooms

Duct shafts
Jumbo lift shaft
Firemen's lift shaft

Section through typical office

- Shops
- Storage
- Truck access
- Lift
- Loading dock

Mechanical and electrical plant rooms

Main lobby

Canopy

Retaining Wall

Old Banana wall

4m to 5.5m thick heavily reinforced concrete raft

1500mm diametre bored piles (total 222 average 18m deep)

Road level

58m

14.5m

12.6m

Two banks of 8 lifts
Jumbo lift
Toilets

Stairs

Electrical room

Two banks of 8 lifts

Telephone room

Plan for floors 3 to 11

CRANE
Tied into the side of the tower on every sixth floor, this crane is the tallest structure on Canary Wharf. Raised a section at a time as work progresses, it keeps one step ahead of the progress of the building and will be responsible for putting the last section of the pyramid roof in place before the end of the year.

AIR CONDITIONING
The tower will be fully air-conditioned. The installation serving the upper half of the building will be located on the 49th floor, one level short of the top. Another air-conditioning unit on the second floor will serve the lower half of the tower. Coolers are located in the roof space.

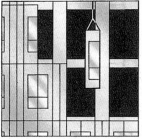

CLADDING
Exterior cladding for the steelwork, in panels each approximately four metres by one, is lowered into place by crane, though the units arrive at the appropriate level in packs, much as in a DIY kit. Panels consist of outside and inside surfaces in a single unit, the stainless steel of the exterior being protected by a blue plastic skin until work moves higher up the tower. A third layer of panelling forms the basis for interior decor.

JUMP LIFTS
The normal practice in the construction of high buildings in this country is for the lift shafts to remain empty until the building approaches completion, at which stage the lifts are installed. At Canary Wharf an innovative transatlantic 'jump car' system has been introduced. The lift machinery is raised bodily by crane every seven floors and three of the shafts, complete with their lifts, are being used to carry construction materials to the appropriate level.

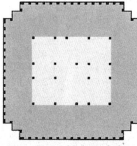

STEELWORK
The steel skeleton of the tower has an outer and an inner structure, like two boxes, one of them inside the other. The outer box is welded steel columns, hollow and with a square cross-section. Each one is three floors high and the cladding is attached to them. The box forming the inner core has columns with an H-shaped cross-section. Both types of column are 'tied' with crossbeams that support the floor at each level.

FOUNDATIONS
The tower is supported by 212 piles, each of which is six feet in diameter and surrounded by a coffer dam like a box of sheet steel. The foundations reach some 25 feet below the level of the dock. To combat the upward pressure that is caused by water movement, eight relief wells pump out water from inside the box.

BUILDING BRITAIN'S TALLEST SKYSCRAPER

PYRAMID ROOF

The tower, with a maximum movement of 13 inches in high winds, will be 'topped out' by the late autumn. Its distinctive roof will be sheathed in louvred blades, which will be textured to channel rainwater over its surface,

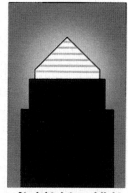

making it self-cleaning. At night, internal lighting will give the pyramid on top of the tower a spectacular golden glow, visible from across London. For security reasons there will be no public viewing gallery in the building, denying the public some of the most magnificent city and river panoramas in the country.

WORKERS' FACILITIES

In the Canary Wharf workforce, which is currently around 3,000, 600 are engaged in the construction of the tower. There are canteens and lavatories for them on every fifth floor of the

tower to avoid the inconvenience and delay that would be caused by descent and ascent.

ROAD TUNNEL

Those materials which do come by land, including the 28,000 tons of steelwork for the principal tower, arrive on a road built out over the water which goes underground through a tunnel to the heart of the building. Materials are then raised by crane and the 'jump lifts'.

RAFT

On top of the 212 piles is a concrete raft 12 feet thick, which has formed the base

of the tower. Concrete for the Canary Wharf project is mixed on site. The concrete already used would be sufficient to construct a fourth lane for the London orbital motorway.

BARGES

The majority of materials for Canary Wharf come by river from Tilbury, where there is a storage compound. Tugs tow them to the West India Dock, usually in strings of six, each barge being 'called' only as required, and its load lifted directly to the point of use.

THE TALLEST TOWER OF BRITAIN

A Square Plan Topped by a Pyramid

One Canada Square

When the morning or evening sun hits the Canary Wharf tower, even hardened enemies of the design have to admit they are seeing some sort of inspiring architecture. The tower's builders and designers have created a new London landmark. Before construction, when HRH Prince Charles saw the model, it is reputed that he said he would go mad if he had to work in a building like that! What would he think about the tower today, when all the floors have been fitted and occupied? Does anybody really go mad if they work in a state-of-the-art high rise building with views across London and the Thames fitted with 58m² size floor plates, air conditioning, spectacular views and not an impediment to obstruct in sight? When the sun breaks through the morning mist and suddenly illuminates the glistening stainless steel cladding of 1 Canada Square, there is no doubt that the building has some inspiration to people from all over the world. Perhaps it is the greatest to be built in Britain at the end of the 20th century and it must be admitted, not British at all.

The architect Professor Pelli wanted to design a building in as simple and pure a manner as possible. When he presented his detailed design for Docklands Square, the building was then called in the Spring of 1988, he chose a square plan topped by a pyramid, because these are forms familiar to every culture. Despite Pelli's assurances and careful choice of words, the design landed almost on its face immediately. But this had little effect on future construction. With planning permission obtained from the LDDC for a building 257metres high the design came in a 263metres and the final building was reduced to 245metres with 9-metre basement. Apart from that, the design of the tower was faithfully executed. Like a juggernaut it rolled on, despite the problems with contractors, the arrival of the recession in the late 1980s, the coming and going of prospective tenants and the dawn of glut in office floor space in the London area.

Tower Taking Shape

The foundations of the Tower at No 1 Canada Square are supported by 222 piles, each six feet in diameter, reaching 20m below the level of the dock. On top of the piles is a concrete raft which forms the base of the 246m high tower. This concrete slab is 4.25 metres thick. The steel skeleton of the building rises from the raft with an inner and outer structure to support each of the 50 storeys. The exterior cladding panels, measuring approximately 4 x 1metre, were lowered into position one at a time. Much of the material used in the construction of the Tower was delivered by barges from a holding site at Tilbury, in a carefully orchestrated, computer-controlled logistics programme. The steelwork was taken directly underground through a tunnel to the centre of the building for immediate use. Three cranes hoisted the steel and other material into position inside the Tower. Two cranes were tied inside the building itself. The third was tied onto the side of the Tower on every sixth floor. As work progressed, the cranes, which were self-climbing, stayed on step ahead. They helped to put the pyramid on the roof in place at the top of the Tower. The roof is designed with distinctive stainless louvred blades which are able to channel

rainwater over their surfaces, so that the roof is self-cleansing. Spectacular lighting and lasers marked the opening in January 1992.

Because the office building was sited on dry land, construction time for the Tower was cut by a year, as it did not require a coffer dam in the dock before its 222 piles could be bored to a depth of 18 metres. Its 27,500 tonnes of steel work arrived day after day with assemblies of 3 storey high "tree" columns and metre deep spandrel beams, which were bolted into position to send its tightly gridded, windload resisting parameter steelwork up at the same time as the vertical load resisting central core.

As every floor became a continuous ring, so that each panel of the tower's skin, reinforced with a double reveal began to play its part as a fourfold vertical beam. Thus each tree, connecting the beams into vast structural square tubes, emitted extremely thin steel floor joist and over the full 50 storeys, two extra office floors. The building's impressive stainless steel cladding was temporarily covered with a blue protective plastic skin and hauled up three storeys behind the trees. Began in the Spring of 1988, by May 1990, the tower was thought the tallest building in Britain with 60 metres still to go. In November 1990 it was topped out and visible from around 30 kilometres away

Spectacular Open Plan Offices

It was opened in January 1992 and could be seen from the north end of Waterloo Bridge. At night, ablaze with light, it gives the impression of a vast ship steaming over the horizon, some distance away. The high ground level lobby is decorated from floor to 9metre high ceiling in red, grey, green and black marble. The termination of the last bank of its 32 passenger lift at the 46th office floor there is nothing but service floor space. A total, of 120,000 sq metres arranged in deep hollow squares, uninterrupted by columns and is ideal for trading. The fitted floors have cellular offices around the perimeter, each with a spectacular, and open plan offices internally with access to views at the corners of the building. Only above the last office floor is there a variation; the top plant room enclosed in turn by the slotted stainless steel pyramid with its 190 tungsten lights that can be seen from far away.

Seen from Greenwich Park south of the river, its altitude is quite apparent, but so is its distance from the City of London. Arriving at the West India Quay, DLR station, or River Bus terminal and making your way to the Tower it is easy to be overwhelmed by a feeling of this vast unlikely structure as part of the City. The simple shape of the building is obstructed or compromised by many dense structures clustered around its base and further on. The tower is now flanked by two more giant towers along its side on the eastern end, forming a new complex in the heart of the new city of Docklands within London.

Completion on Budget

Olympia & York practiced a new style of procurement in the construction of Canary Wharf. They scoured the world to get the best product at the best price. The cost remained confidential. Hundreds of contractors and work people contacted Olympia & York, when they took over from Travelstead in July 1987. The company oversaw all procurement on the Wharf and processed between 4-5,000 bids for the 700 major trade contractors let during the phase 1 of construction. There were also over 2,000 sub trade and supply packages. The Company was quite successful in that they finished the first phase on budget. Finishing to a cost plan set almost fours previously was a major achievement.

During construction the cost escalated, yet the budget was adhered to. Inflation was running at 19% in 1988 but whenever bids looked as if they were going to come in high, the company went out to a lot of competitors all over the world. The Company also practiced a buying policy that is truly international and on a scale never seen before in the UK. They scoured the home market as well as Europe and North America to get the best price. The Company had a list of firms, predominantly North American and willing to travel wherever work was available. In this way they had a wide remit to troll the sub-contracting market. The Company also welcomed everyone who expressed their willingness to bid, big or small, although on many occasions, decisions were made to the specification of legal people in Olympia & York. The Company had therefore enormous purchasing power.

Contact with Best People

Procurement was not just about going to the lowest price and the best product, but also about making contact with the best people. There are stories of how the Company managed to bring down the cost of materials and products, e.g. the cost of flood-lighting of the tower came from an initial asking price of £800 per sq. metre to nearly a third of the £100 per sq. metre. This was all due to the advantage of having an international spectrum. There were a lot of products available on the international market that would cost the same no matter where they were. It is claimed that the cladding industry in the UK had not yet developed to take on the work on the tower and apparently it was claimed that they had no history of high-rise buildings at that time.

Specified the Price

The way Olympia & York went about getting the price they were prepared to pay was simple. They decided the cost and told everyone upfront what price they were prepared to pay. Then the Company managers worked with whoever took on the job, for example engineers, designers, trade contractors, and so on, in order to get the bid that the Company was prepared to accept. Although the installation went to outside contractors, fortunately the materials and workers came from the UK. The cladding became a British product with Canadian know-how. A similar stance aimed at getting the best possible price was taken for all products and trades. If the market was asking, say £1200 per tonne, the Company would do whatever it took to get them down to say 75% of this price, whether by value engineering, rebidding or sourcing from overseas.

Severe Penalties

Another source of much speculation was the Company's conditions of contract. They were extremely strict with severe penalties for contractors that did not perform. One management contractor described the Company as a sword hanging over the contractors head, (sword of Damocles). Other stated it was a stick to make firms perform, but the Company's treatment had always been fair and even handed. With nearly 3,000 major trades and sub trades on the project the law of averages applies, and that meant not only that everyone went away happy. But the Company was fair, even when the contractors were late as long as they gave a good product; they were still on good terms. The Company also created bonus incentive scheme for workers and contractors. The Canadians also bailed out more than 20 trade contractors that got into problems on the Wharf.

TRANSPORTATION WATERWAYS FOE WHARF

Concrete, Steel and Soil Afloat

Major Challenge of Logistic

The waterways in and around the old West India Docks gained a new lease of life as construction of Canary Wharf moved into full swing in May 1988. Finding answers to the transportation issues with such a huge development created a major challenge for the developers' logistic team. But the solutions resulted in revitalised waterways, more contracts for local companies and much less inconvenience to residents. In all up to 80% of construction materials was transported by water.

It takes massive quantities of materials to build on the scale of Canary Wharf. To bring supplies by road would have stretched the East London road network to breaking point. By using barges and ships Canary Wharf took off the road about 16,000 spoil lorries and 30,000 lorry loads of concrete which would have snarled up the roads for about two years. Although river transport was by far the most expensive method, the developers felt it was well worth the extra cost. They wanted to demonstrate their commitment to maintaining a harmonious relationship with the community, not only during construction, but in the future.

Use of Barges

An added advantage derived from more widespread use of barges was that normal barge loads could pass freely underneath the Blue Bridge, at the eastern entrance to the docks. The few ship movements which necessitate the raising of the bridge were restricted whenever possible to times of the day when the volume of traffic is at its lowest to avoid delays to motorists. However, there were still occasions when the bridge had to be raised at peak times when tidal conditions made it impossible to do so. For its own use, the developers acquired a river launch, which was used for bringing visitors from Central London to the Isle of Dogs.

In the mid 1950s there were 4,800 lightermen then at work on the busy River Thames and the Docklands area. In the 1980s there were less than 300 working on the familiar Black Tower barges. After seeing the traditional loads of sugar, timber and wine dwindle, the on sight start of Canary Wharf in 1988 was a boom to every person on the river. People naturally complained about the nuisance caused by the construction work. It was really the best thing that happened to the River in a long time.

Barges are called by different names up and down the country. On the Thames the name lightermen originated when ships, unable to get to a berth, were lightened-up by the barges drawing alongside. For four years essential building materials to build Canary Wharf were transported along the river. Four tugs ranging from 150 to 750 horsepower, were supported by a flotilla of 80 barges. Every day, except Saturday, they travelled the 2½ hour stretch from Tilbury Docks and then back, pulling six barges roped together at a time. When the project became more demanding the number of barges was increased to 12 a day and run just like a shuttle service. Similarly materials were transported for the construction of the Limehouse Link Road.

No Regular Hours

Canary Wharf as clients were very demanding, but lightermen had never worked regular hours and they had to work with the tides. If wanted they could work continuously 24 hours per day and on Sundays. The Thames barges carried up to 280 tonnes of steel. Larger barges carried 800 tonnes of sand and ballast, not to mention piles, tower cranes and toilet pods! According to the workforce it was really a successful project. There was nothing hazardous to transport, everything was trouble free, even labour relations at the docks went very smoothly, despite apprehension by Olympia & York, the owner of Canary Wharf at the time. It is said that if they had brought the materials by lorries on the congested roads, they would still be building the wharf many years later!

LABOUR AND UNIONS

Unions and Employers Can Work Together

Shining Example

It has been said that Canary Wharf construction was a shining example of how employers and unions can work together. The praise is attributed to the industrial relations managers of both contractors and to Olympia & York and also to the Union leaders. These people have been credited with the way they kept industrial unrest of the site for a period of four years. Without the co-operation of the Unions and the patience of the IR officers, there would have been trouble on site. Also a major effort was made to sign a Canary Wharf Agreement with the Unions concerned at the beginning of construction.

There was only one dispute, the unofficial steelwork strike in 1989. It appears that the shop stewards of the Unions attempted to bring all steel erection on London sites to a standstill. They failed but managed to score minor propaganda. It is said that the strike was politically led and was the only dispute that was not resolved through the procedural code of practice under the Agreement. It came about when the site shop stewards formed a series of committees; these Committees attempted to raise issues among the workforce and partially succeeded.

Procedural Code of Practice

Olympia & York employed more than 4,000 workers and staff at the peak of phase one of the construction. It was the only UK big site to have signed a procedural code of practice that operated above the requirements contained in the existing national working rule agreement that pleased the industry for the past 60 years. The success of industrial relations has been attributed to this factor. Another major factor was the great effort put by the industrial relations managers and officers who combined to make the project a role model for fellow construction professionals whether they may be employers or trade unions. In this way it is stated that Canary Wharf can prove to be a model for employers and unions. It claimed to have been the biggest industrial-relations success in Europe.

No Official Disputes

The fact that the co-signatories of the Canary Wharf agreement did not have to deal with any official disputes, gives an indication of its success. It had been reported that a lot of work had gone into solving potential disputes, before they had escalated and there were a number of health and safety major issues to be dealt with. It is claimed that even before the steelworkers walked out, moves were under way to bring industrial unrest to London Docklands construction. In 1989 the Construction Safety Campaign was criticising Olympia & York about lack of adequate medical facilities on site. After some debate a local independent doctor was appointed whose support was that Olympia & York had in fact installed first aid facilities that were quite impressive and more than up to the standard required on construction sites.

Health & Safety

During phase one construction only one death was reported, a steelworker who died in 1989. While everyone recognised that one fatality was too many, the safety record on Canary Wharf has been reasonable in comparison with projects such as the Channel Tunnel, where seven men were killed on the English side and a further three on the French side. Overall Olympia & York's site accident statistics for 1990 revealed that there were nearly a total of 300 accidents, mostly with 1100 minor injuries. All the buildings on site had first aid cabins attended by full-time nurses. An ambulance staffed by a team of paramedics was also available in case of emergency.

Union officials reported the success at Canary Wharf was due to the efficient and conscientious team working together in the interest of the project and also to the great effort made by the industrial relations managers and officers. Both site management and unions emerged after the first four years with a great deal of credit.

Canary Wharf Environment

While the development of Canary Wharf had the single most significant impact on the regeneration of Docklands across the board, it had a particularly crucial role in establishing standards of landscape. The design, specification, construction of the public realm at Canary Wharf is unmatched by any commercial development in this country.

Every little detail of the spaces between the buildings was designed to form a coherent whole, from hundreds of fully grown trees imported from Germany and richly cultivated flower beds, to road signs, handrails and benches. When it opened in 1992 you could be forgiven for thinking yourself to be in a well-established leafy quarter of Central London. Birds twittered in mature trees and insects flitted through the luxury flower beds. Fountains and sculpture jostled for the attention of lunchtime office workers and visitors who relaxed on comfortable wooden benches around beautiful lawns and round flower beds. Only when the visitor looked up at a building 15 storeys or more, did they realise that they are in a brand new development completely separate from the City of London.

Landscape Architects

A major part of Olympia & York's overall concept that more than one third of Canary Wharf's 28.5 hectare must be cultivated and designed by top USA landscape architects. The meticulously designed gardens, squares and water front promenades help soften the tall building edges and lend it a more human scale. They also contribute to the threat that ties the different buildings into a coherent centre. The design of the public urban space is being based on not just present development but future expansion of the new city. The importance of this has resulted in a great deal of attention that has been paid to detailing and a great deal of money has been spent on quality. The focus on detail can be seen by the natural materials and finishes, particularly bronze and a lively mix of stones which dominate the exterior spaces. Every curve and fold has been made as precise as possible and almost every joint and interface seamless.

Gully gratings are in bronze, even the public benches, fashioned from Indonesian teak to a design and are secured with brass brackets. The whole design is dynamic. Everywhere materials, colours and texture vie for the space available. Almost at every corner, there is something of interest. In the squares the water gurgles, the edge detailing of stone balustrade turns into seating or the rhythm of a horizontal railing changes from straight to undulating to mark its end.

Stone Masonry

The monumental masonry is apparent in the stonework of Cabot Square. Random sized slabs of granite radiate in concentric rings from the 16m-diameter base of its central fountain and follows a crown to aid drainage. A New York stone masonry company has executed this arrangement. Handrails on the steps are solid but simple and burnished bronze, which can only improve with wear. The concentration of detail is also clearly evident in the roadway, which changes from asphalt to rough hewn and then polished granite to the paving stone grid. At the squares four corners, step cascades lead down to more intimate tree-lined spaces and provide a screen masking the sound of traffic. This theme continues into two large water courts franking the main piazza. To the north, rain landing features a square of 6 white blooming horse chestnuts and a temporary exhibition area over set laid in a traditional fish scale pattern. The sudden version is a grand sweep of pink granite steps overlooking the dock. This sunny area also acts as a small amphitheatre.

Dockside Promenade

In addition about one kilometre of dock level promenade lines the development. There is not a great deal of interplay with the dock, but arrogant backward swept railings can be leant on. There are also waterside trees and benches to relax in. The railings are one element of a set of specially commissioned street furniture. A family of aluminium street rides of all shapes and sizes pepper the development marking out public areas. All road signs are similarly co-ordinated to reasonable standard. Slender glass and stainless steel bus shelters and phone kiosks successful blend of British, French and American styles are sprinkled along the roadside with linked bicycle stands and rubbish containers.

Fanciful Pavilions

Vital ventilation outlets, staircase heads and service machine rooms were turned into a series of fanciful pavilions, again in classical styles and executed in bronze and stone. But most impressive of all is the quantity and quality of the flower beds and trees. More than 400 fully grown trees of twenty species have been planted in concrete decking. Some of the largest including the English oak, London plane, lime and horse chestnuts are 50 years old and up to 7 metres high. In addition there are more than 6,000 shrubs and hardy perennials. More than 90 different varieties made up a dense but informal ground cover in tended beds. Even the grass for the lawns has been specially selected for healthy growth in the shade of tall buildings and trees.

One of the smart new pillar boxes at Canary Wharf.

A not-so-humble bollard, designed by Skidmore, Owings and Merrill.

Enlightenment... one of SOM's elegant lighting designs.

BENCHMARK...

One of two designs commissioned from Rod Wales for phase one of a development which is setting new standards.

Iseppe Lund's gate is one of the unique features at Canary Wharf.

Canary Wharf development continued with the largest urban planting project ever undertaken in the UK commencing in November 1990. The 10-m high London planes were supplied from a nursery in Hamburg and planting began on the outer ring of Westferry Circus. Above is the fountain at Cabot Square.

Fire Alarm System

Rewriting the rules of fire engineering, proper air conditioning, high speed lifts and electrics that can be expanded to meet emergencies and about are but a few of the ways Canary Wharf has changed the UK building services environment. The 50 storey tower of Canary Wharf is equipped with every high tech device imaginable to protect the fabric and lives of nearly 12000 people who occupy it. The question which is always asked - 'how will people get out in case of a fire? Olympia & York employed one of the best team of consultants to answer the question and also the consultants were watched by the local building control offices to ensure the safety of the building.

At the slightest hint of danger, the last word in fire alarm and public address systems spring into action, commanding people to go to the exits or stay put. On go the sprinklers and the offending smoke is sucked out of the new sealed-off floor more quickly than apparently you can vacuum your living room carpet. This is the claim of the designers. The whole system is apparently automatic and served by its own dedicated fire-rated cabling. When the fire brigade arrives on the scene, it will immediately be able to pinpoint the trouble area. This is because each safety device is controlled by a specially designed central computer system housed in an aptly named fire command centre in the basement of the tower.

Huge display panels depict the safety mechanisms on each floor. When any device is activated, the corresponding light on the panels start flashing. In the event of fire, the Company assist the local fire brigade by sending its own fire experts to the scene. The British Standards was not written for fairly high rise buildings such as the Tower and the fire brigade had to make the standards fit the building rather than the other way round. This was achieved by implementing a whole package of fire defence mechanisms that enabled the Company to install standard staircases and means of escape.

Phased Evacuation

Central to the fire defence strategy of all the Wharf's buildings is the concept of phased evacuation. Rather than design to attempt the buildings with adequately spaced exits to get everyone out in a few minutes, all have been structured so that they are safe enough to evacuate people floor by floor. Every floor of the Tower has been built as a separate fire compartment, with a two-hour fire rating. This passive resistance is supplemented with a host of active measures, including sprinklers and smoke extraction systems. The most controversial aspect of the scheme was the developers technique on how to deal with smoke which is the greatest threat to life in the event of the fire. Once a fire alarm is activated a number of mechanical systems come into play. Fans at the top and bottom of the four corner cases are activated. Each of these blow air into the corners creating a positive pressure. This acts like a balloon. The raised pressure forces fresh air through the leakages and blocks smoke coming from the fire floor, but that might not be enough, so the smoke must be extracted from each floor. The central air ventilation ducts are automatically closed down, isolating the air ducts from the smoky floor. The ventilation system effectively goes into reverse and fans suck the smoke into the shaft and out through the top of the building.

Tenants Sprinkler Equipment

All the buildings are equipped with sprinkler valves on each floor which provide the backbone from which tenants install their own sprinkler heads during fitting out, a compulsory part of their lease agreement. The sprinkler systems are fed from duplicated sets of pumps in the basement. The four pump sets run on emergency generators and are supplied from a reservoir fed by mains water. Each set serves a different zone in the building. Another water reservoir serves the permanently charged two wet riser shafts for use by the fire brigade, which can gain access to the building via two protected shafts. Once again the wet riser pumps have standbys in case of failure. There are also dedicated water storage tanks serving those fire reels at various points throughout the buildings which is supplemented by the domestic water supply. Olympia & York's approach looks like filtering into other large developments. Fire drills are held regularly and tests are carried out by the fire brigade of all the buildings on the Wharf.

Tower's Life

You might feel weak at the knees when you get into one of the Tower's lifts and a trip to the top of the Tower can be slightly disconcerting It takes 46 seconds from stepping into a lift in the concourse till you are on the top floor. A speed of six metres per second for the fastest 12 lifts - they are extremely fast. 2 x 32 passenger lifts are arranged in four banks of eight, each serving a quarter of each floor level. Lifts to the lower floors operate a more sedate speed of 3.5 metres per second. In addition there are two goods lifts and firemen's lifts. The lift cars are linked by intercom to the security room that is tied into the Wharf's central management computer system, beneath the Docklands Light Railway System.

Jump Lifts

The tower is the first UK building to use jump lift technology which enables the lift to be used even as the shaft was being built. One of the goods lifts was built in this way so that it could transport materials. The jump lift was installed section by section to keep up with the structural steel and was fitted with its own temporary machine room. Normally this machinery is removed once the lift shaft reaches its full height. However, for the Tower, the 30 tonnes of lifting machinery was left for permanent use.

CANARY WHARF TUBE STATION

The Elegance that followed the storm

More Prestigious

Technically, Canary Wharf is only the second largest station on the Jubilee Line Extension - North Greenwich is dimensionally larger but Canary Wharf looks more spacious! It is probably the most prestigious and certainly the most important destination. Without it, the Extension would probably not have been built. Canary Wharf is also the busiest station. It was designed to handle a peak passenger flow of 30,000 people per hour, which makes it as busy as Oxford Circus station. This will happen when the new city is at Canary Wharf if completed by 2010. Currently it is handling around 10,000 passengers per hour, 80% normally go in and out of the station through the western concourse - the entrance closest to the Tower at One Canada Square.

Built inside the Dock

As you travel on one of the five escalators from the west entrance to the ticket hall, you will see the whole length of the huge open hall. The east entrance also provides five escalators. The hall is 240 metres long by 39 metres wide and has been built on what previously was the bottom of the West India Export Dock on the south side of Canary Wharf. The dock was built long, deep and rectangular by the famous engineers of early 1800s and looked a perfect place in which to site an underground station. Except, of course, it was a working dock for 190 years and was full of water. Draining the dock required the construction of a cofferdam comprising 5,000 tonnes of sheet piles, a canal and a couple of temporary bridges. Once the fish had been rescued, work began on removing the silt, which had been deposited by the Thames spring tides for two centuries. Amazingly, nothing of interest was found which related to the thousands of ships, which had used the dock over many years. The dockers did not drop deliberately or accidentally anything valuable over the sides of the ships! There were no bodies or bombs dropped during the London Blitz of 1940.

Once the bottom of the dock had been reached - some eight metres below the former water level - 148 concrete diaphragm wall panels were installed to a depth of 27 metres below the dock bed level to create the permanent walls of the station enclosed box within the rectangular dock. This box, which then had to be excavated, is where the trains run and is reached from the ticket hall either by one of the nine escalators, or in the case of disabled passengers, a lift.

In total, 600,000 tonnes of soil were taken out of the dock and removed from the site. This could have meant a staggering 100,000 lorry journeys to and from tip sites in Kent, with very serious consequences for the traffic and local people. However, not one kilogram of muck left the site along the public highway. Everything was taken by barges along the Thames. Each barge was capable of carrying up to 900 tonnes at a time, in a similar way when the Canary Wharf complex was constructed. In 1993 when the project started, 5,000 tonnes of sheet piles, 23 metres long, were delivered to the site by ships from British Steel at Scunthorpe.

Design Modifications

Canary Wharf station was central to the planning of the Jubilee Line extension. But what was not foreseen was that Olympia & York, the Canadian developers of the £4billion scheme, would go into liquidation in 1992. Not only did this mean that the whole project was put on hold until the ownership of Canary Wharf was sorted out, but it also meant that the second phase of development was put on ice. This had significant consequences on the design of the station. Modifications were made in design and construction which meant a loss in time. The station should have finished in 1996 but was not completed until 1999.

Open and Airy

Canary Wharf station feels open and airy and very modern. The escalators span-like bridges between the various levels and pass through openings n the roof and ticket hall slabs. You can stand on the surface and see the trains running 25 metres below. The large glass canopies let natural light into the ticket hall. Every one of the 400 curved panels of glass is unique in shape and contour. They were made in Italy by the firm, which also produces windscreens for the Ferrari! The whole station not only looks elegant but also requires minimal maintenance. The area around the station has been landscaped as a beautiful park.

Right. Canary Wharf Station during Construction, looking from the mezzanine level through the vast west entrance awaiting the glass canopy.

CANARY WHARF TODAY

From Dereliction to Financial Dream

Standard for the Capital

In the early 1980s it was little more than desolation and depression. Twenty years on, Canary Wharf is London's most impressive complex, with offices, shops, restaurants and beautiful waterside locations. It is a shopping centre, sought after financial hub and it has got more bars and restaurants than a small town. It is at the heart of year round activities and is topped by the tallest building in the UK. Canary Wharf dominates the London skyline as a standard of the capital's progress into the 21st century and a reminder that the future is hi-tech, high ambition and all commerce. Viewed from Greenwich Park with the sun setting to your left, is an impressive piece of architecture as anyone can wish to see. People still tend to think of Canary Wharf as something alien. A little detached from the South East of London and not much more than a complex of offices and lifestyle apartments. It is not like this. In its own way and not just physically, Canary Wharf has forced itself into the perception of Londoners, largely due of course to the extension of the Docklands Light Railway and the Jubilee Line. It is no longer an overbearing architectural monster.

The Canary Wharf dream dates back to the early 1980s when Docklands was largely derelict. In 1981 the Conservative Government created the London Docklands Development Corporation to buy and control development in the area. By 1985 the Chairman of Credit Suisse First Boston was declaring an interest in having a back office in a converted banana warehouse on the Isle of Dogs and this modest ambition slowly grew to becoming a Wall Street on the water. Later that year a consortium including the Bank announced its plans for Canary Wharf and sent shockwaves both through the City and the local residents. It was the biggest single regeneration project many people had ever seen and it was right on their doorsteps. It was an ambitious scheme and what it needed was funding. Olympia & York became interested enough to some hiccups took over the whole project in 1987, paying £73million.

Financial Difficulties

Despite their initial difficulties Olympia & York persevered and declared it was going to build a modern city covering 93 acres including Heron Quay and Port East with over 12 million sq ft of commercial space. Plans were drawn up and the idea for 1 Canada Square the 50 storey tower, the tallest building in the UK was mooted. On 11 May 1988 building began. In 1989 there were signs of trouble that everything was going down and pear shaped. Olympia & York had borrowed 2.5billion dollars from a global consortium that the company's assets were said to be £7billion and it had a reputation for success. In 1990 Olympia & York borrowed a further half a billion and doubts started to grow about the company's financial position. Even so Canary Wharf opened in January 1992, three years after the construction began. But the problems with one of the early tenants and difficulties in leasing space led in May 1992 to Olympia and York going into administration. In 1993 a restructuring package resulted in the formation of Canary Wharf Ltd to handle the whole project.

More Banks Move into the Wharf

Two years later Canary Wharf Ltd was sold by the banks that formed it to an international property corporation, a sale estimated to be worth £800 million. The building was generally in abeyance and there were still problems in letting space. Then in 1996 Citibank decided to move into Canary Wharf. It was a big break and work started in February 1997 on the 560,000 sq ft Citibank building. Later that year work began on Canary Wharf riverside, the first large development since 1992. In 1998 with the Corporation of London worried by what was happening on Canary Wharf and steady leakage of city institutions to the new development listing regulations to allow the skyscrapers in the square mile, HSBC announced that it was going to move to new headquarters in Canary Wharf. The place was well and truly under way. What has happened is startling.

When the tenants moved into 1 Canada Square in the early 1990s there was still empty floors and a new housing estate feel to it. Canary Wharf was not much more than a slightly well-groomed building site and developers fantasy with few shops or cafes. These facilities were most important to journalists who had previously dropped from the paths of Fleet Street into the Holborn pubs. It was rather depressing. A handful of years later, as we have entered into the new Millennium, it is no longer something to sneer at or indeed ignore. It is all it says on the tin, a giant spider of an office complex that is constantly spawning new eggs, a shopping centre and there are 200 shops and restaurants that easily rival the edge of town developments, a mecca of gourmet restaurants and even an entertainment centre. There is even a weekly newspaper "The Wharf" and a high quality magazine called "Canary" dedicated to keeping abreast of the latest news. Most important of course is that it is just minutes away from the City, via the DLR or the Jubilee Line extension. It is a landmark that may last for a long time.

Canary Wharf's Cabot Place - the central retail area takes pride of place under a dramatic glass dome. The restaurants are on the top floor.

Workers and visitors enjoy a wide range of foods, from fast food to international cuisine.

A full range of retail facilities including restaurants, pubs, cafes and support services are available on various floors of the development at Cabot Place East and West. The second floor is exclusive to restaurants. With thousands of people working at Canary Wharf the place is very busy, especially on a hot summers day.

Westferry Circus overlooking the Thames is one of the major public spaces of Canary Wharf offering a lawn and garden at its centre, where people can relax and enjoy the intricate landscaping.

Canary Wharf has its own DLR station housed in the glass-enclosed concourse. The sky-roofed pavilion is a masterpiece, multi-level food and shopping thoroughfare that brings Canary Wharf to life with people.

CANARY WHARF MASTER PLAN

Space for the Giants of the Banking World

HSBC Tower

At the end of 1998 work started on a new landmark building at Canary Wharf to house one of the world's largest banking and financial services organisations, the Hongkong and Shanghai Banking Corporation (HSBC Holdings plc). This is an organisation with assets of nearly £300 billion, 5,500 offices worldwide and employer to about 130,000 people in 81 countries and territories. The group expanded mainly by establishing offices throughout the world until the mid-1950s, when it began to create or acquire subsidiaries. This culminated in 1992 with one of the largest deals in banking history, when HSBC acquired the Midland Bank.

The project was on the cards for two years but the sheer scale of Canary Wharf's biggest deal shocked the City of London and turned down the revamped NatWest Tower. The low key announcement contrasted with two years of intense negotiations between HSBC Group and Canary Wharf company. The deal has enabled HSBC to bring all staff to a modern, pleasant and convenient environment. It also brought various business units to work more closely together in order to improve the services offered to customers.

The HSBC Tower at Canary Wharf has brought under one roof its 8,000 staff who were at ten offices scattered throughout the West End and City. The 1.1 million sq. feet building is around 700 ft high with 41 storeys, including 3 trading floors of 50,000 sq. ft. There is a promenade level and three basements providing more than 300 parking spaces. Completion took place during 2001. The principles established by HSBC's founder, Thomas Sutherland, have stood the group in good stead since 1865 and look set to continue as the bank becomes a major player in the continuing success of Docklands in the 21st century.

American Bankers

About the same time the total occupancy at Canary Wharf was nearly 98%. The Bank of New York exchanged contracts to become the new top tenants at Canary Wharf, occupying 100,800 sq.ft over four floors 40, 41, 48 and 49, of the 800ft landmark tower for moving its 500 staff from the West End during 1999. The move meant the original Canary Wharf development, which in 1992 was in the hands of receivers because of poor tenancy take up, was virtually full five years later. Bank of New York was founded in 1784 and is the oldest bank in the US still operating under its original name and no doubt must have had continuous dealings with shipping lines and merchants operating in the Port of London for nearly two centuries. The bank provides a complete range of banking and other financial services to corporations, businesses and individuals worldwide.

The Bank of New York joined a growing band of financial sector organisations at Canary Wharf, including the Bank of China International, Bank of Montreal, Barclays Capital, Bear Stearns International, Citibank, Coutts & Co, Credit Suisse First Boston, Edward Jones, Euler Trade Indemnity , Financial Services Authority, Morgan Stanley, etc.

Design of Twin Towers

Looking east from the Millennium Wheel at South Bank, it is possible not only to have a clear picture of the famous No 1 Canada Square Tower, but also of the considerable changes that are taking place around it. The two sister towers reached completion at the end of 2001. One was designed by Professor Cesar Pelli's, the American designer for Canary Wharf Phase 1, for the Citigroup, and the other by Sir Norman Foster Partnership for HSBC. Both towers were initially proposed by Canary Wharf's Canadian developer, Olympia & York, and are slightly smaller at 42 storeys are just as imposing in their steel and cladding. But while from a distance of about 5km, these are the obvious signs of present expansions at Canary Wharf, a visit to the Isle of Dogs shows a great deal more dramatic development. Some six hundred thousand square metres of office space have been constructed. The Canary Wharf Group, the owner of the site, predicts that by 2005, there will be 1.3 million sq. metres and a working population of 90,000. Unusually, all this building and that for Phase 1 development is planned and projects managed by the client Canary Wharf Group. They believe it is the best way to ensure that buildings are developed and built on time, ready to start collecting rental income.

Other Developments

Apart from the two new towers, construction work has been proceeding for a dozen new buildings and underground shopping malls. These include buildings alongside and connected to the new towers and new developments on Herons Quays to the south and at Churchill Place to the east of Canada Square. These buildings are designed by different groups of architects and engineers, but retain Canary Wharf's quality finish to provide the tenants; most buildings are already signed up, with some of the best office accommodation in London.

Millennium Masterplan

The masterplan for Canary Wharf has placed the Wharf at the hub of international action of the future and has been hailed as the city of the 21st century. In 1999 the Canary Wharf Group produced a progress report on its plans for another 3.5million sq ft of extra office and retail space. The landscape has since been dramatically stamped with more steel and glass to house 100,000 workers by 2006. There will be more glass-covered retail centres below ground.

The people who work on the south side of the development look onto Canada Square Park and Jubilee Park. Employees have the convenience of an underground link with the Jubilee Line station. Behind the Citigroup Tower lies the south skyline and offers magnificent waterfront views. The view from Heron quay shows at the centre the eleven storey building designed by French architects on sheets of glass. Another development is 15 Westferry Circus which continues the crescent shape of the Circus and was ready for occupation in 2001. The grand River Thames as it snakes away from the City around Westferry Circus offers some of the best views in London.

Canary Wharf's central axis is aimed directly at the City of London. Caboot Square is surrounded by giant office blocks, yet remains both light and airy.

TOWERS AT CANARY WHARF

Newspaper Industry Revolution

Fuelled by the requirements of new technology the press barons of Fleet Street in the City were turning their backs on the birthplace of newspapers with its cramped printing conditions and over-manned and out-dated equipment. News International's imposing fortress established in Wapping in 1984, proved a salutary experience. Despite the demonstrations by its former staff and clashes with the police, it demonstrated that the long awaited revolution in the newspaper industry was possible. Almost overnight the costs of producing the Times, the Sunday Times, The Sun and the News of the World were cut by around £80 million. Persuaded by such financial considerations, the majority of the national newspapers obviously felt it was a step in a direction they could not ignore.

The Financial Times, the Daily Mail and the Guardian, along with the Daily Telegraph were soon after on their way downriver where the newspapers interests lay in not what the papers said, but what the papers had to do. With the newspapers moving to Docklands and the building of the Daily Telegraph printing works at Millwall Dock, the bosses admitted the decision to leave Fleet Street was painful for the company, but there was no option.

"The Sky the Limit"

In Fleet Street, the Daily Telegraph had to print their papers on machines, which were only capable of producing 15,000 copies an hour. Their new Docklands machines could cope comfortably with 60,000 an hour. In fact the sky was virtually the limit. The papers were rolling off computerised presses housed in their printing hall, with a generous area unthinkable in Fleet Street. Ironically, despite being called the Daily Telegraph works by satirists, the Company's printers had already landed the contract to print a rival, left of centre paper, the News on Sunday. The management was adamant they were interested in business affecting policies. They later changed their name to Westferry Printers.

The same rationale seemed shortly to pervade the thinking of most of the newspapers moving into Docklands. Fed up of operating at a huge disadvantage compared to the trend setter, News International, they were determined to compete at their level. The Financial Times announced its plan to move to Docklands. Its investment of £75 million eventually was located in the former East India Dock area, producing a 56-page colour paper, allowing journalists to direct-input their stories. The Guardian built their offices in the Isle of Dogs, leaving behind its antiquated presses in Grays Inn Road in the City.

Meanwhile, the Mail and Evening Standard Group obtained planning permission for new printing facilities south of the Thames in the Surrey Docks. It was a huge relief for the management who were struggling under the weekly strain of producing around 26 million papers on old out-dated machines. The Mail's new £100 million plant was fully operational in 1988.

Redundancy Costs

But the process of modernising the printing industry and activating new technology was being achieved at a heavy cost. Initially the printing unions continued to fight News International at Wapping but lost their cause at the end. Other papers paid big money to avoid confrontation. For instance the Financial Times offered up to £45,000 per voluntary redundancy to achieve the 400 job losses. The sums differed but generous pay-offs were the name of the game as part of the process of change to new technology. But whilst it was clear in 1986 that the printing side of the newspaper industry was going to be Docklands-based, plans for the move of the editorial staff took a little longer. The Daily Telegraph staff moved to a building at South Quay Plaza, only 10 minutes walk from their printing works. They later moved to Canary Wharf Tower when completed in 1992.

Relocation Incentives

Late in the 1988s the eyes of the newspaper world were gazing at the Mirror Group, which has been careful not to show its plan. Finally it committed itself to closing down its printing works in Holborn and moved to the Canary Wharf Tower after the move of the Daily Telegraph. The United Newspapers, publishers of the Express and Sunday Express, however decided to remain in the City for the time being.

It was hardly surprising for these newspapers to move. The early 1980s relocations were given a package of incentives, which included a number of year's rate-exemptions, tax relief on new buildings and ideal working environment. Today, Fleet Street has become only a shadow of its former self, merely another historic landmark on the tourist's map, while mainstream journalism moved downstream to the water city of Docklands.

The New Fleet Street - Amongst the first to spot the potential of London Docklands was the newspaper and magazine publishing industry. The picture shows the Daily Telegraph Offices at Canary Wharf Tower.

Big Communication Business

Most national newspapers and magazines you read have more than likely originated or passed through Docklands on their way around Britain and the world. Once famed for its imports from all comers of the earth, Docklands today export news and media with extreme speed worldwide. This new big business communication industry based around the greatest modern commodity, information technology, replaces the precious cargoes of the past. East of Tower Bridge is in fact home to five national daily newspapers and five Sunday papers. Wapping and Canary Wharf alone boast four dailys.

In Surrey Quays, the Harmsworth Press produces some 20 million Daily Mails, Standards, Metros, and Mail on Sunday each week, while Wapping presses thunder out up to 80,000 copies of the Sun and Times papers every hour. Westferry Printers at Millwall, print 2.5 million newspapers every night for the Telegraph, Guardian, Express, Star, Financial Times and The Sport, at a rate of 360 papers a second! Maintaining Docklands nautical connection, over sixty titles on this subject are produced by these printers, Europe's biggest, including Lloyd's List and as part of the Docklands community, The Islander.

Canary Wharf Tower full of Journalists

The vast majority of the press gang live in the new Fleet Street Tower of Canary Wharf and One Canada Square. More than 12 floors of the 50 floors of the Tower is occupied by national newspaper groups, from the five floors of the Telegraph (11-16), the Independent's two floors (18-19) to the Mirror's five floors (19-24).

From Bliss for Brides in Beaufort Court on South Quay to huge computer titles, Docklands is also home to numerous magazines, Prime, Best and Your Home start at Marsh Wall offices. Northern and Shell produces 550,000 plus copies of OK! and the Arsenal and Liverpool football clubs magazines. Limeharbour is also home to The Builder Group, which churns out Building, Property Week and other construction titles. The New Civil Engineer is based at Heron Quays. Next to Northern and Shell is the UK's biggest corporate publishers, Barkers Trident, which also has offices in Manchester and York and branches in New York and Dubai, producing anything from home equipment catalogues to newspapers for airshows at home and overseas. Apart from the newspaper people, there are advertising agencies including the well-known Ogilvy & Mather in Cabot Place and Warman & Bannister marketing in Marsh Wall.

Reuters' Global and BT Satellite Dishes

At Leamouth, where the East India Company operated nearly 400 years ago, Reuters' Global Technical Centre is a true 21st century electronic trading post for sending by computers financial information and 15,000 news stories, pictures and graphics each day to 20,000 receiving satellite dishes in Europe. At peak times financial data is transmitted at 6,500 updates a second, with the NASA centre directly controlling some half a million terminals in 120 countries.

At North Woolwich the Royal Docks, BT's Earth Centre on the old Standard Telephone cable site, brings TV pictures from all over the world. The 12 satellite dishes take new feeds and pictures from Sky's West London studios and ITV live sport shows into every home. Built initially in 1984, just at the start of the Docklands regeneration, the station provides financial data services for banks across Europe. The TV company Planet 24 also operates from Docklands.

Westferry Printers

When everybody in Docklands have gone home and after the pubs have closed, the wheels of Westferry Printers, Europe's largest on the shore of Millwall Outer Dock really start grinding. The company produces 2.5million newspapers a night from its 12.5 acre plant. It started early in the 1980s as printers for the Telegraph, but now operates independently to produce numerous titles, including The Daily and Sunday Telegraph, Daily and Sunday Express, Daily Star, Guardian, Observer, Financial Times and The Sport. Each of its 18 presses produces 17 newspapers per second, with newsprint travelling through the presses at 24mph! Each reel of newsprint stretches 8 miles (10.8km), produces 24,000 newspapers and lasts for 20 minutes. Around 500 reels of paper are used each night, with an electricity bill of nearly £4,000. Nearby at Westferry Circus operates the famous Reader's Digest with 500 staff producing the magazine, car manuals and DIY books and the stereotype prize-winning notification letters circulated at homes throughout Britain!

Filming in Docklands

Docklands have been used for many years for filming, particularly the use of the riverside warehouses. At the end of 1999, after being tipped off by the New Millennium Experience Company, reporters and photographers were rushed down to North Woolwich, just before the completion of the Millennium Dome. Their mission was to infiltrate the latest Bond movie. The "World is not Enough" was being filmed along the Thames, Royal Docks and at the Dome. The photographers were briefed specially to capture the beautiful Bond bad girl and to snap the thrilling Bond stunt that would open the film. The story was that Bond's powerboat would chase the Bond girl's vessel up from the MI6 building at Vauxhall Bridge to the Millennium Dome. The girl landed safely on the Dome site and pounced ballerina-like into a hot-air balloon and rose skyward. Bond, however, crash-landed his boat, made a grip for a rope on the rapidly rising balloon, lost his grip and fell groundwards onto the Dome's roof and got a stiff ticking off from the bad girl. It was truly exciting stuff for the public. The film opened in time for the New Millennium.

LONDON'S OFFICE MIGRATION EASTWARD

After the Big Bang Came the Big Demand

The Big Bang of 1986

The City's Big Bang in October 1986 restored to the office market levels of demand and rental growth that were last seen in the heady days of the early 1970s. The problem for estate agents was where to find space because what was available and what was likely to be available for the next two years was already spoken for. The boom in the office market looked like taking a long time to dissipate, which was good news for the property industry and Docklands. It seemed doubtful that the City would be able to cope with the demand, even though the City Corporation had indicated more liberal planning policies. Research also revealed that demand for new office space in the whole of London could be much greater than has been anticipate.

Docklands Business Community

The Docklands dream was rapidly taking its shape in reality by 1987. Finished buildings were replacing architects and Engineer's drawings and daily more people were commuting into the Isle of Dogs on the so called "futuristic" light railway. Keys to the successful working of the developing business community were, effective advertising by the LDDC, and the establishment of a number of specialist companies to offer the new arrivals communications services, as well helping to voice abroad the success story of London's new business centre at Canary Wharf.

A number of glossy and informative magazines and papers were published, including the Docklands News financed by the LDDC, Docklands Digest, Docklands Business World and Docklands Property Guide. The last one was primarily for advertising by Estate Agents. The communication companies were also able to offer a wide range of marketing services to the local businesses. These included design, print and photography, the production of promotional material, specialist exhibitions, consultancy and direct sellings. The first Docklands Property Exhibition of 1988 for commercial and retail property was held at the junction of Docklands and the City, the World Trade Centre in St Katherine Docks and was repeated a number of times.

Property Promotion

The exhibitions were seen as an invaluable vehicle for both of two important groups: the developers and the estate agents. They promoted their interests in Docklands as well as providing a window on the area for those companies that were considering establishing here. The exhibitions had the full backing of the LDDC and attracted major corporate sponsors. What attracted business and these companies was the London Docklands Enterprise Zone at the centre of the Isle of Dogs which was the fastest growing part of it. There were companies down here, which were going through some of the most exciting periods of their existence. Newsworthy events were occurring every day. Companies also offered services for the organisation of conferences and seminars, all of which would be geared o the client's precise needs. Another group of companies provided public relations consultancy, including all aspects of media relations, promotions and sponsorship management, design and editorial services.

Business Efficiency Centre

The year 1988 was a major period of consolidation for the Isle of Dogs. Several important landmark schemes were coming to fruition with further improvement of roads and infrastructure. Many phases of commercial development in the centre of the Isle were nearing completion. Schemes such as Glengall Bridge, Harbour Exchange and South Quay Plaza contained a mix of retail elements, providing shops, pubs, banks and restaurants comparable to a high street shopping facility. These developments surrounded the Business Efficiency Centre created by the LDDC earlier and situated close to the DLR Crossharbour Station. The Centre was thriving, containing 20 tenanted companies offering different services to existing and prospective businesses. About 2,000 people a week visited the LDDC Showroom and Visitors area for information. Also the success of the nearby Docklands Light Railway Shop reflected the huge amount of public interest in the railway and its location opposite the Greenwich Foot Tunnel made it very convenient for regular passengers as well as numerous tourists and day visitors to Docklands and Greenwich.

Modern Telecommunications

Modern business requires a sophisticated level of infrastructure for its telecommunications. Docklands bid to develop into a prime financial centre, attractive to the full range of city office users, required the same level of telecommunication services to be provided as found in the City. This meant high speed digital techniques which are now a business requirement, including direct access to a high digital exchange via fibre optic cable able to send very fast strains of constantly changing data to provide access between computer terminals in different locations and of course with satellite services around the world. Today, Docklands has the visible presence of two 40ft dish aerials of Mercury Communications in the West India Dock and two similar aerials of British Telecom at North Woolwich in the Royal Docks. These are the prime means of contact with the satellite which allow Docklands to have instantaneous worldwide communication. The old Docklands service was adequate for voice, but not for the other high speed data links.

Docklands great advantage however, was the capacity it had to install new cable and equipment from scratch, in contrast to the historic congestion of the City of London. British Telecom further converted one of the Poplar exchange units to a digital system in 1987. The introduction of fibre optics for business users followed shortly after, about the same time direct links for the other sophisticated high speed telecom services become available. The timing of the introduction of high speed digital techniques in telecommunications was in line with that of office development and suited the major commercial users.

An impressive view of South Quay office blocks from millwall Dock, c1995.

East India Dock development at Blackwall has a mix of office, leisure and retail areas.

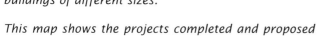

Harbour Exchange is one of the largest office developments on the Isle of Dogs and consists of eight buildings of different sizes.

Glengall Bridge development across Millwall Dock provides shops, pub, bank and restaurants comparable to a high street shopping facility.

This map shows the projects completed and proposed on the Isle of Dogs, c 1988.

The revitalised and new office developments around Millwall Docks on the east side of the Isle of Dogs, c1999.

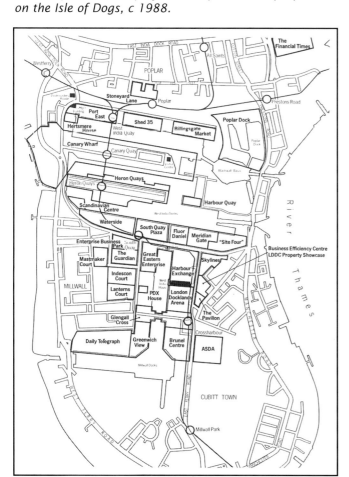

Risks and High Potentials

The scope for development in Dockland was described by the LDDC as exceptional. This could be seen, not just in the overall scope of development, but also in the wide choice that developers had in regard to the size, type and design of their project. This showed that developers were faced with an unusual freedom in terms of supply. On the other hand there was a large competing supply of almost inevitable feature of the market. On the downside of the situation, the developers were also faced with more than the usual uncertainty. Development in Dockland carried their fair share of risk, but also the potential of high rewards.

Market Analysis

Analysts in attempting to assess high demands were, firmly entering speculative territory. This was the case where research had to go beyond facts in order to make forecast. Demand for costing in Dockland was particularly difficult for two reasons. Firstly, local demand was almost non-existent. In most markets elsewhere, local demand can be relied upon as a source of demand. An analysis of companies making up the local economy, the changing fortunes and space requirements normally provide useful indications as to the likely future demand. In Docklands this approach was entirely irrelevant. Secondly, in the mid 1980s we were still in the early stages of redevelopment of Dockland, no pattern of demand had yet been established, at least in the commercial sector. Exceptions were London Bridge City in Southwark, which had established itself almost effortlessly as a City office location, and the newspaper world, which was moving almost in its entirety to large sites in Docklands. The most crucial demand sector was the office market.

Offices the Key to Development

Many mixed commercial schemes had retail, leisure and residential elements. For the majority of speculators, offices were however the main component on which their viability hinged. On the basis of the plans during the late 1980s, Offices held the key to successful regeneration of Docklands. As the largest, nearest and trend-setting office market, the City held the key to the future of Docklands as an office location. Views were varied on the future of City markets. The demand of the City office market was characterised by a number of factors. Office demand in the City had risen sharply since 1984, coinciding with the run up to the deregulation of the Stock Market in 1986.

Upsurge in Demand

Demand by the major players in the financial market, particularly by the large corporations that were mainly responsible for the upsurge in demand. A second factor for demand was the need for new efficient space to allow the full and unrestricted application of modern information technology. This demand coincided to a large extent with the previous source as deregulation had gone hand in hand with the introduction of electronic markets and settlement schemes.

New High Tech Accommodation

The need to update existing office accommodation resulted in a continual demand for new efficient space. The large existing stock of older offices, unsuitable to adaptation, underlined the scope for provision of new space through redevelopment. Vital to future demand was the success of deregulation set off by the Big Bang in 1986. The consensus view was that we have to wait a few years for the dust to settle.

Overspill from City

In attracting overspill demand from the City Docklands had many assets as well as a drawback. Historically, the following were the main assets in the 1980s.

1   Low Accommodation Costs

The guide was the rent which was being quoted for Canary Wharf in the late 1980s. At approximately £20 per sq foot this represented a discount of at least 50% on City rates. This level, compared well with competing locations in London Bridge City, Victoria and West End. Rent in the top M4/M25 location such as Windsor and Uxbridge were at similar levels, as in Docklands.

2   Docklands image

Docklands developed a pioneering image with the rent marketing strategy. A move to Docklands was taking part in an experiment with the confidence or at least the hope that this decision would be justified by the area's successful development into maturity.

3   Waterside Environment

Docklands' prime asset was and is its waterside environment. Miles of it, along its docks and river front. Using this asset to its full advantage was no easy task. It proved an excellent selling point.

4   Choice and Flexibility

Docklands offered enormous scope for development and a wide choice in virtually all aspects of the office building including size, location, specification and design. Relocating office users in the market for new offices, say central London or M25 centres, normally faced a frustrating narrow choice and had to compromise in one or more aspects of their requirements. Building their own offices hardly reduced the constraint and with a slow process given planning controls and procedures. Docklands could respond quicker and more comprehensively to occupiers' requirements. This was a powerful tool in the hands of developers in docklands which they exploited to the full.

5   Minimum Disruptive Moves

Any office move outside central London was bound to be disruptive in terms of the service industry's major asset, i.e. its staff. To minimise such disruption is a prime consideration in moves. In comparison to moves to an M25 location or centres further out, a move to Docklands would only extend commuting times by a relatively small amount.

The bomb which devastated South Quay in February 1996 killed two men and broke the truce with the IRA, left a wide trail of damage from which Docklands took years to recover.

South Quay looking west from the entrance lock, c 1992. Office development on the Isle of Dogs Enterprise Zone continued to grow and became the glamourous home to a growing number of city firms.

Today's business community in Docklands has grown from those humble beginnings of low rise buildings, such as those chalet-type offices along Heron Quay on the Isle of Dogs, c 1986.

Queues at Sales Offices

Residential development was an outstanding success story in Docklands. Queues at sales offices were a common site for both upmarket riverside conversions in Wapping and assisted housing schemes in the depths of Surrey Docks. At least two examples suggest the Docklands housing market catered for a wide range of demands. At the cheaper end of the market were the assisted housing projects. With an ageing and deteriorating stock, the Dockland boroughs had an opportunity to provide suitable housing for those on their waiting list and other local residents. This type of demand was responsible for approximately 40% of house sales up to 1988. In contrast to this local demand, there was an influx into Docklands of those affluent young professionals from the City with an eye for a good investment and not to be bothered with the apparent contradiction of jumping on the Docklands bandwagon, while fulfiling their wishes for homes of individuality and character. Both markets established very quickly, and judged by the levels of demands and prices, the residential sector was the most consistently successful in Docklands.

Affordable Housing Schemes

In the assisted sector, the provision of new local authority housing was limited. The LDDC was not a housing authority, i.e. it was not allowed to fund house building, whereas the local authority had restricted housing budgets. There was therefore a strong emphasis on home ownership. The key to the provision of assisted housing by the LDDC lay in its powers to acquire land. For sites considered suitable for this purpose, the LDDC sold land to house builders subject to certain conditions which forced developers to provide housing in their scheme specifically aimed at local residents. One means of achieving this was by giving local residents the right to buy during a limited period, up to six weeks, where after any remaining units could be offered in the open market.

A further provision was to set maximum prices, well below the market prices for that part of the scheme to be offered to local residents. This was the so-called affordable housing scheme. In addition housing association, although held back by lack of funding, were in the market offering occupiers a combination of equity and rent which reduced the level of their initial payment. Normally, assisted housing formed only part of the larger residential scheme, with the balance available on the open market and with an overall price level at the lower end of Docklands scale. The various types of assisted housing were mainly found in Surrey Docks (Southwark), Beckton, (Newham), Wapping and Isle of Dogs(Tower Hamlets). In the open market the strong demand and steep price increases were not just the size of a fashion as one might associate with the 'yuppy' label frequently attached to it. Demand in fact was very soundly based and supported a continuing higher rate of profitable development.

Centre of Employment

One factor behind this positive demand outlook was that London had continued to prosper as a centre of employment during the 1980s. Demand for homes in London area was therefore strong. The opening of a large area for residential development in Docklands had therefore found a ready market. The proximity to the City, the high profile marketing of the area, the attraction of waterside living and the opportunity to provide unique accommodation through conversion had all contributed to the attractions of Docklands. Not surprisingly, the main demand was in those parts of Docklands nearest the City, such as Wapping, Limehouse and South Bank. These were also the areas with the highest potential for interesting warehouse conversions. The superior locations and amenity qualities of these areas were reflecting in the highest residential values in Docklands. The top values were on the waterfront with prices falling away sharply as the water views diminished.

Lofty Views and Luxury Living

In Docklands the coffee, tea and spices have moved out to make way for a new urban breed called the loft dwellers. Their origins appear to combine the custom built artist studios of 19th century Paris and more recent Bohemian pioneers who first moved into the derelict warehouses and factories in the Soho area of Manhattan. It is possible that to the new breed of dwellers, loft living is not just an alternative to the average house or flat, it is more of a commitment to a distinctive way of living, which is taken very seriously indeed.

In Docklands, lofts became a serious business commanding both big money and big art. No longer was demolition seen as the panacea for all new architectural initiatives. The 19th century warehouse and factories were recycled and their potential was harnessed for those lucky enough to buy their way into almost unlimited space near the centre of London, with numerous window views. No longer the loft dweller thought in terms of rooms, square feet became a more important reference specification. It is a somewhat ironical thought that many loft dwellers are living in a 2,000 square feet space that in their parents, and grandparents, days was the oppressive workspace for perhaps 200 people and dockworkers!

Beautiful Penthouses

Penthouses were usually amazing, but if you had well over £1 million to spend, then the Boiler House Penthouse, next to Tower Bridge, was available in the late eighties. It is a triplex apartment situated on the southern half of the seventh floor and the entire eighth and ninth floors of the building with about 350m2 of living accommodation and 125m2 of terraces. The addition of a gallery has made this an exciting three storey home. Views from this apartment are unparalleled with each bedroom leading onto a paved terrace via a sliding patio door. There are four double bedrooms each with an ensuite bathroom, overlooking the river and the City adjacent to Tower Bridge. The estate agent described it as "it has to be seen to be believed!"

Papermill Wharf - stunning riverside apartments in historic Narrow Street with three tier penthouse and within walking distance of Canary Wharf.

Apartments overlooking Limehouse Basin Marina, some with river views, part of a large development of six buildings

Gun Wharf - Grade II listed converted warehouse next to Wapping Station.

Residential Market for the Adventurers

For several years Docklands' residential property market provided handsomely for trailblazers adventurous enough to realise the great potential of the place. Buying purely for speculative purposes and seeking a quick billing, grew to such a number that the market became dampened by speculators trying to take their profits. On some estates there were many homes that had never been lived in on the market, and in order to clear the backlog of houses for sale some punters had to lower their sights. Some estate agents were not sorry to see the demise of the rank speculator. It was considered that empty houses on an estate looked bad and it slowed down the development of the community. So when the gold rush was temporarily over, the rise in prices resumed at a more realistic price.

Individual Characteristics and Prices

It should be pointed out that the Docklands market split into several component parts. Starting in the west, on the north side of the Thames is Wapping close to the City. Travelling east, this leads to Limehouse and then the Isle of Dogs and further east is the massive Royal Docks and Beckton. On the South Bank in Bermondsey, the developments were around the old Courage Brewery and Butlers Wharf in the shadow of Tower Bridge. Further east is Rotherhithe and then the Surrey Quays. They all covered about eight square miles. Each of these areas displayed their own individual characteristics and prices varied markedly. Wapping and Bermondsey were most expensive. For a riverside apartment, with a view of Tower Bridge, you wouldn't get much change from half a million pounds. The most expensive were the penthouses. The warehouse conversion became the ultimate in chic housing. By and large, the more expensive developments avoided the rampant speculation which was evident in the cheaper new developments. By the end of 1980s decade the market settled down. The speculators had had their day and people were selling their deals not their homes. There was a recession beginning and several developers went bankrupt.

Investors from Hong Kong

In the Isle of Dogs, the proposal for Canary Wharf remained the joker in the pack! But once the financial centre went ahead and had the support of the City's banking community, prices started to rise. Water views were very important, even if it was only a canal. About this time another type of speculator emerged; the ex-patriot buyer. The investors from Hong Kong and Singapore rented out their properties for three years and then sold them. They were really interested in new developments.

South of the river, the Surrey Docks was an area that people underestimated. There was a large rise in the residential market, while the massive potential of the Royal Docks began to be thought about. Existing developments in both areas proved popular, but prices were initially a long way to go to catch up with other areas of the Docklands market.

Blossoming of Butler's Wharf

Butler's Wharf proved to be a prime example of the potential that the renaissance of a derelict inner city area can realise. Money and talent were not lacking, but the progress of the development was slow during the first three years after purchase of the 14 acre site. But it began and became a new focal point for the capital, which could in time become as famous as Covent Garden in the West End. The Victorians who built the complex, the 19th century warehouses, "Larders of London" in the shadow of Tower Bridge on the south bank of the Thames would have been impressed with the dedication which was applied to restoring life to these conservation areas.

Unlike St Katharine Docks across the river, the area around Butlers Wharf has retained the flavour of Docklands trade that used to exist here. Shad Thames, the famous 'Canyon' with its lattice work of iron gangways connecting warehouses on the waterside to those behind, evokes the Victorian age possibly more than any other street in London. Not only are there the attractions of the warehouse buildings, but just across the river rises the City. The view of London is probably only equalled by few places from the south bank.

Basic Land Use Strategy

Some 17 listed warehouse buildings form the heart of the scheme. The developers aimed to create a new community, where people can live, work and play - a community in the inner city that does not shut down at night or cater only for the very rich. The planning consent, granted by the LDDC, the planning authority for the area, laid down the basic land use strategy. Of the 1.2 million square feet of space within the area, roughly 45% was residential, the rest being divided among shopping, offices, studio workshops and leisure facilities. At the heart of the area is a new centre for designers, the Design Museum created by the Conran Foundation. Its unique collections and exhibitions on design have attracted industrialists, artists, students and the public. It has influenced the character of the area and style of the goods sold in the local shops.

To give the area variety of residents, the London School of Economics built a hall of residence here to provide lower cost housing. Another way of achieving this was to sell properties to buyers on an 'equity sharing' basis. Under this arrangement the buyer pays for, say half of his house, while renting the remainder until he can raise the cash to buy the whole property.

More Covent Gardens

Old Covent Garden is a good example to Londoners of what can be done if existing buildings are refurbished and turned into modern uses with care. If you are looking for a place without too many of the tourist crowds, Butlers Wharf provides the quieter Victorian venue.

Russia Court and Finland Quay seen from Greenland Quay.

New housing at Greenland Dock enjoy the local facilities of Docklands Sailing Centre. Watersports such as sailing and canoeing make wonderful confidence boosters for youngsters.

Social and private housing along the Surrey Canal.

In July 1988, HM The Queen Mother, looked at housing schemes in the Surrey Docks accompanied by the Chairman of the LDDC, Sir Christopher Benson and the Mayor of Southwark, Rita Sergeant. The following month the Council dropped its opposition to the LDDC.

Top New stylish social housing at Hythe Point, Surrey Docks, south of the River Thames. **Bottom** Innovative self-build schemes in Docklands provided low cost housing for local families and others. Maconochie's Wharf, the first on the Isle of Dogs, is the largest self-build development in Britain. The houses vary in size, shape and layout but the uniformity of materials used -timber, while bricks and slate roofs - give the development a pleasing uncluttered feel.

Maconochi's self-build housing on the Isle of Dogs.

THE SUCCESS STORY OF SURREY DOCKS

The Development cost the Taxpayer very little

Revival of Rotherhithe

Where the memories start to meander like the soft loops in the River Thames past Tower Bridge, there lies on the south bank the former barge berth of Lawrence Wharf. This great wharf did not survive the Luftwaffe blitzing during World War II, which saw nearly half of all buildings in the area, destroyed. Today this area has been transformed into a most desirable development of residential homes for those in pursuit of a luxury lifestyle.

This part of Rotherhithe started to blossom during the 1980s. At the same time great tracts of land from Greenland Dock, the anchor point curving up to Rotherhithe Village has undergone a massive metamorphosis. National and international building companies moved in soon after the formation of the LDDC to create a new living environment for the future. The Danish developers of Lawrence Wharf already were responsible for the riverside Greenland Passage, at the entrance to Greenland Dock, Columbia Wharf, Nelson's Dock and Holiday Inn hotel.

Developments with Parkland

Old Rotherhithe Street is an exciting part of Docklands that forms a quieter backwater with the busy traffic being carried along Salter Road. Many residential homes have been built between the river and Rotherhithe Street. Greenland Docks forms the environmental anchor at the southern point of Rotherhithe. Here extravagant house building provides a new waterside living quarter for London, set around the oldest commercial dock in Britain.

Success Story of Docklands

House building in the Surrey Docks, south of the River began in the early 1980s and is sometimes called one of the success stories of Docklands. This is partly because the largest new housing development in the whole of London is tucked away in this loop of the river. The area started with some advantages. After the closure of the Docks in 1969, the GLC built a spine road through the area and comparatively little new infrastructure was needed. Initially there were some problems. The local authority, Southwark Council had made strenuous efforts to attract the giant Trammell Crow trade mark into the area which was a large wholesale trading centre, after the Port of London Authority had filled in the docks to create the development site. Unfortunately much of the distinctive character of Docklands had already been destroyed by the infilling of the docks.

Tesco Shopping Precinct

After the formation of the LDDC in 1981 the Southwark scheme fell through and the LDDC vested their 132 acres (53 hectares) of land. Negotiations between Southwark Council and the LDDC also broke down. One of the first acts of the LDDC was to arrange for the world of property housing trusts to buy the dilapidated Downtown blocks and renovate them and manage the flats with funds provided by the Corporation. In 1985 the LDDC dug out part of the recently filled in docks to try and return the water which had made it a distinctive part of London. The Surrey and Canada Water was restored and linked by a 6metre wide canal. Soon Tesco the giant store was attracted and developed a neighbourhood shopping centre on Canada Water. Tesco was persuaded to double the size it originally envisaged for its own store, which at one time had the fifth largest turnover in the country. Tesco took a third of the space in the centre and High Street names like BHS, WHSmith, Boots and Top Shop.

South Dock Marina

Associated Newspapers built a plant of one million square feet to print the Daily Mail, bringing 1000 jobs to the area. The Scandic Crown, now The Holiday Inn became the first new hotel in Docklands since the opening of the Tower Thistle Hotel in St Katharine's Dock in 1973. There were new parks and London's largest working marina at the South Dock.

Danish Developers of Greenland Dock

The development of Greenland Docks was one of the first to be tackled making full use of the waterside all around the dock. A developer produced a framework and Greenland Dock turned out to be immensely popular and brought in £72million for a spend of a quarter of that. As it was built the ISLF Danish Company and other developers stepped in. Surrey Docks produced a range of housing and tree lined streets and water canals which were immediately sold and very popular. As in Wapping, the Surrey Dock development cost the taxpayer very little because there was no need for huge infrastructure development. Owner occupation rose from 3% to more than 40%. Profits from sale of land enabled the LDDC to invest over £10.5 million to help the Council refurbish over 1500 Council homes. When the LDDC handed back the area to Southwark in December 1996, the population had risen from just under 6,000 in 1981 to 16,000. The Corporation provided land for 4,000 of the new homes built. Further west along the river the commercial activities at Hays Wharf, east of London Bridge, was available for development in the beautiful Hays Galleria of fashion shops, cafes and restaurants overlooking the River Thames.

Hays Galleria

One of the most spectacular warehouse conversions in Docklands is undoubtedly that of Hays Dock on the South Bank, where a new tourist attraction in the formed of a glazed "Galleria" with shops, bars and restaurants forms the space between the original restored warehouse blocks. The Hays Galleria is part of a major renewal area, known as London Bridge City, which includes office blocks, the refurbishment of a number of historic buildings and the construction of a new river pier and riverside walk for the public. The new headquarters of the Mayor of London has been constructed adjacent to this development.

An aerial view of Surrey Quays in 1995 looking north west, shows complete transformation of the whole peninsular into housing, marina and sports centre. The white building in the centre is the Mail's £100 million printing plant which was fully operational in 1988.

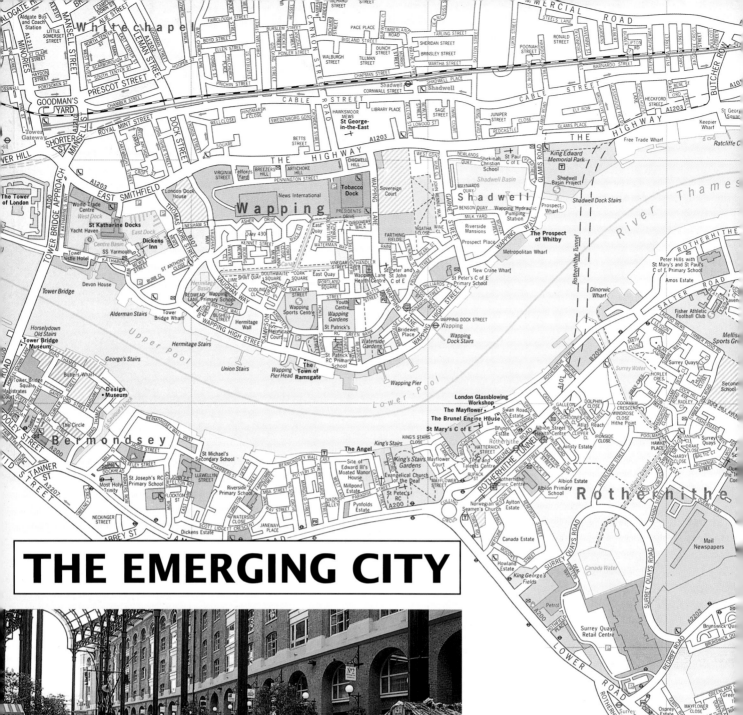

THE EMERGING CITY

Hayes Galleria at London Bridge City.

Anchor Brewhouse, Butlers Wharf and Design Museum at Bermondsey.

Scale 1:10 000

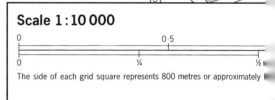

The side of each grid square represents 800 metres or approximately

⊖ Underground Station	△ Police station
🚢 RiverBus pier	△ Fire station
• Bus stop	⊞ Hospital/health centre
P Parking	⊞ Library
← One way street	PO Post office
ℹ Tourist information centre (open all year)	⊠ Post box
ℹ Tourist information centre (open April-October)	† Church
☎ Telephone	○ Sports centre / club
T Toilet	

London Docklands

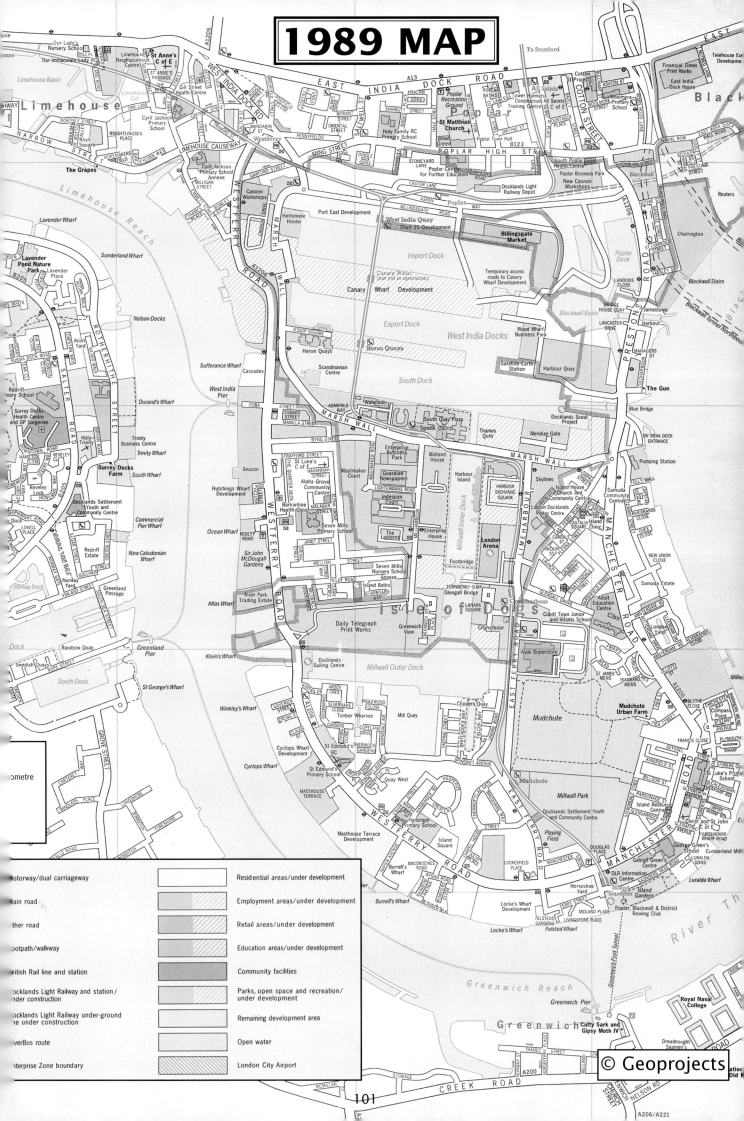

1989 MAP

© Geoprojects

High Standards of Properties at Competitive Prices

Modern Conveniences

If you have ever been searching for a property to rent in London you will undoubtedly come across the ageing furniture and 1960s kitchens, which your friendly agents would describe as 'full of character'. Docklands with its combination of high quality new properties and completely refurbished remarkable warehouses offered high standards at competitive prices and often incorporating interesting and unusual architectural features, as in converted lofts. First of all, kitchens are fully fitted with washing machines, fridge freezers and the majority have dishwashers as well. Put into perspective if one compares a four bedroom modern town house in some developments in Battersea , south of the river, built by the same company in the Isle of Dogs overlooking the River or the Docks the price difference is almost double. They are both finished to the same high standards yet in Docklands in the late 1980s the price was £225 per week whilst Battersea cost £400. If one compared this with Kensington the price was even greater with the same house being £700 per week. In Docklands the quality is so high that even a one-bedroom flat at £120 per week would have every conceivable gadget. Where else would one be able to rent a two bedroom, two bathroom flat with a jacuzzi for around £200 per week in the mid 1980s!

Health Clubs and Water Sports

Astute young executives in the City with their ability to sniff out a bargain had already been renting in Docklands for a few years because of the boom there. Travelling to work can take about 10 minutes rather than the 45 for some of the more established letting areas, such as Kensington and Chelsea, although the atmosphere is quite different. The scope of the facilities Docklands can offer also encourages tenants to enjoy a lifestyle hard to match elsewhere in London. Squash courts, tennis courts, gymnasiums and swimming pools are all available. There are also all forms of water sports from windsurfing to water-skiing, rowing to dinghy sailing. These facilities are not only used by the beginners, but also those up to champion standard with the prestigious powerboat championships taking place in the Royal Docks. The new Docklanders also enjoyed the privilege of driving and parking as they pleased. Unlike the rest of London every property has a parking space or garage and wheelclamps are an unknown phenomenon in the area.

Historic Pubs and Sites

Docklands also has some of the most historic and famous sites in London, including the Tower of London, which is within easy walking distance of the western dock development in Wapping and developments around Horselydown Downs Square, south of Tower Bridge. A wide range of properties are available in these areas, from small apartment flats to luxurious riverside warehouse conversions. St Katharine's Dock with its delightful combination of winebars and restaurants overlooking the marinas create a village atmosphere, reminiscent of some of the more secluded parts of Chelsea.

The Prospect of Whitby pub is one of the oldest and most renowned pubs in London Docklands. Situated at the eastern end of Wapping, it has stunning water views making it an extremely pleasant "local" for the residents of developments in Wapping High Street and along Wapping Wall.

Stunning Waterside Views

Price ranges are reasonable for apartments or studio flats to two-bedroom flats on the waterfront. The developments, further east on the south side of the Isle of Dogs, have undoubtedly the best view in London. Not only do they look out on the busy River Thames, but also offer stunning uninterrupted views of the former Royal Naval College at Greenwich, the Royal Observatory and the Cutty Sark. Again the rents are reasonable. The developments and security, stunning views and high standards of interior provide lovely homes for the City market. Now that the Docklands Light Railway operates to Lewisham, their front doors are linked to the City in about 15 minutes.

Community Spirit

Another unusual aspect of living in Docklands is the amazing community spirit, which has gone into each new development. The area has always been renowned for its close knit community and it is pleasing to see this re-establishing itself. Communal barbecues take place on a regular basis throughout the summer and it is this friendly community spirit and extremely competitive rental prices that makes Docklands the place to live. The message is so why not come and enjoy 21st century living near the heart of London!

Contributions of Estate Agents

Occasionally in a lifetime, a surprising innovative service is born which changes forever the way things used to be. The evolution of City estate agents and their move into Docklands in the eighties was one of those times. It takes a special dedication to blaze a new path in any field especially field as complex and dynamic as that of new homes and office marketing in Docklands. It took a daring commitment to defy the old image of East London. They had an unprecedented vision of the rising market in the area.

"The evening mist closes the riverside with poetry"

Dramatic Change in East London

Docklands has been the most dramatically changing and improving section of London during the past few decades and is still one of the prime areas in which to invest in residential property. Developments and refurbishment have been carried out into high standard buildings, providing luxury homes with sustained demand, prices have enjoyed exceptionally good increases, especially with the success and letting of Canary Wharf accommodation for commercial purposes. Docklands have seen most of the price trends and fluctuations to date. In the early 1990s the hope-for price boom never materialised and there was a slowing market. However strong price increases started in the second half of the decade.

Quaint Wapping and Bermondsey

With the newly opened Jubilee Line extension and the well established Docklands Light Railway and London City Airport, prices have continued to increase to make docklands residential property a superior investment. Wapping is probably the most well known part of Docklands and certainly was the best short term investment in the 1980s. Apart from the advantages of good transport facilities and opening of the Tobacco Dock shopping in 1989. The area has quite an historic setting. An exceptional feature of Wapping and Bermondsey are the superb warehouse conversions. Amongst the former derelict remains of former Victorian warehouses there are now imaginative and stunning apartments available. Inexpensive and hitech modern homes nestle side by side offering the pioneer purchaser many choices. Shrewd buyers also invested in less expensive properties around St Saviour Dock, south of Tower Bridge. This soon had the same high standard facilities as Wapping and reached its potential within 2-3 years to become one of the most fashionable sections in Docklands.

Docklands, however has become more than just the domain of the 'arty' section of the population and a place for those people looking for a sound property investment. Increasingly, many Londoners, especially City executives and those seeking high quality modern living in specialist accommodation convenient for the City and West End are coming home to Docklands.

"Whistler's Poetry"

Whistler in the 1870s described Docklands "the evening mist closes the riverside with poetry, as well as with a veil, and port buildings lose themselves in the dim sky and the tall chimneys become campanili and the warehouses are palaces in the night." Similar sayings or words have been used by many developers in the Docklands area over the past 20 years. The same developers state that there is no excuse now for Londoners not to be full of health and beauty with so many residential complexes coming out in Docklands with major recreational facilities. Perhaps you fancy a swim in an indoor heated pool - and a workout on an exercise bicycle and rowing machine before you set off for the office in the morning. Then what about a game of tennis and a sauna when you get back, or if you want to work from home the use of a conference room complete with photocopier, fax machine and telex are available in some of these large developments, such as the Cascade, one of the early developments on the western side of the Isle of Dogs. They have huge balconies, 50ft long providing sweeping views all around the development towards the City, the South East and North.

Mooring Facilities

In some of these developments there is a place to moor your boat, in addition to all your recreational facilities. Some projects in the Surrey Docks have 200 berth marina complexes. There are also yacht clubs associated with large scale developments on the Surrey side. The attraction is to business people who want to entertain their clients against a backdrop of spectacular water views. After all Mr Grant Ware Travelstead the 6'2" tall Kentuckian headed the initial consortium to build a massive commercial home for his empire at Canary Wharf, gambling at that time with approximately US $4 1/2billion.

The Cascades Apartments described in a brochure: "Cascades takes the cadence of water music for its theme, and evokes gentle ripples of humour with light-hearted symbolism."

Warehouse conversion in Narrow Street, Limehouse. Buyers were charmed by the enchanting interiors created by top designers and Dockland's pioneer developers.

Sir Thomas More Court, Wapping, one of the most sought after canal-side homes in London.

Stylish waterside homes overlooking Shadwell Basin, Wapping, less than a mile from the City.

Timber Wharf homes, Isle of Dogs, gives the impression of an oasis of tranquillity!

Clippers Quay: A waterside community with moorings, surrounding the former graving dock at Millwall.

City Brokers and Bankers

Wapping is the part of Docklands nearest to the City of London. Property values in Wapping are high; matching the best London has to offer, with an array of properties of character, with good transport links. The district has beautiful riverside walkways and history-laden pedigree. The assets include proximity to the City business location. Tower Bridge setting and water are always a seller. The new dwellers are City brokers, bankers and insurers who slip back to their waterside pads after their daily toll. There are many international business people too, renting and returning to the area in between assignments. The properties are used as pied-a-terre by semi-retired rich folk of all ages - the riverside during the week, the country at weekends, or vice versa.

Millionaire's Row

There is a line-up taking in big family houses tucked away along the ornamental canal and superlative warehouse conversions along the High Street and Wapping Wall. Modern and renovated serviced blocks with all modern conveniences include the Free Trade, Atlantic and Dundee Wharves. There is no shortage of gems: St Katharine Docks boasts a millionaire's row of villas, cute cottages on Dock Street and apartments overlooking the marina at City Quay. Some buyers consider Wapping as the quintessential London urban village, rather than Wimbledon or Hampstead, which are described as essentially suburban. Young professionals love both the area and the short journey to the City or Canary Wharf. The supply of riverside warehouses in Wapping is beginning to dry up. The majority of developments are modern offers, located just off-river in many cases.

Isle of Dogs Mixed Residents

The Isle of Dogs is the commercial centre of Docklands, just a few hundred metres from the new riverside luxury developments. East End children still play in Docklands most mixed property market. The total cost of dock building at the beginning of the 19th century was about £7 million, which would just about buy an investment portfolio in the Wharf micro-market at West India Quay. The continuing stream of workers to the Wharf - currently over 40,000, soak up the supply of new developments. Away from the busy business centres, there is a tranquil atmosphere anchored by expanses of water, riverside walks and green open spaces everywhere on the Island. The residential mix still varies despite the influx of white-collar workers. Actors live around the corner from retired lightermen, foreign executives rent next to families who have been there for generations, but such such groups are largely segregated into council and private schemes. Modern riverside apartments, many with porterage, fitness facilities and all modern conveniences, dominate the area. Family housing tends to be clustered in the centre and foot of the island. There are few warehouse conversions, mainly the expensive sugar warehouses on the North Quay.

Upmarket Shad Thames

The upmarket cluster of converted warehouses around Shad Thames is one of London's cutest neighbourhoods and its desirability increases with every new attraction to open in the area. It is the most bustling and cosmopolitan district along the river. Remarkable arrays of Victorian warehouses have survived, now almost all transformed into plush apartments. Eye-catching blocks plus the gap between the originals. There are virtually no houses in Shad Thames. The New Concordia Wharf offers a wealth of original features topped off with impeccable river views.

Predominantly affluent single people and childless couples of all ages live here. City gents stroll across Tower Bridge to the office. Designers, photographers and media personalities have their living and workspaces. Foreign business executives live the good life in plush corporate lets. Many celebrities also live here.

Greatest Residential Area

The central area of Surrey Quays is the greatest residential of all dock areas, conveying a real community feel and with the Jubilee Line Extension, Canary Wharf is the next stop. Billed as a designer suburb of London, the leafy avenues and smart new housing attract the highest proportion of families in Dockland. An increasing proportion of the 25,000 residents are young professionals looking for a relaxing atmosphere away from the hubbub of business. Much of the riverfront is dominated by new apartment blocks. There are also four and five bedroom modern town houses with gardens. Rare warehouse conversions are largely restricted to the area around old Rotherhithe Street.

PROPERTY MAPS & CONTACTS

Location Information (Maps not to scale)

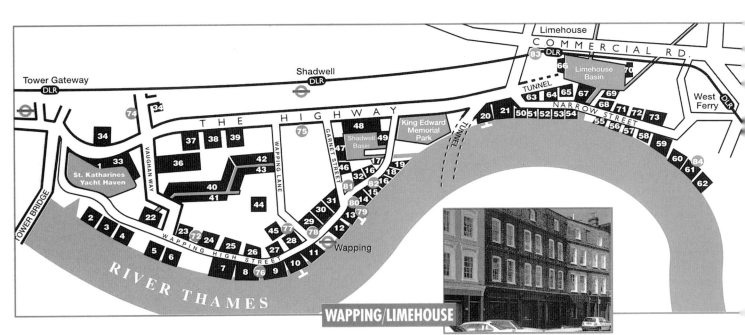

WAPPING/LIMEHOUSE

Wapping

DEVELOPMENTS (Tel no = New)

1 Ivory House
2 Presidents Quay
3 Millers Wharf
4 Tower Bridge Wharf
5 Capital Wharf
6 Pierhead
7 Olivers Wharf
8 Orient Wharf
9 Aberdeen Wharf...... 020-7407 3669/ 456 6800
10 St John's Wharf
11 Gun Wharf
12 Towerside

13 St Hilda's Wharf
14 New Crane Wharf
15 Great Jubilee Wharf
16 Thorpe's Yard 020-7690 9990
17 Monza Building.......... 020-7407 3669
18 Pelican Wharf
19 Trafalgar Court
20 Free Trade Wharf
21 Atlantic Wharf
22 Hermitage Waterside
23 Hermitage Court
24 The Schoolhouse
25 Dundee Court
26 The Sanctuary
27 Bridewell Place
28 Gun Place
29 The Carronades

30 The Falconet
31 Prusoms Island
32 Prospect Place
33 The City Quay............ 020-7481 9898
34 Royal Tower Lodge
35 Sceptre Court
36 Quay 430
37 Telfords Yard
38 Breezers Court
39 Pennington Court
40 East Quay
41 Spirit Quay
42 Discovery Walk
43 Waterman Way
44 Portland Square
45 Chimney Court
46 Riverside Mansions

47 Newlands Quay
48 Maynards Quay
49 Peartree Lane

Limehouse

50 Keepier Wharf
51 Phoenix Wharf 020-7456 6800
52 Commercial Wharf
53 Old Sun Wharf
54 Chinnocks Wharf
55 Victoria Wharf
56 Papermill Wharf
57 Blyth's Wharf
58 Duke Shore Wharf
59 Dunbar Wharf
60 Molines Wharf 020-7456 6800

61 Limekiln Wharf
62 Dundee Wharf
63 St George's Square
64 Eagle Wharf West
65 Regent's Gate
66 Limehouse Basin 020-7423 9
67 Goodhart Place
68 Victoria Lock
69 Quayside
70 Commercial Wharf 020-7531 9
71 Sovereign Place 020-7539 3
72 The Water Gardens
73 Ropemakers Fields

ESTATE AGENTS

74 Felicity J Lord 020-7481
75 Blue Chip 020-7709
76 FPD Savills 020-7456
77 Phoenix Property 020-7702
78 Carleton Smith & Partners .. 020-7488
79 Docklands Accommodation
   Agency 020-7702
80 Oliver Jaques.................... 020-7702
81 Property Liaisons................ 020-7680
82 Knight Frank 020-7480
83 McDowalls 020-7790
84 Cosgrove Estates 020-7537

SHAD THAMES/BERMONDSEY

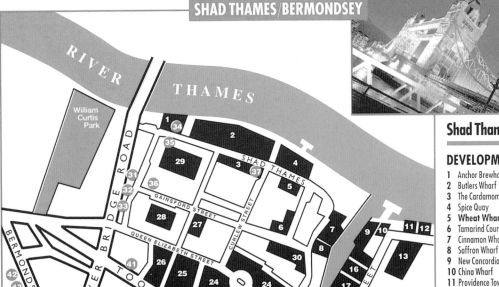

Shad Thames/Bermondsey

DEVELOPMENTS (Tel no = New)

1 Anchor Brewhouse/Boilerhouse
2 Butlers Wharf
3 The Cardamom Building
4 Spice Quay
5 Wheat Wharf 020-7407 3669
6 Tamarind Court
7 Cinnamon Wharf
8 Saffron Wharf
9 New Concordia Wharf
10 China Wharf
11 Providence Tower
12 Springalls Wharf
13 Jacob's Island
14 Hobbs Court
15 Little London
16 St Saviours Wharf
17 Vogans Mill
18 Unity Wharf
19 Lloyds Wharf
20 Scotts Sufferance Wharf

21 Dockhead
22 Christians Warehouse
23 Millennium Square
24 The Circle
25 Raven Wharf
26 Boss House
27 Horselydown Mansions
28 Tower Bridge Piazza
29 Horselydown Square
30 Butlers & Colonial Wh..07000 46

ESTATE AGENTS

31 Chestertons.............. 020-7357 7999
32 Alex Neil...................... 020-7234
33 Duncan Allen 020-7407
34 Rive............................... 020-7407
35 Hamptons....................... 020-7407
36 Cluttons......................... 020-7407
37 FPD Savills 020-794
38 Michael Kalmar & Co 020-7407
39 L Spring 020-725
40 John D Wood 0800 01
41 Felicity J Lord 020-7407
42 Daniel Cobb 020-735
43 Williams Lynch 020-740

106

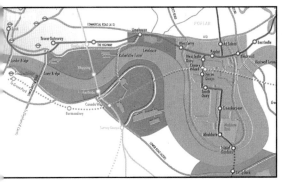

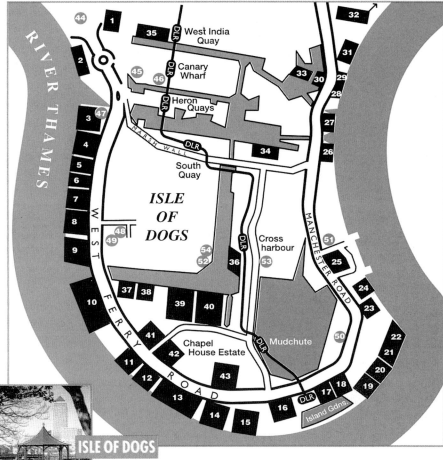

© Guide Magazines 1999.

LONDON DOCKLANDS

Key to main transport links

- MAJOR TRUNK ROADS
- LT UNDERGROUND STATIONS
- DLR NETWORK
- DLR EXTENSION
- EAST LONDON LINE
- JUBILEE LINE EXTENSION

e of Dogs

DEVELOPMENTS (Tel no = New)

remiere Place
anary Riverside 020-7512 9393
ascades
he Anchorage
Millennium Harbour .. 020-7537 7502
cean Wharf 020-7512 9955
tlas Wharf 020-7456 6800
rnhem Wharf
ld Bell Gate
yclops Wharf
asthouse Terrace
Maritime Quay 020-7537 7122
urrells Wharf
aconochies Wharf
ockes Wharf 020-7512 9955
orseshoe Close
ralda Gardens
umberland Mills
aledonian Wharf
bitt's Wharf
ymouth Wharf
ompass Point
illennium Court 020-7536 0956
illennium Wharf 020-7531 9997
ndon Yard
alleons View
erhead Lock 020-7538 9359
ldharbour
ncordia Wharf

30 Jamestown Harbour
31 Vantage 2000 .... 020-7531 6518
32 Virginia Quay 020-7536 0671
33 The Boardwalk 020-7987 2200
34 Meridian Place
35 Port East Apts 020-7537 0000
36 City Harbour
37 Kingsbridge Court
38 Quay View
39 Mill Quay
40 Clippers Quay
41 Ironmongers Place
42 Barnfield Place
43 Lockesfield Place

ESTATE AGENTS

44 Alphabet City 020-7345 9666
45 Knight Frank 020-7512 9955
46 Lincoln Radley 020-7512 9388
47 Alex Neil 020-7537 9859
48 Elizabeth Pryce 020-7987 9065
49 Gaynor Walker 020-7364 0500/1
50 Merrydown Kent 020-7538 8722
51 Property Matters 020-7538 0102
52 Phillips Residential 020-7363 0606
53 Sand Property 020-7308 9943

SOLICITORS FOR PROPERTY

54 Alexander Johnson 020-7537 7000

ISLE OF DOGS

SURREY QUAYS/ROTHERHITHE

Surrey Quays/Rotherhithe

DEVELOPMENTS (Tel no = New)

1 Cherry Garden Pier
2 Princes Tower
3 Hope Wharf
4 Elephant Lane
5 Brunel Point
6 Princes Riverside
7 King & Queen Wharf
8 Globe Wharf
9 Sovereign View
10 Pageant Steps
11 Southside Quay 01277 262422
12 Canada Wharf
13 Lawrence Wharf
14 Trinity Wharf 020-7237 8408
15 New Caledonian Wharf
16 Greenland Passage
17 Rainbow Quay
18 Swedish Quays
19 Baltic Quay

20 Greenland Quay
21 Howland Quay
22 Brunswick Quay
23 Aland Court
24 The Lakes
25 Finland Yard
26 Canada Waters 020-7394 9589
27 Wolfe Crescent
28 Hithe Point
29 The Pumphouse 020-7407 3669
30 Bywater Place
31 Lavender Dock 020-7702 3434

ESTATE AGENTS

32 Kinleigh 020-7231 3800
33 Winkworth 020-7237 9119
34 Burnet Ware & Graves 020-7232 0333
35 Alex Neil 020-7394 9988
36 Burwood Marsh 020-7394 1999
37 Oliver Jaques 020-7231 5050
38 Property Liaisons 020-7252 0111
39 Cluttons 020-7237 7575
40 Seagers Residential 020-7394 9200

Property Maps and Estate Agents

This map shows all the new properties privately developed In the four areas of Docklands, namely Wapping and Limehouse, Isle of Dogs, Bermondsey and Surrey Quays including Rotherhithe. The Jubilee Line extension was opened in 2000 and serves the South Bank, Surrey Quays, Canary Wharf, in addition to the Docklands Light Railway that has been extended to Lewisham.

Unity Wharf Mill has a wealth of original charm and character and overlooks St Saviours Dock, Bermondsey.

An apartment in an original warehouse conversion in a historic part of Docklands, Narrow Street, Limehouse.

Pelican Wharf in Wapping offers unique Thameside apartments next to the Prospect of Whitby pub with the only private floating river terrace with deep water moorings in London.

Right across the dock water from Canary Wharf and linked by a footbridge, is West India Quay. Among the apartments available here are the Port East Penthouses in the beautiful Grade I listed buildings, c 1802. Floors of solid oak in living areas, sandblasted brick walls and original exposed ceiling beams are among their features.

Princes Tower, Rotherhithe - Three bedroom flat with impressive reception and balcony offering views over the river to Tower Bridge.

Vogans Mill, Bermondsey - character two bedroom flat in a warehouse conversion.

CONSERVATION AREAS IN DOCKLANDS

Designation of Conservation Areas

The regeneration of London Docklands was initiated primarily for economic and social reasons but in the process it created an opportunity to conserve the maritime architectural heritage of London. Efforts were made to invigorate the historic urban fabric with new activity and to enhance the character and appearance of both areas of special architectural interest. The unique historic warehouses and buildings had been neglected and many had been demolished. These buildings served the docks and wharves of the Port of London for a number of centuries. The buildings that survived after 1980 represented the last chance and it needed a great deal of dedication for some to be saved for posterity as a record of the greatest port in the world "possibly".

It was not always easy to convince the owners of derelict buildings that their property must be preserved. However through a combination of grants and legal restrictions, resulting from planning permissions granted for conversion and change of use, the vast majority of Docklands' surviving historical buildings, many of which are dotted along the Thames riverside have been saved.. Furthermore the designation of 17 conservation areas in Docklands has ensured a stable planning environment and allowed landowners and developers to have confidence and reasonable certainty of the status of their land or buildings. They have also provided for the public local community an assurance that areas are being protected and any environmental improvements will take that into consideration.

Architectural Heritage

Substantial sums of money have been spent on a number of listed buildings in Docklands, including the Grade 1 listed Georgian warehouses on the north quay of the West India Docks built 1802. More than £20 million was spent in a major programme of works to ensure the structural stability of these buildings and to protect them from further decay until their recent conversion into luxury apartments and the housing of the Museum in Docklands. All the conservation areas in Docklands contain buildings and waterscape of architectural, historic and environmental interest. Six of the designated areas have been classified as being of National significance, and identified by Government as being of outstanding architectural or historic interest. Much of the old riverside areas of Wapping, Limehouse, Bermondsey and Rotherhithe are in fact protected by being included within conservation areas.

The regeneration which has taken place in such areas has been with conservation in mind. New buildings within these areas are expected to blend with their surroundings, although in some circumstances modern architecture does clash with old Victorian warehouses. Although the conservation aspect was of prime importance, new buildings and alterations and extensions to existing buildings within conservation areas have had to follow high standards of design and had to make positive contributions to the character of the area for the future. New buildings have been encouraged as a means of filling gaps in street frontages and riverside, completing the enclosure of urban spaces and

helping to eradicate dereliction. Additionally environmental improvements have been carried out in conservation areas which include landscaping and enhancement of roads. The preservation and enhancement of the conservation areas has ensured that the regeneration process has been woven into the existing urban fabric to enrich the architectural heritage for future generations.

Regeneration of Thames Riverside

The transformation of London's river from a double band of warehouses and smoky factories to the most desirable real estate in the capital is almost complete up to the Isle of Dogs. Very soon, there will be no more land or buildings available for residential developments on the bank of the Thames, near the centre of London. In the space of just 20 years, the riverside has completely changed. In the early 1970s, barely anyone lived on the river downstream of Chelsea, except for the Archbishop of Canterbury, at Lambeth Palace on the South Bank. The ships that used to be moored three deep on the wharves on the Pool of London had long gone. The docks were closed, the cranes stayed idle and the warehouses that sucked in raw materials from all over the globe, and supplied the world with manufactured goods stood empty, and unloved up to the beginning of 1970s. At that time it seemed that nothing could be done with the whole area and the warehouses and that it would remain a wilderness forever. But an extraordinary thing happened, a few visionaries saw the potential of the old wharves as big spaces to live in and the stories of some of these conversions are given on the next pages under the conversion of historic warehouses.

Pumping Station Site for Orchestra

State of the art technology is the main reason why a world orchestra would make its home in Docklands. In the 1980s when many orchestras were under financial threats, the Academy of St Martin-in-the Fields was to build and move to a purpose-built recording studio, rehearsal hall and concert hall complex in the former Hydraulic Pumping Station overlooking Shadwell Basin and near the historic pub of the Prospect of Whitby in Wapping. This Station used to provide hydraulic power for the operation of locks and cranes in the Port of London. It was considered that a new Docklands home would be the perfect solution, principally for building a state-of-the-art recording studio for orchestras to use. They would be able to expand to be commercially viable. In the absence of subsidies, they would be able to hire out the studio, which would be of great help. The rehearsal rooms would also generate income. Observation platforms could be provided for the public to watch the orchestra rehearse. For Docklands residents too, a new home at Wapping would mean that music would be a regular feature of expanding social life in the area. The Academy of St Martin-in-the-Fields aimed to mount an international fundraising campaign for about £5 million to convert the Station, but unfortunately the project did not take off.

WEST INDIA QUAY HERITAGE WAREHOUSES

Housing the Docklands Museum and Luxury Penthouses

"Industrial Cathedrals"

The West India Quay warehouses on the Isle of Dogs, built to store bonded sugar, coffee, rum, juices, hardwood and spices from the West Indies, were so nationally important at the beginning of the 19th century that the Prime Minister of the time laid the foundation stone in July 1800 and another Prime Minister performed the opening ceremony two years later. In the 1980s grandiose plans from major developers to bring them back into modern day use as Port East foundered when the costs of working such unique warehouses were detailed. It was a price too high even for Olympia & York, the developers of £4 billion Canary Wharf, who struck a deal with the LDDC which involved the contractors Trafalgar House.

English Heritage Code

Fortunately English Heritage had laid out such a strict code of heritage quality for the five storey buildings that renovation costs were likely to be three times the normal. Flagstones, 200 years old, lifted out a few years ago were carefully numbered and emergency repair work was carried out under the eagle eyes of English Heritage Inspectors.

During 1990s, the biggest planning debate in the history of East London was fought over proposals to convert Europe's finest warehouses into a £40 million waterside live and work accommodation. Developers started secret talks with the former LDDC's planners. Warehouse pioneers and conservationists demanded a public enquiry over the future of what was described as the "Industrial Cathedrals" warehouses on the North Quay of the former West India Export Dock. They were protected by the Department of the Environment as Grade I Listed buildings and are the finest remaining Georgian warehouses in the world. They were last used in the 1970s as the West India Docks were finally closed after nearly 180 years.

Spectacular Apartments

Finally the contract to bring the massive warehouses back into use went to the fast growing company owned by a Canadian, Manhattan Lofts Corporation, which has transformed part of the City centre living in London with luxury loft conversions. Tower Hamlets Council Planners and other bodies have gone for the developers' simplistic designs to restore and renovate the old warehouses but the plans for them were still spectacular and the scheme was the biggest the firm had undertaken. The LDDC's planners were pleased by the stunning concept of the re-development which had satisfied English Heritage and Local Community groups. A joint consortium of contractors carried out the construction work.

Shops and Hotel

The scheme includes shops and restaurants on the ground and first floors and so called luxury loft apartments on higher floors. On the east side, a 30 storey massive tower built for a hotel. On the west side is the 110,000 square feet Museum of Docklands. During 2000, spectacular loft apartments were for sale at sky high prices which were snapped up, not surprisingly, considering their heritage and position alongside the gleaming Canary Wharf. The West India North Quay has its own station on the Docklands Light Railway and it is a short walk from Canary Wharf station on the Jubilee Line extension. It is less than a minute away from the Docklands Highway and Limehouse Link, linking Docklands to the City and West End.

Glorious History

The original warehouses on the North Quay were designed by the architect George Guilt and were built by the contractors Adams and Robinson ready for the opening of the West India Import Dock in 1802. In 1814, iron columns were inserted by the engineer John Rennie to strengthen the floors for storing the heavy bags of sugar. The Import Dock, financed by the rich London merchants, was the first cargo handling dock in London. It was the world's largest water structure of its kind for the next forty years.

By 1808 the North Quay transit sheds and warehouses were handling 125,000 tonnes of sugar each year in barrels, the cargo worth millions of pounds on the London Stock Market. The quayside was lined with flat-bottomed ships from the West Indies, unloading sugar and molasses into the warehouses. Early in the 20th century the sugar was arriving in 200 lb bags and the work of unloading was carried out at such a furious pace causing such bleeding to the dockers' shoulders that the area was named "Blood Alley".

Museum of Docklands

Other imports from the West Indies included rum, cocoa, pimento and juices as well as exotic hardwoods such as lignum vitae, logwood, mahogany and rosewood for the English furniture trade. Just before World War I, the Port of London Authority replaced the wooden transit sheds on the quayside with two-storey brick reinforced concrete buildings which were demolished in the mid-1980s. The sugar warehouses were bombed during World War II and only two of the original nine warehouses survived. The raw sugar blazed for almost a week destroying the warehouses and Canary Wharf spirit shed on the south side of the dock; it was the biggest fire in London since the Great Fire of 1666. After the war, the berths were used mainly by Jeppson Heaton shipping company for general imports and exports on their services of nine vessels a month to and from the Mediterranean ports. The quayside was closed for shipping early in 1970. The history of the dock is told in the Museum of Docklands, housed in the first of these two warehouses.

Free Trade Wharf at Shadwell takes its name from the two listed riverside warehouses which were built by the Honourable East India Company in 1796. The listed buildings have been converted into residential and commercial premises along a mall, with adjoining luxurious leisure and fitness facilities as part of the new apartments on the west side. The Prospect of Whitby pub is nearby.

Luxury lifestyle living in the Sugar Warehouses, built by the West India Dock Company in 1802, at West India Quay, Isle of Dogs. The Grade I listed building has been painstakingly preserved and enhanced with modern wood, steel and glass fittings to give a superb fusion of 19th century architecture and modern environment. The penthouses facing Canary Wharf are adjacent to restaurants, a health and fitness club and a multi-screen cinema complex at Port East.

CONVERSION OF HISTORIC WAREHOUSES

The Treasure Troves of Docklands

Protection of 19th Century Warehouses

A survey carried out by the Department of the Environment culminated in 1983 with the listing of most of the 19th century warehouses as buildings of architectural and historical importance giving them statutory protection. This provided a new and exciting form of renovation project for housing bringing large numbers of people to Docklands and providing a powerful symbol for the regeneration. It also provided a stimulus for the development of surrounding sites although there had been a number of conversion schemes carried out on warehouses before the coming of the LDDC. Most of the renovations took place between 1980 and 1990. The earlier ones included surviving warehouses and small granaries in Rotherhithe dating from 1790s.

Oliver's Wharf

An early scheme and one of the first warehouses to be converted into housing in the early 1970s was Olivers Wharf in Wapping. This was one of the many large imposing warehouses built along the Thames during the second half of the 19th century following the Customs Consolidation Act of 1853, which allowed its use as bonded stores. This building was unusual in that it was the high Victorian Gothic tradition rather than the more usual classical structural style. Within this building the large open floors with high ceilings gave the opportunity for spacious accommodation with the added excitement of wide river views and beautiful lighting effects from reflections from the water.

New Concordia Wharf

An early scheme carried out in the 1980s was the conservation of New Concordia Wharf in St Saviour Dock in Bermondsey. Here considerable attention was paid to detail with new elements being in sympathy with the original. One of the difficulties of adapting such as this to housing was providing it with the necessary level of fire protection. Here the architects determined to retain the original interior structure, which comprised iron columns supporting timber beams and joists with timber floorboards. The iron columns were coated with mastic material which swells when heated and provides insulation to stop the columns cracking by heat. The large timber beams were such a size that charring during a fire provides protection to the remaining timber which retains its load-bearing capacity. The floor joists and boards are of such a slender size that they could not provide fire protection. In order to overcome this the floors were provided with concrete slabs laid on top of the original boards. The electric wall cranes on the dockside were also retained and although only dating from 1930s they were considered of visual importance in the historic building.

Gun Wharf

Once certain developers had pioneered the principle of converting warehouses into housing, other companies began to look for similar opportunities. Barratt of East London were one of those carrying out the refurbishment of Gun Wharf at Wapping. This building although very much in the late 19th century tradition was mostly built in the 1920s with two bays being added after 1937. The interior structure comprised steel stanchions encased in concrete supporting the concrete floors already giving an acceptable level of fireproofing. In this building the loading bay flaps on the riverside were used as balconies.

Vogan Mill

On the south bank St Saviours Dock in Bermondsey once formed the mouth of the now vanished River Neckinger. This narrow and historic waterway had warehouses rising sheer from the water on either side giving an intense of enclosure. These warehouses near New Concordia Wharf underwent a programme of refurbishment by several developers. Warehouse conversion in this area included St Saviour Wharf, a large Victorian building and the adjacent Vogan Mill. This had been in use for 130 years milling peas, lentils and barley and until the early 1980s it was still in use receiving its raw materials by barges which were emptied by vacuum pump. The large white silo which is an important local landmark is newly built. Other adjacent wharves, Unity Wharf and Lloyds Wharf have also been conserved. On the other side of the dock Christians warehouses were also converted into housing by Bovis. The Lucoms, projecting boxes fitted with hoists and used to load goods into the loopholes below, were retained and used as extensions to the upper flats.

Butlers Wharf

Upstream St Saviours dock is the vast Butlers Wharf complex of Victorian warehouses. The most dramatic part of this complex is the section along Shad Thames where the buildings rise sheer from the back edge of the pavements on both sides of the street, which is crossed by bridges at several levels giving it the appearance of a canyon. Sir Terance Conran as Chairman of the development group has, beautifully renovated the original Butlers Wharf building designed by Tolley and Dale and built 1871-73. The bridges have been beautifully restored and the warehouses have created magnificent residential group of buildings next to Tower Bridge.

Free Trade Wharf

Another major development scheme for important early warehouses at Free Trade Wharf at Shadwell were also beautifully refurbished. These were built in the 1790s by the East India Company to the designs of Richard Jupp. The warehouses comprised a pair of brick buildings with arcades facing each other across a courtyard running from the highway to the River Thames. The development was entered from the street under the storm arch surmounted by the Coat of Arms of the East India Company.

London Bridge City

An impressive redevelopment was the London Bridge City on the south bank between London Bridge and Tower Bridge. St Martin's Property Group originally acquired the site in 1981, following the acquisition of the properties of Hays Wharf whose association dated back some 300 years when in 1651 its founding father Alexander Hay landed goods on the site to the east of London Bridge.

Proposals and Funding

In the heart of Wapping, hidden behind 20 foot walls, a remarkable transformation took place in the late 1980s. It was the fruit of many years planning that resulted in the transformation of the skin floor warehouse into a shopping and leisure complex twice the size of Covent Gardens' famous market hall or plaza. It was in 1977 that the skin floor was bought from a property company. The building, which is sandwiched between News International and Wapping Lane, was in a sorry state and had been bombed in the Second World War. The original developer had planned for a shopping centre but he could not raise the cash to make it a reality. Then came the idea to use this site for medieval jousting competitions. It was reckoned that the City business people would want to come and watch such a spectacle. This suggestion fortunately did not materialise and the developers went back to establishing the building as a shopping and leisure complex for the East End.

The Focus of Development

It was only after there had been a substantial influx of new money into Wapping through the activities of the London Dockland Development Corporation and the house builders. As such a good change of attitude towards development in Docklands made the developers raise cash to realise their plans.

To restore and convert the skin floor was going to cost a minimum of £20 million. The first stage of the works had to be to preserve as much as possible of what was left of the original building on this site. Negotiations with the LDDC produced £1 million grant towards the cost of repairing this structure while a further £2 million urban development grant was made available from the Department of the Environment. The rest of the cash was provided by the developers and their building contractors. As had so often proved to be the case, with docklands developments, it was the contractor and not the property developer who was prepared to take the risk.

Remarkable Warehouse

The skin floor is a remarkable warehouse building. Built between 1811-14, revolutionary structural techniques in the application of cast iron were used in its construction. It was built on the north side of Tobacco Dock, now filled in apart from an ornamental canal. One of the hi-tech buildings of its day, it was described as the largest, finest and most convenient warehouse building of its kind in the world. Originally called new tobacco warehouse, its present name, the skin floor, implied it was used by the fur trade. But this also refers to the name given to the tobacco leaves or skins that were stored in casks on the ground floor of the building in the long bays watched over by Customs officers. The bays with their dramatic spans, achieved by the imaginative use of cast iron columns, are recalled in the drama by the eerie, massive bowel vaults beneath the dock. These vaults seemed to stretch on forever beneath the building and in the cold dark air echoes were muted by the bare earth floor. Here was stored barrels of wine and brandy with perfect temperatures for maturing. brick, stone and granite, the vaults feature elegantly chamfer columns with intricate brick vaults. The columns rest on slabs of granite, and

these in turn rest on beech piend piles, kept damp by a specially designed system which redirects water from the roof down to the piles. The problems with the architect team had was how to create modern retailing space where both levels are equally attractive to shoppers and to comply with the stringent requirements relating to work on any listed building. To create a visual link between the upper and lower levels the design had punched holes through the ground floor to let light into the vaults with a gallery round the edge of the void at the upper level. These courtyard areas are open to the sky - a gap in the roof was left so natural ventilation is provided.

Design to Suit Retailers

To lessen the effect of ground and basement levels and in addition to the courtyards, the entrances of the northern and southern end of the building feature staircases which direct shoppers readily to the vaults or the upstairs floors if they wish. Such a design would make the centre more attractive to the retailers. At design stage, the question was asked what sort of shops would Tobacco Dock have? It was forecast that as much as 35% of the scheme would be let to restaurants, food and wine shops, to create the feel of the place for visiting tourists, local residents and workers from the City and Docklands itself. The precinct would be a speciality shopping centre where small traders sell quality goods, often fashion-orientated. Adjacent to the building parking for 500 cars plus coaches was provided.

Failure of Businesses

It was predicted that it would be popular from the word go. St Katharine's Dock has very little else to offer the estimated 25,000 residents, the developers claimed, in the way of shopping and Tobacco Dock should prove a welcome addition to Wapping and Docklands as a whole where there was still an acknowledged dearth of speciality shopping. Equally tourists would find the place worth a visit. In addition to the shopping attractions a full-sized replica of a tall pirate ship was installed in what was left of Tobacco Dock itself, just to the south of the building. Also there was a detailed working model of London Docks as it used to be in heyday for tourists to enjoy and study. Unfortunately shortly after it was opened, trade was not as expected. It was claimed that the prices of goods were too high and not within the spending power of the local people who lived in the Council flats in the area. The shops closed and the precinct basically also closed and that is the position in the year 2001. The only successful business which was carried on was a bar and a coffee shop afronting the dockside. Although the retailers did not succeed the remarkable skin floor has been preserved for the nation.

It was Tobacco Dock that brought down the contractors Harry Neal. They were going to be paid for £65 million of the work on site when the development was sold. The project was not sold and Tobacco Dock Development Company went into receivership. Unsecured creditors were paid only £11 million from £70 million debts.

Illustration on Page 114
Announcement by Tobacco Dock Company circa 1989

TOBACCO DOCK
London's Shopping Village

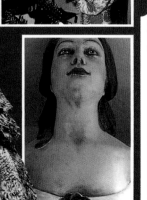

- Open seven days a week
- Speciality shops and restaurants from around the world.
- Late night shopping Monday to Saturday.
- Generous car parking.
- Minutes from The Tower of London.
- Over twice the size of Covent Garden Market.
- Street theatre and entertainment.
- "The Sea Lark", 'Treasure Island' Adventure Ship.
- "The Three Sisters" – The Pirate History Ship.
- Perfect for a family outing.
- Irresistible tourist destination.
- Unique Georgian Malls and Arcades.

The West India Quay Warehouses house a Museum of Docklands and many loft homes. There is a festival of shopping and dining and a hotel with spectacular views to Canary Wharf.

Ivory House at St Katharine Dock, historic building with original features and unique apartments overlooking the marina haven.

Butlers Wharf and Courage Brewery are excellent conversions to residential and commercial accommodation adjacent to Tower Bridge in Shad Thames.

Hays Galleria shopping precinct in London Bridge City and the facades of the listed warehouses of Hays Dock in the background.

New Concordia Wharf outstanding converted warehouse at the entrance to St Saviour's Dock in Bermondsey.

Whitechapel Art Gallery

The development of the arts in London Docklands is important not just for the tourists and visitors but for the thousands of residents and visitors in the area, the size of Oxford. Visual arts have traditionally flourished in Tower Hamlets with possibly the largest concentration of artists in the country established in a wide area around Whitechapel Art Gallery, many of whom live and work within East London.

In 1989 the LDDC appointed an arts development manager with the objective of raising the cultural profile in two ways: by encouraging major art organisations to relocate in London Docklands and by promoting a variety of events throughout the area. Initially, a series of events was piloted, to provide guidelines for the future. Exhibitions, open-air concerts and theatrical performances were some of the events organised. The Space Arts Centre, housed in a converted church off Westferry Road, is a music, comedy, film and art venue, with relaxed surroundings, for the local community on the Isle of Dogs.

London Arena

The London Arena on the Isle of Dogs stages popular entertainment, pop and sport. When Luciano Pavarotti first came to the arena in June 1989, he hit the headlines when 11,000 people came to see him. A series of concerts by Pink Floyd attracted an audience reputedly of 65,000! Pop concerts and ballet have been organised successfully ever since. The programmes have also included some business events, and on the sporting front there have been wrestling, boxing and go-karting events.

Design Museum

Close to Tower Bridge is the Design Museum, which opened in July 1989 in a gleaming white riverside building at the magnificent Butlers Wharf, surrounded by some sculptures. In the first six-weeks, 25,000 people made their way there, some using the Thames Riverbus. With a series of changing exhibitions, the museum aims to attract the general public, designers and artists. National and international designs are exhibited regularly. In the Review section, new products are continually being added, while the study collection takes a historic perspective of design of everything from the humble chair to the typewriter. The restaurant "Blue Print" on the first floor has a large terrace overlooking the River, and an associated lecture theatre.

Trinity Buoy Wharf

Trinity Buoy Wharf is a secluded riverside location at Blackwall, poised at the confluence of the River Lea and the Thames, directly opposite the Millennium Dome. It contains a range of historic buildings, including London's only lighthouse, which is Grade II, listed. Until 1988 it was used as a storage and workshop area, belonging to the Trinity House Company. Equipment were made and tested there and the lighthouse, built 1864, was used for training keepers for over a hundred years. The history of the buildings made it a fitting place for creative activities.

Through the Incentive Fund,, projects were encouraged for the development of artists' studios, rehearsal working spaces and general cultural functions. Just before their demise in March 1998, the LDDC established a trust to safeguard the future use of the site and selected the Urban Space Management to organise a raft of cultural developments.

Sculpture and Public Art

Public art was an ingredient in the regeneration of London Docklands and the area is surprising rich in fine examples which often go unnoticed. A map of the area pinpoints 50 pieces of public art, varying from wooden statues to glass panels. The map gives information and location on the sculptures which are attributed to many artists. They can be visited by walks in Docklands. Please see the author's book "London and Dockland Walks".

LDDC Arts Incentive Fund

For the world outside Docklands, a message of resurgence came from performances, exhibitions and venues. The LDDC employed high profile innovative arts activities to draw attention to area and highlight the potential of its historic buildings for longer term art use. In this context the programme was to have a wider regeneration remit. To deliver this programme, the main vehicle was the establishment of a modest Arts Incentive Fund. As with its education fund, it required funding partners so that the organisations benefiting had a chance to build the relationships that would last beyond the LDDC's lifetime, and it too offered a shrinking proportion in the final years before its demise. The fund distributed over 100 grants up to a maximum of £15,000, ranging from support for visual arts exhibitions, contemporary dance and theatre.

The Design Museum at Butler's Wharf, Bermondsey

During 2003 it was proposed to close the Arena for redevelopment.

Top: London Arena, on the Isle of Dogs, one of London's top sports, conference and pop venues.
Right: A replica of the gateway into the West India North Quay opened by the Mayor of London in July 2000.

Top: The great operatic tenor Luciano Pavarotti in a performance at the London Arena

Right: "Young Girl" on view at an exhibition of contemporary art at Trinity Buoy Wharf art centre.

Below: The Spice Girls first appeared at the London Arena for the Brit Awards of 1998.

London's only lighthouse at Trinity Buoy Wharf.

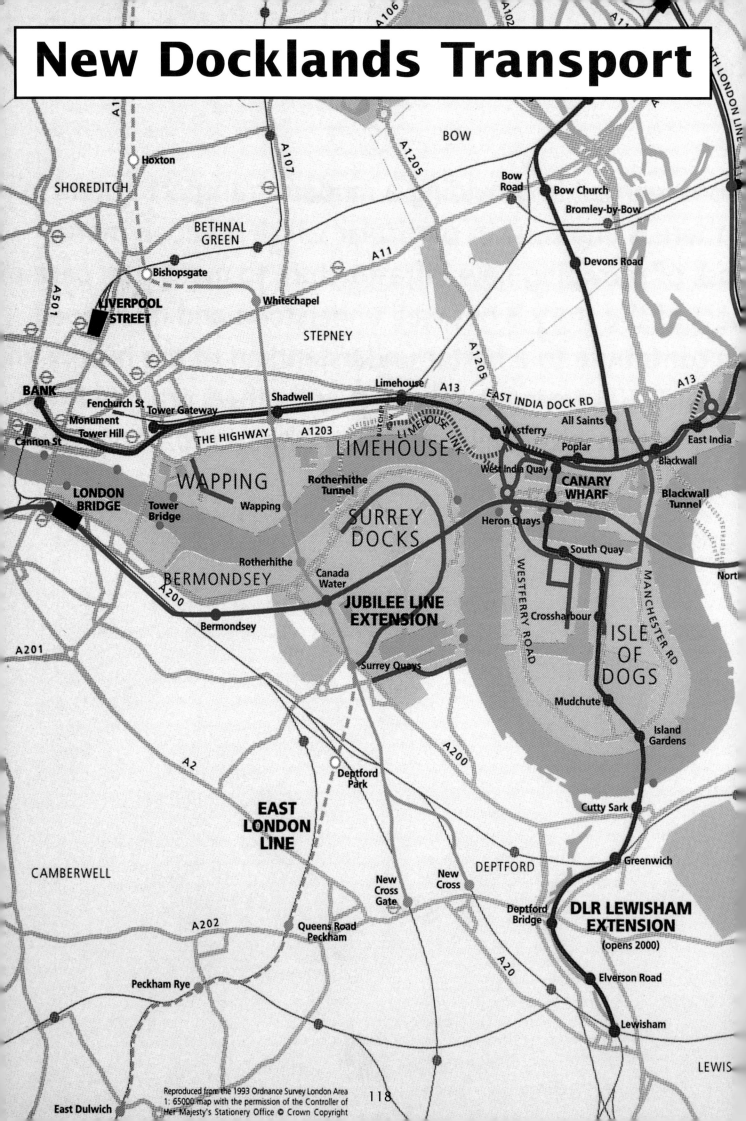

New Docklands Transport

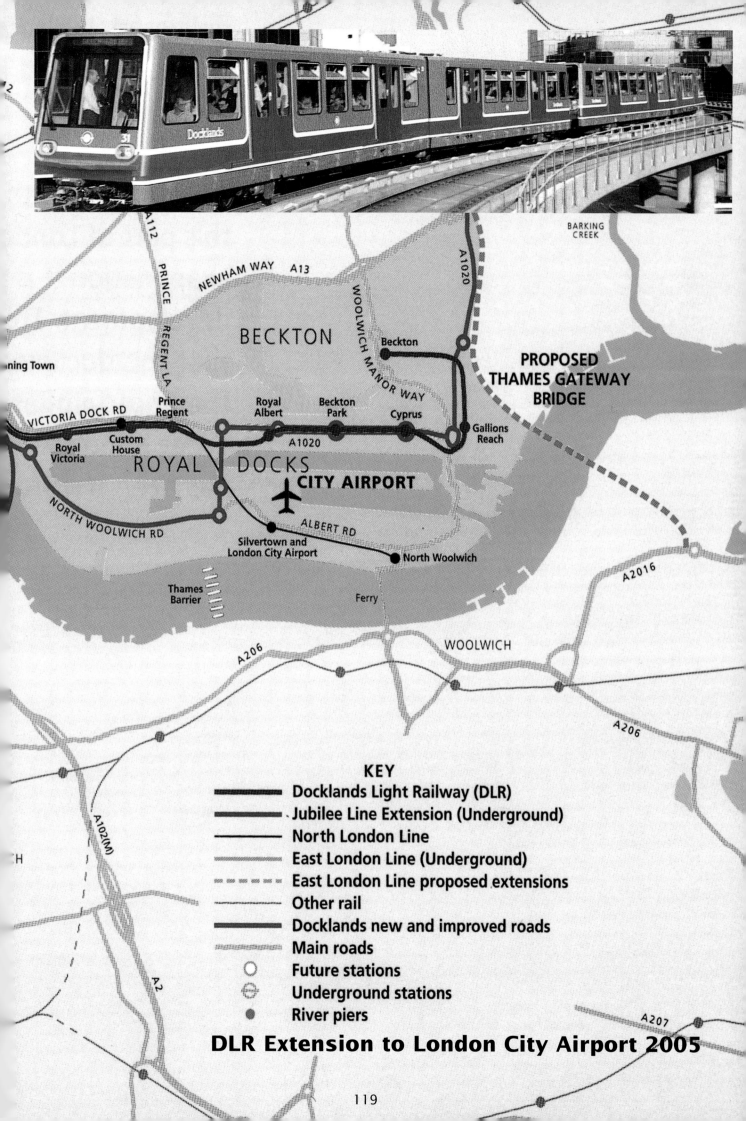

KEY

Docklands Light Railway (DLR)

Jubilee Line Extension (Underground)

North London Line

East London Line (Underground)

East London Line proposed extensions

Other rail

Docklands new and improved roads

Main roads

○ Future stations

⊖ Underground stations

● River piers

DLR Extension to London City Airport 2005

Small Scale Transport Schemes

The Docks and their surrounding communities had always been isolated from London's transport network. For the area to be successful in attracting investors and developers, it had to be more accessible and to be perceived to be accessible. The record of much planning and debate, but only limited implementation and achievement of those plans in the 1960s and 1970s, led the LDDC to promote different approaches. The first steps were to make a rapid analysis of the proposals for relatively small projects within the Enterprise Zone on the Isle of Dogs. These were proposals, which the Corporation could deliver quickly unlike the major schemes such as the Tube line, which, though very important to Docklands, had a faltering history. The early proposals therefore were focused on the Isle of Dogs Enterprise Zone, where inadequate roads and bridges inhibited development and regeneration projects. Two early examples of these small-scale transport schemes were the red brick road and Docklands Clipper Bus.

Poor Dock Estate Roads

Accessibility within and around the Enterprise Zone in 1980 when at the time of its designation in 1982 was very poor. The existing dock estate roads were inadequate for development purposes and public transport was non-existent. Difficulties were also experienced by frequent breakdowns of lifting road bridges over dock entrances and which had ceased to be maintained since the closure of the Docks. The old Millwall Cut bridge, which is now Marsh Wall, for example, which had to be opened to allow boats to get to the timber yards on Millwall outer dock, would often get stuck. Traffic was then forced to go all the way round the outside of the Island on Manchester Road and Westferry Road. Proposals to open a new Asda superstore on the Island were also being hindered by these access problems.

LDDC Red Brick Road

The LDDC therefore conceived the idea of red brick road. These were a basic network of 7.3metre roads, designed to serve all the major sites in the Enterprise Zone. The first phase of these roads was opened in 1983. As well as serving Asda these roads allowed the Corporation to focus on the development of sites around what would become Millharbour, which were the first sites to be made available for regeneration. At the time the maximum potential development considered feasible for the Island was a low-density business park. The red brick roads were envisaged as being adequate in providing local capacity for the Island and were to be supplemented at a later date. Red bricks were used for these roads as they looked attractive and conveyed an early statement about the potential of the area and assisted in calming traffic to travel at reasonable speed. They also offered potential way of dealing with repairs by allowing individual areas of brick to be taken up to allow works to services as necessary.

Docklands Clipper Bus

Another early transport move was to set up and subsidise the Docklands Clipper bus, high profile frequent shuttle bus running between Mile End tube station and the Isle of Dogs. It provided an early signal for the change of prospects in the area and fulfiled a vital role as a public transport feature.

Government Approval for DLR

At the same time as these minor improvements were being made, debate was going on how to improve the quality and capacity of public transport. Following joint analysis and discussions with the GLC and London Transport a report on Public Transport Promotions Provision for Docklands was submitted to Government in June 1982 recommending the construction of a new automated light railway with a cost estimated at £65million. In October 1982 Government approved the proposal with cash limited for the project at £77 million and set a target opening date of 1987. The first London Docklands Railway Bill was deposited in Parliament in November 1982, and Royal Assent was received in 1984-85 and the Docklands Light Railway (DLR) opened to the public on 31 August 1987.

PROMOTING NEW TRANSPORT

The Delays, Problems and Moving On

Local Opposition and Funding Problems

It has always been acknowledged that an adequate transport infrastructure would be the key to successfully regenerating an urban district. Promoting and developing such new transport systems can often be complex and protracted. Many Government departments and groups are normally involved and only rarely is there a correct solution from the outset. Selection of an appropriate scheme is a long and involved process with planners, engineers and decision makers having to weigh many conflicting interests, factors and opinions of pressure groups. In urban areas like London Docklands, the need for new transport was opposed because it caused considerable disruption and inconvenience to the local community and was unwelcome to those most affected. It, therefore, took a long time to create the transport infrastructure and was the subject of much criticism by investors and developers.

Another factor to bear in mind was that initially the transport projects relied entirely on public funding, though later this was changed under the Private Finance initiative. The competition for public expenditure was fierce and not forthcoming prior to the formation of the LDDC. For nearly twenty years the history of transport proposals was far more about schemes which were not funded or implemented, or were much delayed.

Arrival of Canary Wharf

The more pragmatic and sustained effort adopted by the LDDC in its early days bore some results. But it was not until the mid 1980s, however, that the potential scale of development was established with the arrival of Canary Wharf. It was the progress of this massive development proposals which crystallised transport requirements for Docklands. They paved the way to future funding and rapid implementation, with substantial contributions by the private sector. During the 1980s and 1990s, this arrangement resulted in the building of most of the paper plans made in the 1960s and 1970s. The LDDC backed by the central government funding and the vision and financial contributions of Canary Wharf Company and other entrepreneurs helped to translate past aspirations into real projects for the 21st century London.

One of the major criticisms of the LDDC during its period of operation was the delay in its transport programmes. They blamed it on the long lead-time needed for implementation of road and rail schemes. They argued that it takes much longer to plan, fund and execute transport plans than it does to plan and complete a building development scheme. On average a major development can be planned and built within 3-5 years. Phase 1 of Canary Wharf took 3-4 years. It was said that a major road or rail scheme takes up to 5 years at the planning/funding stage, 1-5 years at the Public Inquiry/Parliamentary stage, and 2-5 years to build, a total of up to 10-15 years in all. The initial DLR took about 5 years to complete and the Jubilee Line about 15 years. Generally the LDDC could not predict the scale of development at Canary Wharf until 5 years after its establishment in 1981.

It was impossible to complete the major infrastructure ahead of commercial development on the Isle of Dogs. Even with the fast track approach, the lead times for transport schemes could not match the development boom in the Enterprise Zone. Because of this delay, other measures were implemented to provide additional transport in the short term. New bus services and the Riverbus along the Thames provided support, but unfortunately the latter did not survive for long due to lack of public support.

Olympia & York Concern

When the Canadian developer, Olympia & York began the development of Canary Wharf in 1987, the thought uppermost in their minds was transport. One important transport link was already reasonably well advanced in the shape of the Docklands Light Railway (DLR) but it only needed a brief inspection to appreciate how inadequate DLR specifications were. It was built cheaply on the cautious assumption that something like 15,000 people would use it each day. Olympia & York realised that it would not be able to cope and suggested delaying the Line's completion until it could be upgraded. The answer was that this was impossible, as the date for the official opening by the Queen had already been set July 1997. There was no going back. This decision proved rather disastrous, as the DLR after its opening could not cope with the number of passengers. Commuters hated it initially and prospective tenants were weary of moving to Canary Wharf. This was not the only matter to have gone wrong in Docklands.

Later after London City Airport opened, jet operations were finally approved, even though it should have been clear from the start it would need to cater for the British commuter jets. The arguments over the Jubilee Line extension from the West End to Docklands were not resolved in the early 1990s A new road to link the top end of the Isle of Dogs and Canary Wharf with the City was proposed. Finally in August one of the Transport Ministers spent a week in Docklands using what public transport was available, including the DLR, which was out of action for most of the time. He came up with that great remedy "something needed to be done"! Having an effective and sensible Docklands transport has a bearing on the development of the country as a whole.

Emergence of Docklands 1989

Docklands in 1989 was nothing less than a new emerging city within London. The plans for new rail and road links recognised that Docklands was far more than just a successful experiment in inner city regeneration. In 1984 when some roads were being built to serve the Enterprise Zone and work started on the Docklands Light Railway, the best anyone dared to imagine for the Isle of Dogs was about four million square feet. In 1989 when construction was advanced on Canary Wharf and more than twenty million square feet of commercial development were forecast, considerable effort was made to ensure that transport infrastructure kept up with the remarkable pace of development in Docklands.

DOCKLANDS LIGHT RAILWAY

Putting London Docklands on the Map

Connection to Rest of London

When it was first suggested at the beginning of 1980s that a light railway system be built through East London, sceptics said the idea was crazy and few people believed it would actually happen. Critics denounced the scheme saying that the railway would be a "white elephant" in the middle of nowhere among derelict land. Eight years later, the cry changed; it was a "Micky Mouse" railway, and why on earth didn't they build it bigger?

The £77 million Docklands Light Railway (DLR) when completed in July 1977 became the pride of the East End, bringing people to the new financial centre of Canary Wharf on the Isle of Dogs. It created about 100 jobs for local people and for the first time East London had a transport system to connect it to the rest of London. The first few months of operation had not been without their problems and breakdowns but these were gradually overcome.

Extension to Bank

Work began in 1988 on the 1.5km extension to Bank in the heart of the City and was completed in 1991 allowing passengers access to the Central, Circle, District and City lines. The construction was funded partly by Olympia & York the developers of Canary Wharf and partly by Central Government. The journey to the City from Canary Wharf took about ten minutes. During the tunnelling for the railway, the Museum of London archaeologists found at Fish Street Hill, a Roman well containing the stones and pips of cherries, sloes, plums, apples, grapes, figs and blackberries. The seeds of herbs, lentils, peas, cereal bran and hazel nuts were also found, as well as many bones of fish, birds, lamb and perhaps the earliest find of a black rat in Britain! A shaft, which was sunk at Bucklersbury, revealed the remains of Roman timber buildings, of a jewellers workshop with ornamental metal work including a fine pendant, studs, buttons and other items were recovered.

Extension to Beckton

A bill to extend the railway a further 7.2km to Beckton was approved in December 1988 and was completed in 1992, serving the growing communities in Beckton and South Newham. The Docklands Light Railway became a major Docklands success story. Its popularity could be measured in the number of people travelling on it. Shortly after its opening, it was estimated that the number of passengers was just over 150,000 per week. Weekends were proving to be a particularly busy time as people from all over the country, as well as overseas visitors were coming to Docklands to see just what was happening and to experience "travelling light".

Extension to Greenwich and Lewisham

London Borough of Lewisham first proposed extension of the DLR southwards under the Thames to Greenwich and Lewisham in 1985. The extension was widely supported by the public and a number of organisations, including the London Boroughs and the LDDC. Despite the scheme's many benefits it was impossible to obtain Government approval until November 1990. An enabling Bill was laid before Parliament, promoted by London Transport. The approval was subject for the new line to

be funded entirely by the private sector. Justifications for the extension came from major benefits that it will bring to London as a whole. The extension provides a strategic cross-river public transport link for London, benefiting southeast, the Thames Gateway, Docklands and the City. It relieves road traffic congestion, in particular on Tower Bridge, Rotherhithe and Blackwall Tunnels. Also for the first time the Line is a direct link between the Tower of London and Greenwich, which together were visited by over 5million tourists a year.

Consortium for Design and Construction

The route of the new extension follows an alignment judged to have the least adverse environmental impact with five new stations south of the River and two replacement stations on the Isle of Dogs. The transfer of ownership of DLR from London Transport to the LDDC in the middle of the House of Commons proceedings caused some uncertainty. As a result Royal Assent was not received until May 1993. But in the end there were very few significant changes to the scheme as originally promoted. The next stage was to determine how the project could be funded by the private sector. Responsibility for the project within Government was transferred in August 1993 to the Private Finance Unit of the Department of the Environment. Joint product office was established to take the scheme to market. A 25-year concession was awarded in September 1996 to the City Greenwich, Lewisham Rail Link consortium for the design, build, financing and maintenance of the extension. The extension came into operation early in 2000.

The total cost of the project was £260 million, including cost of private finance, the bulk of which was provided through a bond issue on the capital interest, with 10% coming from subordinate debt and equity funding, 25% as compensation from Central Government for the effect of capping rail fares in London and 5% from local contributions. This is a much higher percentage of private finance than achieved for any other public sector project to date in Britain.

Extension to City Airport

In March 1999, Docklands Light Railway Company sent out 4,000 letters as the first part of a public consultation exercise for its proposed £80 million extension from Silvertown to London City Airport. The Government called for construction companies to invest in the project, based on the success of the Lewisham Extension, as a public/private partnership. Three routes for the extension were considered. DLR's favoured route leaves the existing Beckton branch at Canning Town and using the former Silvertown Tramway alignment to the airport.. The 4.4 km route would operate from Canning Town to North Woolwich, with stations at West Silvertown, Pontoon Dock, City Airport and North Woolwich. Much of the route between the lower Lea crossing and the Airport would be on elevated viaduct. Trains to City Airport could be running by 2005.

Future developments include an extension to Barking and Dagenham Dock.

DLR STATION AT THE WHARF

Feeding the Canary

During the 1990s Canary Wharf DLR station was rebuilt to feed and cope with the crowds of passengers expected on completion of the development. Space on the site was a premium. Difficult access and lack of working space are normally problems on construction sites, but rarely such justification as at this station in the heart of Canary Wharf. It was dwarfed by the towers going up just feet away and good relations with the neighbours were essential! There was barely a scrap of storage space for materials; deliveries had to be timed almost to the minute.

Three new tracks were built at the station and the existing two were demolished. This allowed a better layout with platforms on both sides of the tracks. The central third track terminates at the Wharf so that extra rush hour trains can start and finish there.

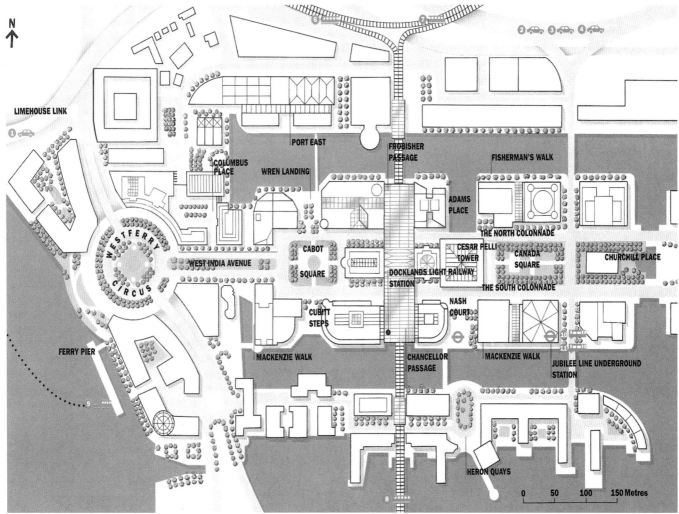

Putting Canary Wharf on the map of Docklands; two major stations give the development the transport arteries it needs. The above is the plan of the Wharf as presented by Olympia & York in 1989.

123

RE-EVALUATION OF TRANSPORT PLANNING

The Essential Contribution of the Private Sector

Lifting Aspirations

The signing of the Master Building Agreement between the London Docklands Corporation and the Canadian developers Olympia & York for a 12.2 million sq ft (1.1million sq.m) financial centre at Canary Wharf on 17th July 1987 changed the potential and demand for transport in Docklands overnight. With the coming of Canary Wharf, forecasts of the ultimate employment in the Isle of Dogs increased in 1986 from 12,000 to 50,000. This total continued to increase as subsequent proposals for other sites emerged encouraged by the vision of Canary Wharf. Understandably the transport planners involved were concerned how to accommodate this dramatic increase in the local workforce.

Although the initial DLR scheme was designed to allow for capacity increases, it had not been expected that this increased capacity would have been needed so quickly and to such a huge scale. Between 1985, when Travelstead's scheme was first proposed and 1987, all the transport plans for Docklands were re-evaluated. The new business Centre brought with it a unique opportunity to lift aspirations and seize benefits which would never otherwise have been achieved. During this re-evaluation major decisions were taken which included the upgrading and extension of the DLR, the need for a second rail link and the establishment of a direct road link to the City.

DLR Upgrading

The first step in the upgrading of DLR was to increase the railway from one to two car trains and to extend the system into the heart of the City at Bank. In November 1985, following pressure and commitment of financial contribution to the construction by Canary Wharf, the Private Bill for the Bank extension was deposited, receiving Royal Assent a year later in 1986. The contracts for the extension and upgrading, involving the lengthening of platforms and strengthening of structures was let in July 1987 shortly before the opening of the line. Tunnelling work started in 1988 and the extension opened in 1991.

These and other changes to DLR would ultimately increase its capacity to over 12,000 passengers per hour in each direction, over seven times the initial design figure! The contracts for changes were let at a time when the contracts for the initial railway were still running up to July 1987. The significance and difficulties of the overlap between the new and old contracts was not properly understood or addressed at the time. Invariably the lack of resolution of interface responsibilities between the different contractors led to contractual disputes and major problems of operation. The allocation of responsibility for non-performance of the system was not defined. These issues gave London Transport and the DLR Company enormous problems for many years to come.

Increased Forecasts

The improvements made to DLR were not sufficient to provide adequate access to Docklands in the long term. The forecasts made in 1989 of the final employment for the Isle of Dogs increased substantially from 50,000 to 125,000 to 150,000. In addition to this capacity requirement, it was considered that more choice was needed for public transport users.

Underground Tube Line

An old proposal for an Underground tube line was finally resurrected in 1989 to provide high capacity rail services to East London. Initially, the line was an extension of the Bakerloo and later a new line running from Waterloo to North Greenwich. The final proposal was the Jubilee Line extension from Green Park to Stratford. The Bill was deposited in November 1989 and Royal Assent was granted after a long period of debate in 1992. Olympia & York played an important part in the final decision. Without their long campaign and part funding of the new line, there would not have been strong Government support for the proposal. Although London Transport and the LDDC played an important role in planning and justifying the scheme, it was almost entirely in the approval stage due to Olympia & York that the line was constructed.

Financial Contribution by Developer

The most important factor was the willingness of Olympia & York to make substantial financial contributions towards the cost of providing public infrastructure in Docklands from the early stages of their development of Canary Wharf. For the Bank extension to DLR this amounted to £75 million, about 40% of the total cost, and for the Jubilee Line project the contribution was £400 million of the original estimate of £1 billion.

When Olympia & York went into liquidation during 1992, the Jubilee Line project was halted, as Government would not commit the go-ahead without the promised private contribution by Canary Wharf. After long debates and negotiations, the creditor banks brought the system out of Administration in Autumn 1993, who committed the Olympia & York contribution. The Jubilee contracts were let and the Line was opened by January 2000, to serve Docklands and the Millennium Dome.

Docklands Highway

Although rail transport was vital for Docklands' success, improvement of the road network to the Enterprise Zone was seen as vital. With the demise of the Greater London Council (GLC) in 1986, the LDDC, rather late, pressed for a series of roads, which came to be known as the Docklands highway. This would provide a 24km (15miles) of new and improved roads from Limehouse to the Royal Docks. This scheme included the construction of the expensive Limehouse Link, a new dual carriageway tunnel under the Limehouse Basin providing the connection to Central London and the lower Lee Crossing at Blackwall and further east to the A406, M11 and M25, ten years after the establishment of the LDDC. The improvement of the A13 vital road through docklands is being completed.

A new six-car, 1040 passenger Jubilee Line Transport train at Stratford Station. Each car has audio and visual information systems, closed circuit TV monitoring and an emergency intercom to the operator.

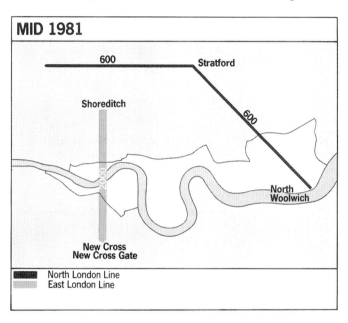

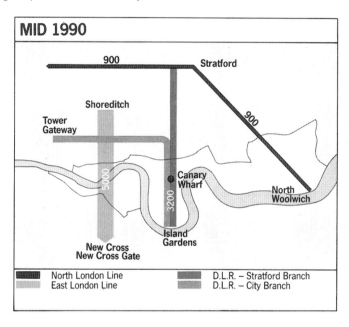

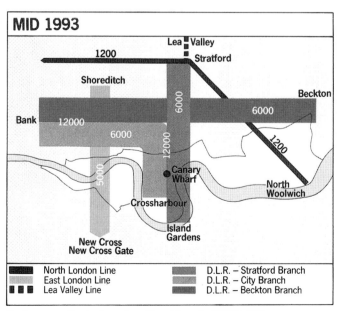

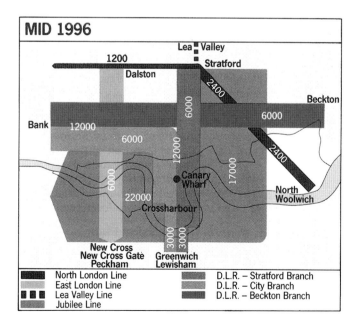

Rail capacity in London Docklands 1981-97

Recent massive development of transport network in East London. The charts show Peak Hour Capacities Passengers per hour. Widths of rail lines indicated are proportional to their capacity.

THE NEW JUBILEE LINE

London's Great Mass Transport

London Underground Railway

In 1865 London built its first underground railway. The Capital has changed enormously since that first Metropolitan tube was constructed. Its population has grown to expect a freedom of travel to traverse the city and the suburbs quickly   The latest underground is the Jubilee Line Extension to south and east London. There are already twelve tube lines which are inter-changing to provide most of London with a rapid transport system. The latest line runs between Green Park and Docklands to provide a much needed link between the West End, South East London, Canary Wharf and Stratford.

Docklands infrastructure problems were much publicised throughout the 1980 decade and the inaccessibility of the Isle of Dogs, particularly became an old chestnut for those determined to knock the area at all costs. However, these difficulties were at last addressed and significant developments were afoot.   The property developers, London Docklands Development Corporation and the Docklands Boroughs realised that for the regeneration of the old Docklands to be successful, transport links had to be further enhanced, if investment from the private sector was to be maintained.

Most Important New Transport System

The extension of the DLR to Bank in the heart of the City was being completed in 1991. An extension to Beckton was planned, as was an extension south of the river to Lewisham via Greenwich. Perhaps the most important transport system was the proposal for the extension of the Jubilee underground line.   It was predicted to transport 20,000 people each way per hour, and would link directly with the tube system. This would finally lie to rest the misconception that Docklands was in the middle of nowhere. London Transport brought a private bill before Parliament for commencement of construction in 1992. The Department of Transport recommended that the developers had to pay for part of the cost.

This new railway line provides a lifeline as a high capacity fast connection between Central London, the Isle of Dogs and the important gateway of Stratford. Journey times from Canary Wharf to London Bridge is about 8 minutes and between Canary Wharf and Waterloo about 12 minutes.   The line has other important implications in bringing the underground to areas of London previously unserved, such as Bermondsey and North Greenwich.   The construction of the tube gave an opportunity for imaginative new station designs. Other features include the incorporation of platform door to improve safety and comfort on the underground stations, which have been the first for the tube network.

British Transport Commission Plan

The story of the Line goes back to the London Plan of 1949 produced by the British Transport Commission. In the years that followed, the main priority for London Transport was the construction of the Victoria Line. While this was being built in the mid 1960s, discussions started on a new line from Stanmore to Charing Cross which was opened on 1st May 1979 and named the Jubilee line in recognition of the Queen's Silver Jubilee in 1977. During the 1970s, further proposals were prepared for extending the line south of the river, which were incorporated in the London Docklands Strategic Plan of 1976. After further reviews by the GLC the plan was abandoned. During 1985, however, the proposals for Canary Wharf were taking shape and causing a re-think of the transport to Docklands.   The start of the Wharf construction in 1988 was giving considerable impetus to development in the area and it was considered to be essential for a further high capacity link to Central London. After several attempts at solutions, the East London Rail Study, commissioned by the Department of Transport recommended practically the present route of the new tube with possible future extensions to the Royal Docks, Woolwich and Thamesmead.   A Parliamentary Bill was deposited in November 1989 and Royal Assent was received in 1992.

Contribution by Canary Wharf

An important part of the package for the scheme was a large contribution of £400 million by the developers of Canary Wharf, Olympia & York, in recognition of the benefits that would arise.   However, when the first payment of £40 million became due in April 1992, the developers went into liquidation. As a result of High Court decision, Canary Wharf came out of Administration and the banks were able to organise a loan from the European Investment Bank to fund the contribution and Government finally gave the go-ahead for the scheme in October 1993. The railway was completed in time for the opening of the Millennium Dome at North Greenwich in January 2000.

Fit for 21st Century

London Transport promised to give Londoners an Underground railway in the Jubilee Line extension fit for the 21st century and was given a welcome boost with a clutch of awards for various stations of the Line.   The new Canada Water station in Surrey Quays received The Concrete Society's Certificate of Excellence for the way in which 35,000 cubic metres of concrete was used for the construction of an underground station the size of St Paul's Cathedral.

Relics of HMS "Warrior"

But Canning Town station got its own prized award by having a section of the iron clad hold from the warship HMS Warrior which has been installed in the new station at Canning Town, where she was built in 1860. The 180 ft high main mast of HMS Warrior dominates at present the skyline of Portsmouth Harbour where the ship has been on public display since 1987.   Introduced during peace time, the Warrior served for ten years in the front line of the Channel Fleet but was never needed in war. Her reputation is therefore not founded on famous victories or battles. She was the first iron-clad battleship and the most powerful ship of her day and responsible for maintaining the 'Pax Britannica'! A special ceremony to commemorate HMS Warrior's links with Canning Town was carried out by the Archbishop of Canterbury at the New Jubilee Line extension during the year 1999.

Archaeological Excavations - The construction of the new tunnels for the Jubilee Line at London Bridge were host to painstaking excavation by archaeologists search for the remains of Roman London beneath the station. Pottery of a small lamp in the shape of a foot and evidence of roads and buildings were found.

Canary Wharf Station - An aerial view of Canary Wharf looking east, August 1998. The two glass covered entrances of the station (right) are in the heart of the vast London Docklands re-development area of the station, reinforced concrete box built inside the former dock.

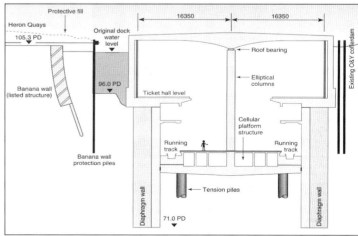

Canary Wharf Station entrance, cross section and construction. This station is the jewel in the crown of the Jubilee Line. Its vast scale and stunning architecture are breathtaking and appropriate for the new fast-expanding financial centre of London (dimensions in mm).

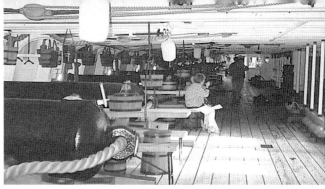

All 650 seamen lived, slept and ate on this deck.

Dr Carey unveils the plaque. The captain and senior Quarter Master of HMS Warrior stand at attention in their period uniforms.

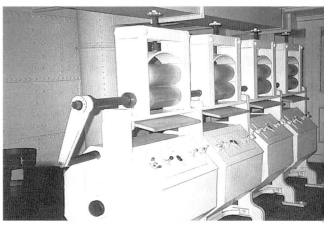

HMS Warrior was the first ship to have washing machines on board.

Bottom: "The Warrior" built at Canning Town in 1864 now on display at Portsmouth. A section of the iron clad was installed in the new station as shown above.

One of HMS Warrior's twenty six muzzle loading cannons.

The site as it was in 1895 when occupied by the Thames Ironworks.

The Thames Ironworks football team in 1895, before they became West Ham United.

Southwark Station is a brand new station on JLE. Introduced after intense lobbying by the local MP Simon Hughes, it serves the local residential and business communities also the New Globe Theatre and Tate Modern. It links the mainline at Waterloo East and is expected to attract 7000 passengers during the peak period.

Canning Town Station - provides a seamless connection between the Docklands Light Railway, Silverlink, Metro and local bus services. Shoe-horning three sets of railway lines between the River Lea, the A13 and Silvertown Way, the station was built beneath high voltage electricity cables.

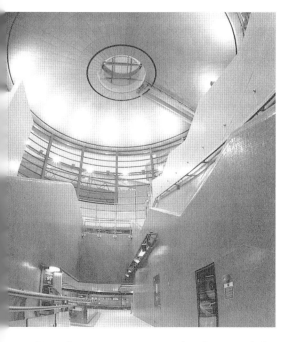

Canada Water Station - The design of the station involved a central glazed "drum" at Canada Water to link all three levels of the station.

North Greenwich Station - The giant Cathedral-link station is on the Greenwich Peninsula and it is intended as the focus for redeveloping the area of South East London. During the year 2000 it served as the main terminus for the Millennium Dome.

Stratford Station - This grand station forms not only the terminus for the Jubilee Line but also provides an important link to, Docklands, Central Line, British Rail and Tunnel Rail Link to Central London when completed. Subways link the tube and mainline.

London Bridge Station - The Jubilee Line extension station was constructed beneath the existing bus station at the front of the mainline station. It has direct links with the Northern Line, Thameslink and the mainlines and is expected to be used by 17,000 passengers per hour.

DOCKLANDS HIGHWAY FROM CITY TO ROYALS

The Most Expensive Road Link in the UK

Docklands Highway Agreement

In 1986 the LDDC unveiled a strategy for a network of new roads, running largely east to west through the Docklands area north of the Thames, designed to provide improved access to key development sites. The highways took seven years to complete and covered mainly the Royal Docks where major developments had not yet taken place. There was a substantial amount of criticism of the delay from developers, particularly Canary Wharf where their first phase development of eight building was opened in January 1992!

To help build these highways, the LDDC went into agreements with the local boroughs. Under the Accord with Tower Hamlets, the Council made its land available for construction of the Limehouse Link Tunnel and Poplar Link Road, and the Highway Authority agreed not to oppose the major road schemes, in the Isle of Dogs and Limehouse. In return the LDDC agreed to provide new housing accommodation and to assist housing refurbishment for Council tenants to a far greater extent than the direct housing loss due to road schemes. In total 556 households were re-housed. The LDDC also agreed to fund a £35million package of social, economic and community projects to benefit Tower Hamlets residents.

Compulsory Purchase

To implement construction, the LDDC used its Compulsory Purchase powers when it was not able to buy land by agreement. Only one public enquiry was held in Newham. In Tower Hamlets the public enquiry for Limehouse Link brought opposition from local residents and landowners. Approval of all main Compulsory Purchase Orders was given by the Secretary of State for the Environment in 1989. In addition, the highway schemes were governed by the local statutory planning procedures. However, the LDDC made their proposal for the Limehouse Link to the Secretary of State for the Environment without involving Tower Hamlets Council. The Secretary of State decided not to call in the planning application and the LDDC was granted planning permission.

Limehouse Link

Limehouse Link is a critical part of the highway network, providing the important connection of Dockland to the City of London and the West End. As well as improving access to the surrounding East London road network, it has brought significant traffic relief to the area of Limehouse which, combined with traffic management measures secured improved environmental conditions for local residents and future developments. A number of options were identified to build the link between the Isle of Dogs and the City. The scheme built is a two-land dual carriageway, with an underground junction at West Ferry Road. The alignment of the western end is determined by the presence of Rotherhithe Tunnel approach ramp from where it curves along the northern edge of the Limehouse Basin. Here the tunnel depth is dictated by the navigable depth required for the connection between Regents Canal and the Thames. From here the route runs through an open area, Ropemakers Fields between existing housing, it then crosses Limekiln. The tunnel then widens to accommodate slip roads leading to and from Westferry Road and Canary Wharf. It continues under the Docklands Light Railway and West India Dock Road before rising to the surface to connect with Poplar Link Road. The total length is 1.8km with 1.5km in tunnel; the route is generally 6-8metres below ground.

Accord with Tower Hamlets

Planning permission for the road was granted in July 1988 after the Secretary of State for the Environment decided not to call in the Planning Application. The Public Inquiry into the Compulsory Purchase Order was held in October 1989 and lasted four weeks. To minimise disruption for people living along the line of the road, the LDDC signed an Accord with the London Borough of Tower Hamlets. The Corporation undertook to provide replacement housing and to refurbish existing accommodation for those tenants directly affected. The construction was to be done to a fast track programme, allowing less than two years to tender stage. A tunnel box had to be designed to carry loads resulting from future development over land. There was no precedent for construction of this type of tunnel in the variable ground conditions of East London. The difficult water bearing strata at the site dictated structural design of the tunnel.

Link Specifications

The tunnel consisted of a rectangular box for ease of construction, with twin bores 10metres wide separated by a central wall. A width of up to 22metres was needed to accommodate the slip roads for the underground junction. The box was 7.8metres high, providing a clearance for services overheads and depth for service trenches below the road surface level. Construction between the external walls and roof and floor slabs were pin jointed with dowels for temporary support of the slabs during constructions. Skin walls constructed inside the tunnel box after casting of the base slab supplemented them. The tunnel has a design speed of 60km per hour with a medium central line radius of 189 metres and gradients on the approach ramps of up to 6.8%.

Ground conditions and the relatively shallow tunnel depth dictated that construction should be by cut - and-cover method. In order to minimise the construction corridor width and ground movements "top down" construction was used. Diaphragm walls were built on each side of the tunnel to 4metres depth below base slab level, to form the external walls of the tunnel box. Ventilation extractor fans, power distribution and other services are housed in three service buildings framed in reinforced concrete housed over the tunnel portals and a fourth building east of Limehouse Basin. During construction noise and vibration levels were controlled under Section 61 of the Control of Pollution Act 1964, but the residents still complained bitterly about the nuisance and the Corporation was taken to Court.

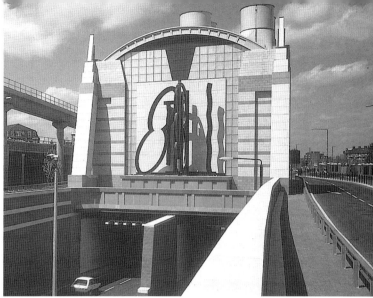

The western entrance of the Limehouse Link tunnel at Wapping.

The eastern entrance to the Limehouse Link tunnel at Poplar.

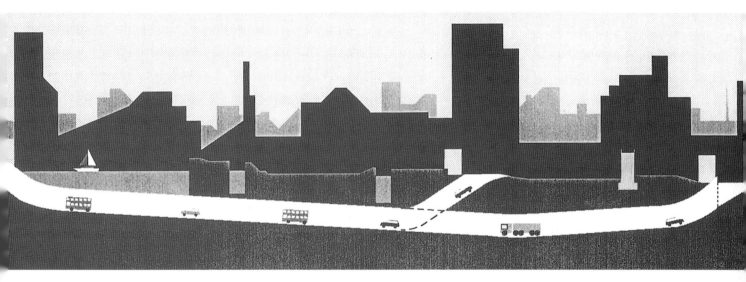

Reaching from the Highway in Wapping to just north of Westferry Circus, the Limehouse Link underpass provides a crucial transport route for motorists travelling between the City and Canary Wharf.

Aerial view looking east from Shadwell Basin to Canary Wharf where the Limehouse Link was constructed.

Poplar DLR station footbridge spanning over Aspen Way north of Canary Wharf.

Diaphram Walling

The Limehouse Link was the largest cut-and-cover construction contract undertaken in the United Kingdom. Work started on the underground dual two-lane 1.8 kilometre road in November 1989 and was fully open in November 1993, providing access to Canary Wharf, the Isle of Dogs and the Royal Docks. The contract, finally at £263 million, was initially awarded to well known civil engineering contractors Balfour Beatty and Fairclough as a joint venture, the client being the LDDC. It proved to be the most expensive road building in the country.

The initial works required the site to be cleared to a depth of 1.5 metres to remove the foundations of old buildings, as shown in Figure 1. Following the construction of guide walls, diaphragm walling sections 1.2 metres wide and up to 24 metres deep were excavated under bentonite using grabs suspended from crawler cranes. Reinforced steel cages were then lowered into the excavated trench and the bentonite fill was replaced by concrete to form the tunnel side walls. Following the installation of the diaphragm walling, well-pointing was carried out to relieve the deep water aquifer. Bored piling (Figure 2) was installed in the wide section of the tunnel to temporarily support the roof slab during the construction of the tunnel beneath. Excavation was then continued inside the diaphragm walling to the soffit of the tunnel roof. This was done using conventional digging machines (Figure 3). Cross propping of the diaphragm wall was necessary during the excavation process to minimise ground movement.

Concrete Roof Slab

The 1.5m thick reinforced concrete roof slab rested and pin-jointed to the diaphragm walls. This was then cast in 4.2 metre bays along the length of the tunnel and a series of 8.4m openings left for access beneath the tunnel roof. Excavation then commenced under the tunnel roof from one of these openings, using tracked front-end loaders. These machines transported and deposited the excavated material back to the opening where it was grab loaded into dumping trucks (Figure 4). Once the next opening was reached all future excavated material was moved forward to that opening to allow other operations to commence behind the excavation. However, the steel reinforcement and other materials continued to be handled generally through the initial 8.4m opening. These were transported along the tunnel by trailer to the overhead hoists (Figure 5).

Openings of 4.2m were formed in the tunnel roof at 50 metres intervals for access and ventilation. The wall-propping system within the tunnel itself was installed as the tunnel excavation deepened using hoists fixed to the underside of the tunnel roof to place steel tubes of 1350 millimetre diameter horizontal cross props. These props prevented movement of the diaphragm walls and were placed in sequence every 4.2m as the lower the excavation progressed. The reinforced base slab for the tunnel was constructed using conventional concreting methods.

Placing of Concrete

The internal dividing centre and side walls were then constructed with travelling shutters. These walls transferred the load from top to the bottom slab of the tunnel. The side shear walls were stressed to the diaphragm walls so that they operated integrally. Concrete was distributed by a pumpmain throughout the site, from the centrally placed batching plant at Dundee Wharf in Limehouse. Placing of concrete was with static booms for much of the diaphragm walls, the roof and base slabs and internal elements. Cable troughs, linings, tunnel services, drainage channels, ventilation fans were added and finally the road inside the tunnel was built.

Temporary Cofferdam

Construction of the tunnel under Limehouse basin involved the installation of a temporary cofferdam which was then dewatered, allowing the tunnel box to be constructed from the bottom up by conventional methods. Before constructing the coffer dams, 140,000 cubic metres of silt and debris was dredged from the basin. Marine fill, excavated from 26 miles in the North Sea, was pumped into the desilted basin to form a working platform (Figure 7). Sheet piling cofferdams were constructed into the clay below the marine fill (Figure 8). The water table was then lowered by dewatering wells and the material excavated. The concrete tunnel box was then constructed into the clay below the marine fill (Figure 9). Once the tunnel box was completed, the cofferdam was removed and the basin water was restored (Figure 10). The marine fill was then re-used to cover the tunnel roof of the Link so as to act as a load spreading layer. Located in an urban environment the construction was affected by limited access and a restricted working area. The site was little more than the width of the tunnel itself. Issues such as noise, pollution, materials transport and diversion of local roads and services were of concern to the local residents and the contractors.

Transfer to English Partnerships

With the opening of the Limehouse Link and the rest of Docklands highways on 7th May 1993, the Corporation became responsible for managing and operating the 32km road network. This was thought to be the largest privately owned network in Europe, which was made accessible to the public. The Corporation retained responsibility for the operation acting like a highway authority, as it wanted to take a proactive role in minimising disruptions for incoming companies and developers and to ensure that traffic was kept moving safely and efficiently while developers were constructing the major schemes in the area. However on their demise in 1998 the roads were handed over to the London Borough of Tower Hamlets. The Limehouse Link and East India Dock link tunnels ownership were transferred to the English Partnerships, the Government agency which took over in 1988 the remaining assets and liabilities of the LDDC.

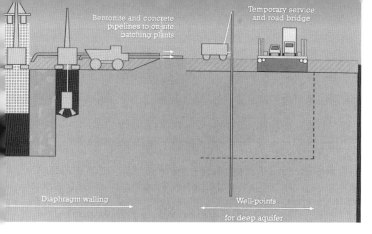

Figure 1 - The site was cleared to a depth of 1.5 metres and foundations of buildings removed.

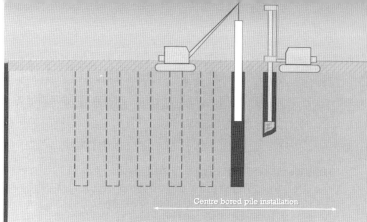

Figure 2- Bored piling was installed for temporary support of roof slab during construction.

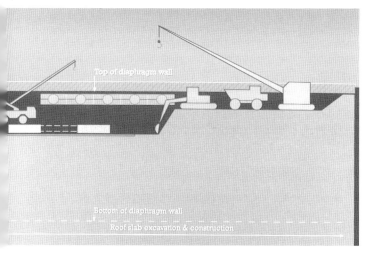

Figure 3 - Excavation was continued inside the diaphragm walling to the soffit of the tunnel roof.

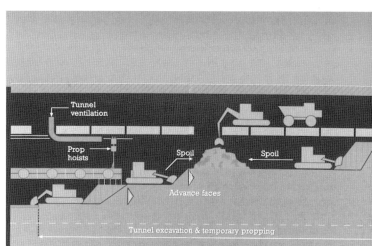

Figure 4 - Machines transported and deposited excavated material where it was grab-loaded into dumping trucks.

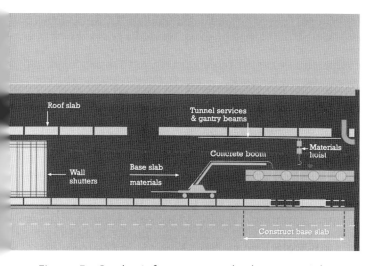

Figure 5 - Steel reinforcement and other materials were transported along the tunnel by trailer to the overhead hoists.

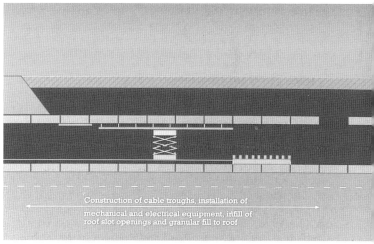

Figure 6 - Construction of cable troughs installation of mechanical and electrical equipment.

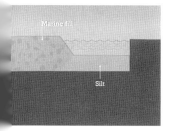
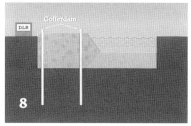
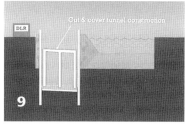

Figure 7 - Marine Fill was pumped into the basin to form a working platform.
Figure 8 - Sheet piling cofferdams constructed into clay below the marine fill.

Figure 9 - Concrete tunnel box constructed into the clay below the fill.
Figure 10 - Cofferdam was removed and Limehouse Basin water restored.

LONDON CITY AIRPORT

Battles for the Skies

The Idea for STOLPORT

The idea for London City Airport emerged as a result of the attempt by the LDDC and investors looking for a project to change the perceptions of the Royal Docks from the 19 century image of docks and ships to one based on modern technology and innovation. Bryman Airways were interested in expanding their services and so the opportunity to develop a STOLPORT (Short Take Off and Landing Airport) which would serve businesses in the City and Docklands. The disused quay between Royal Albert and King George Docks was identified as the best site. It was the right size and its east-west alignment would mean that the traffic using the new airport would operate in the same direction as the traffic using Heathrow, Gatwick and Luton. This would make it easier for the air traffic control authorities to cope with the facilities.

There followed a period of some months during which the contractors and investor Mowlem sought to sell the idea of an airport to the local people. A number of trips for residents was arranged to Plymouth which had a similar facility and in June 1982 the concept was demonstrated in Docklands when a DeHavilland Seven airplane was landed on a cleared area of quayside at Heron Quays, next to Canary Wharf on the Isle of Dogs. The airplane proved to be quiet and some of the opposition to the idea was quelled. Two public polls were taken which indicated some support for the scheme. With the inception of Canary Wharf development in 1985, everyone started to think about the huge possibilities, and it was on the strength of this that the airport went ahead and opened in 1987.

Airport Operators Rivalry

As the new London City Airport was rapidly preparing for its take off in October 1987, the £30million project had already hit some problems. Billed as the new European airport, it was built on the quay between the Albert and King George V docks. It found itself phased with a series of difficulties. Although the 762 metre long runway had already been completed, much of the project was still subject to discussions. The question mark still remained as to who would be allowed to fly out of the dockland site. The two front runners were Euro Express, a subsidiary of British Midland and Bryman Airways; both had made formal applications to the Civil Aviation Authority (CAA) for operating licences. The CAA was to meet in March to make its final decision, but meanwhile rivalry between the respective bidders to turn Docklands into a new entrance into Europe had not always been conducted smoothly.

Publicly all the three welcomed the prospect of working together at the new airport. At that time both Primaspace Bryman and British Midland the parent company of Euro Express were locked into a battle of respective routes. Tensions had not been confined to routes alone, the type of aeroplanes suitable for the new airport, was also the subject of heated debate. Although London City Airport was originally given the go-ahead on the basis that only comparatively quiet DeHaviland Dash 7 turbo prop short take off, and landing plane would be allowed, London wide, the possibility of introducing jets

had already generated fierce argument. Euro Express indicated whilst they were perfectly content with the 50 seater DeHaviland which was quite capable of serving such routes as Frankfurt and Strasbourg, they would like to explore the possibility of introducing jets sometime in the future. More dramatically Euro Express had spent considerable time and money attempting to change the proposed construction of the £130 million suspension bridge which was planned to take the road traffic across the River Thames near the east end of the airport runway. Under the original plans submitted by the Department of Transport, the new bridge would have 420 feet high towers. Euro Express having compiled the detailed feasibility study suggested the structure could be substantially lowered, so allowing jet aircraft with a more gradual rate of descent than the Dash 7 to land completely. But if the two competing airlines seemed to spend time in opposing discussions in one respect they were united. They all objected to the proposed fees for using the airport.

Airport for City Executives

Figures submitted by the airport developers, Mowlem the contractors to the two airlines, showed that the owners were planning to charge higher landing fees than British Airport Authority does at Heathrow Airport. Mowlem was also working out what it would have to charge airlines for renting the buildings and terminal facilities. But as the developers looked for a good return on their investment, the airlines complained of increasing financial strain, which they warned, could become prohibitive. Whilst the developers and airline companies continued to hammer out a working relationship against this turbulent background, the public relations machine was gearing up for the scheduled take off that October from the airport. Already the terminal was nearing completion in 1987 with its ten departure gates able to handle up to 60 flights each day.

Flights to UK and European Cities

At least the airport authority could not look better to the City business executives who would have the option of making their present 15 mile journey from Central London to Heathrow a thing of the past. The business executives flying from London City Airport could expect to reach Paris before their Heathrow counterpart had even boarded the plane. The PR people stressed that it was not only the traveller who stood to benefit, with the Airport promising to generate around 400 local jobs, the developers argued that there was even icing on the cake for long standing docklanders. It awaited to be seen whether those living under the flight path believed in the promises or thought it was pie in the sky! In the 1990s, the runway was extended and the airport has succeeded in operating flights by Bryman Airways to major cities in the UK and Europe.

The Queen opened London City Airport on Guy Fawkes Day in November 1987 and later there was a fireworks display to celebrate Britain's first new airport for 40 years.

Riverbus Service to old Docklands started in 1988, but unfortunately had to be closed due to financial problems.

Docklands Light Railway - winds its way through the heart of the Isle of Dogs.

Lewisham Docklands Light Railway Station opened in 2000.. A new 12-minute service from Stratford to Lewisham, operating Monday to Friday in peak hours; making a 50% increase in peak services to Canary Wharf.

Limehouse Link, the road to business confidence. A convoy of 20 black cabs became the first vehicles to travel through the £263 million tunnel.

Canary Wharf Station
By the end of 2000, the Jubilee Line Extension was completely open and astonished passengers with its grandeur. It is a wonderful piece of civil engineering infrastructure even though it was 20 months late and £1.4billion over budget.

RISE AND FALL OF THAMES RIVER BUS

Transport System for Docklanders

Floating Assets

A hundred years ago Docklands was served by over 6000 sailing barges and lighters carrying a wide variety of cargo from visiting ships in the bustling docks to the numerous wharves along the river. This fleet has since the 1970s dwindled to a precious few which have survived the closure of the Upper Docks to take on new roles, including the delivery of materials by river during the construction of Canary Wharf. A number have been converted to restaurants serving the Isle of Dogs. Others have been restored and are moored in other dock areas. The Felix at St Katharine's Dock by Tower Bridge has served the business community in the City and Docklands, as a corporate hospitality and private dining venue. The solid original pine and oak timbers remain intact and a new bar has been added, creating a relaxing atmosphere that has also been used for numerous successful press launches and parties. Handy for the City and Docklands, the boat can be enjoyed at its mooring on a sailing trip along the Thames and its estuaries, retracing some of its bygone days.

Thames Line

Early in the 1980s the River Thames was supposed to become a vital transport system for Docklanders eager to beat the familiar jam on the Capital's roads and rails. It was estimated that 2.5 million Londoners would travel to work by boat when a comprehensive service is launched. The ferry service would be provided by a new company called the Thames Line which was exercising its public relations during 1987 in order to win the contract. The Company had the right timing but also had to convince Government that they had the right means to do the job and the direction under the London Dockland Development Corporation, the Thames Water Authority, the Port of London and London Transport. Beside this company others submitted feasibility plans. The official specifications required were daunting. The boats had to travel at up to 30mph to compete against the roads, be highly manoeuvrable and operate timber and other bulky rubbish in the water with little or no wash. Within a short time the number of serious contenders were narrowed down to a few.

Thames Line quickly became a front runner largely on the basis that it had two prototype crafts in the water capable of doing the job. It also had on board its team a number of highly committed experts familiar with the pitfalls of previous attempts to set up a River bus service along the Thames. The past failures to harness the Thames for passenger transport had hinged largely on inappropriate craft and under funding. But the most encouraging results were obtained under the GLC prior to their demise in 1986. In conjunction with the Ministry of Technology the GLC ran three Hovercrafts, having obtained good reliability, but Government financial restrictions resulted in the GLC withdrawing its vital subsidy. The essential difference with the latest ferry venture was that Thames Line as a conventional business without subsidies had aimed to make a projected profit. Short haul 50 seater ferries were proposed to operate between Putney and Greenwich. A 50 minute morning and evening service for commuters upstream and downstream from the City were included. Fares were expected to be around 10% higher than those charged on similar journies by bus and tube, but time would be saved on many trips.

River Bus Contribution

The River Bus, which was set up in 1988 and died in 1993, made a small contribution to the regeneration of London Docklands and to its transport system. It could be observed how relatively few passengers it carried compared to buses and trains, but it had a unique pioneering image, which attracted many supporters during its lifetime. There is a long history of attempts to run services along the River Thames, which may help to explain its demise. Passenger traffic on the Thames grew in the 18th century, but began to flow away as more bridges, roads and railways were developed. Steamboats flourished in the first half of the 19th century but the last company went into liquidation by 1886.

Schemes during the 20th century included a boat fleet run by the London County Council between 1905 and 1907 and a water bus initiated during the Festival of Britain in 1951 by a consortium of owners and which with it once the South Bank site closed. Since the end of World War II there have been a number of attempts to run commercially viable transport systems on the Thames. There were a number of reasons why these services failed to survive, among them are lack of integration with bus and rail, lack of riverside facilities, operating difficulties and high costs.

Problems of Operation

The birth of the River Bus was due to the two newly developed riverside areas, namely Chelsea Harbour and Canary Wharf, and appeared in between carrying residents and business people who preferred to travel by boat, rather than journey by tube and bus. The boats were relatively small, with 62 seats and built to high standards of comfort. Staffing was relatively generous to keep the customer service standards high. It was expected that demand for the service would grow as more firms were relocated at Canary Wharf. This was the concept which attracted a Business Expansion Scheme grant in 1988 and which started the Thames Line service. Unfortunately the Thames Line was opposed by the established River Thames operators who run tourist services and there were complaints about the damaging effects and creation of problems for rowers and others, which meant they had to slow down. The catamarans also experienced problems with rubbish floating in the Thames damaging their propulsion equipment and further damage to the hulls from frequent docking at piers.

In February 1994 the fleet of eight River Bus catamarans were sold to a company in Bangkok for tourist use in that city. Since then a number of studies have been looking at different kind of services along the Thames, but nothing has yet been developed for a comprehensive service.

BRIDGING THE GAPS IN DOCKLANDS

Stunning Collection of Footbridges in London

London's New Footbridges

London Docklands boasts a stunning collection of footbridges in the capital. The construction of such landmarks has given Docklands some vibrancy and identity. The clutch of these bridges have also received accolades from many critics and observers. The former LDDC claimed that they had crystallised for some people that Docklands is a success and that they helped make the outside world notice that Docklands is a special place and not the same as the rest of London! The aim has been to 'humanise' Docklands by providing pedestrian and cycle routes. It appears that construction initially grew out of this desire. The first of the area's landmark footbridges was marked by a dramatic cable-stayed span and glass footbridge at Poplar DLR station. The design aim has been fitness for purpose and building something with style and interest.

Canary Wharf Bridges

Two striking new bridges have been built to bring Canary Wharf within easy strolling distance of neighbouring dockside quays, which helped to counter a perception of the huge office complex as an isolated district within the island. To the south of the Wharf, a £2.5 million S-shaped footbridge in two sections links South Quay, by the Britannia International Hotel, with the chalet-style offices of Heron Quays. A simple floating structure joins Herons Quays to Canary Wharf. As well as allowing boats through, the flexible design can be shortened, dismantled and moved any time to provide a direct link across the dock water between Marsh Wall and Canary Wharf Jubilee Line station.

The second landmark crossing, an elegant £1.5 million design pontoon design, joins the north side of Canary Wharf with the West India Quay, spanning the old West India Import Dock. This important conservation area has the imposing blocks of Grade I listed sugar warehouses which have been converted into luxury apartments and a home for the Docklands Museum. Many Canary Wharf workers have therefore access to restaurants and pubs in Marsh Wall nearby. Both bridges were financed by the LDDC and opened during 1995/96.

East London River Crossing

Following an extremely long gestation period, this proposal for a bridge in East London finally went through a Public Inquiry of record length in 1985/86 and was approved by the Secretary of State for Transport in 1988. However changes to the bridge designed to accommodate London City Airport constraints being near the flight path of the aeroplanes necessitated another Public Inquiry in 1990 and the go-ahead for the scheme with the revised bridge, was again approved in 1991. Throughout this time considerable concern was being expressed by opposition groups about the impact of the bridge and roadways on Oxleas Wood and on large areas of housing in Plumstead. The scheme was subjected to two further challenges. A High Court challenge by the London Borough of Greenwich and a challenge from the European Commission who contested the environmental assessment made by the Department of the Environment as the original enquiry did not comply with EEC directives on the environmental assessment.

As a result of this uncertainty, the Government decided in 1993 that while it was committed for the need of a new road link across the Thames in East London as a key element in the strategy to regenerate the Thames Gateway, the current scheme designed and chosen some time ago now failed to meet the high environmental standard applied to road schemes. With the publication of a transport strategy for London in 1996, the original plan for the East London River Crossing was finally scrapped in 1997. In the report consultation was held regarding the Blackwall Crossing, Woolwich Rail Crossing and Galleons Reach Crossing for the Thames Gateway area.

The S-shaped South Quay footbridge spans 180m across South Dock and connects to Canary Wharf. It is made up of two identical cable-stayed sections, one of which rotates to allow boats to pass through.

The West India Quay footbridge is a gently arched 90m pontoon structure which might easily be overlooked if it was not for its day-glow green paintwork. It connects Canary Wharf to the North Quay.

ECONOMIC TRAINING AND JOB PROMISES

Employers Moving Out

The economic situation of Docklands in 1981 was instrumental in starting the regeneration in East London. In common with the rest of London, the area had seen a dramatic decline of jobs over the previous fifteen years, particularly with the disappearance of shipping and the reduction of the manufacturing sector. Associated in part to this decline was the large stock of derelict floor space with unit sizes largely unrelated to market demand and much of it obsolete n terms of modern requirements. These were hardly assets, which could attract new business to Docklands. Government studies at the time also confirmed that inadequate premises were a material factor for many employers moving out of the Inner City to other locations outside London, resulting in loss of jobs and contributing to the air of dereliction as vacated premises were being largely ignored by firms. This was particularly true of the situation in Docklands.

Creating Modern Business

The view was taken that what Docklands required for its long-term employment future was viable companies with potential for growth and not those simply attracted by the prospect of financial help or indeed other handouts as offered by other regions undergoing similar economic changes. As part of this strategy, over 2 million square feet (187,000m2) of empty obsolete dockside sheds and buildings were demolished by the LDDC in the Enterprise Zone on the Isle of Dogs, to provide land for development and subsequent business premises. Such buildings would be let at market rates in order to attract not only new businesses but also to create a nucleus for a modern business environment for the area. Wimpey built Business Park, Indescon Court and The Lanterns were schemes all located in the Enterprise Zone, which represented the first wave of new business ventures in Docklands. They provided modern landscaped accommodation with car parking in a range of unit sizes and at rental levels lower and very competitive, which existed elsewhere. Serviced sites were also made available for those companies that preferred to buy their own plots of land and build their own buildings. Publishers Northern and Shell was an early example.

Outside the Enterprise Zone, companies were provided with business development support programmes and financial assistance under the Inner Urban Areas Act. The LDDC's contributions were not adequate in this direction to provide substantial improvements in employment of local residents.

Docklands Business Centre and Club

In addition to providing development land and financial assistance, the Corporation was determined to develop a working relationship with the emerging and prospective business community. As a result, in April 1983 the Corporation Board approved two major initiatives; the creations of the Docklands Business Research and Information Centre, which later became the Docklands Visitors Centre, and the Docklands Business Club. The Centre provided a comprehensive support service by the Corporation to the investors.

Staffed by specially recruited business managers from the private sector, it offered help, advice, information and counselling services. The Club would stimulate a dialogue between the Corporation and companies on plans and their implementation for a successful economic redevelopment of Docklands. The approach, new in the UK, was based on one which had been tried successfully in the USA. There, City Halls and local businesses had long pioneered such partnerships in jointly redeveloping redundant waterfronts in Baltimore, San Francisco and Boston.

Job Training by Skillnet

Towards the end of 1984 some progress was being made towards economic revival. Re-election of the Conservative Government secured the continued existence of the LDDC. The start of work on key public transport schemes such as the Docklands Light Railway there was the beginnings of local recognition that future jobs would come from the new economic sector unrelated to the past.

This signalled the need for job training locally. However, the LDDC had no formal responsibility or powers relating to education and vocational training. The Manpower Services Commission (MSC) was responsible for funding adult training in the United Kingdom and there was no MSC office in Docklands. It was also found that training was the last activity in the minds of disappearing local employers, parents and adults who became unemployed. The feeling among people was that there were no jobs and no future for them. In these circumstances, the provision of access units proved problematic. Later the Corporation decided that a "training broker" was required to bring together employers, providers of training and local unemployed people. This agency was called Skillnet and as it evolved new issues emerged. One of which was funding as the MSC, and European social fund resources were only available for schemes relating to 18-25 year olds. Overall, the agency did not succeed fully.

Public Scrutiny of LDDC

The LDDC's activities in job creation, training and employment was placed under formal public examination when its officers were summoned to appear before the House of Commons Employment Committee during 1988. Given the Committee's chosen framework, the Corporation's endeavours attracted a critical response. It recommended that the LDDC make more effort to target employment and training initiatives on disadvantaged groups in the local community who might otherwise miss out on the benefits of regeneration. Some progress was made towards movement in this direction. This period, however, coincided with the tail end of the 1980s property boom and the start of the most significant development of Canary Wharf's financial centre, which held the promise of some 50,000 new jobs early in the 21st century.

NEW EMPLOYMENT AND NEW OPPORTUNITIES

Office Jobs versus Dock Work

The Old Docks Professions

At whatever time of day the ship settled into the berth in the Port of London, the ship gangers with their dockers swarmed on to her deck and into her hold. Then began the typical dockers' work. A hundred years ago, any man who was fit and able could present himself at the dock gates in the morning and, if he was lucky and chosen by the foreman, could earn a few shillings a day humping cargo on and off the ships. The system of casual labour in the docks existed because the work was unskilled. Workers who found themselves seasonally unemployed - agricultural labourers, builders, costermongers - could 'fill in' slack periods by getting work at the docks; they needed nothing more than brawn, and endurance.

Of course, there were also skilled and semi-skilled tradesmen working in and around ports. In London, there were "lumpers" mainly concerned with the handling of timber cargoes; "whippers" who worked on coal ships; "lightermen" who sailed the Thames barges; and "stevedores" - regular, as opposed to casual dock workers, who regarded themselves as 'professionals'. The skills these men needed for their work were learned on the job; apart from the system of apprenticeship which applied to trades such as lighterage, there were seven years of training but no formal schemes. As often as not, skills were passed on from father to son.

Since the post-World War II labour scheme and more recently privatisation and the need for ports to become more flexible, have broken down lines of demarcation between jobs. Working in a port today is a multi-skilled profession; a crane driver may need to operate a fork lift truck, drive vehicles onto a ro-ro vessel, or even assist with maintenance or other tasks. Not surprisingly, port authorities have been re-assessing their training requirements and developing new ways of providing their workforces with the skills they need to perform effectively. This flexibility was unfortunately too late for the vanished and remarkable breed of London dockers.

Dock Closures Leading to Economic Void

The closure of the upper docks by the Port of London Authority with the resultant decline of relevant port activities in East London created an immense economic void which had to be replaced with new economic activities. The major aims of the regeneration were the need to provide a new economic environment for the area, to attract new business sectors and thereby to create new jobs and opportunities not only for the local Docklands communities but also for Londoners. The regeneration over the past three decades of the 20th century produced successful outcomes as measured in terms of new private national and international investments, new jobs and businesses. Moreover it has provided a solid foundation for the area to play an important financial part in contributing and supporting London as the financial centre of the world.

In 1981 it was found that about 1000 mostly small companies left behind following the closure of the docks. These companies employed 27,000 workers. They were the remnants of the industries, which had once employed 70,000 people and contributed locally and nationally in the Port of London. The LDDC as an urban development corporation was however not concerned or equipped to handle such employment matters. The Department of the Environment established it for physical regeneration of the area and that is where the primary thrust of their activity was concerned. The remits covered powers for planning and development, land management and infrastructure provision.

Enterprise Zone Factor in Creating Jobs

An early factor in creating jobs was the establishment of the 482 acres of the Isle of Dogs as an Enterprise Zone (EZ) which came into being in April 1982. This had a 10-year life and was to play a key role in the regeneration of docklands. The tax incentives offered attracted investors and new businesses on premises built by the private sector for buying or leasing. The LDDC demolished most of the warehouses and sheds to provide land for development. Low rise buildings of Wimpey Business Park, Indescon Court and the Lanterns were early schemes cheaply constructed.

Thousands Working at Canary Wharf

Outside the Enterprise Zone, companies were assisted with business development support and financial help under the Inner Urban Areas Act. A year after the introduction of the Enterprise Zone, and the success of new house building, the London Docklands Development Corporation established the Business Information Centre to prospective customers and the Business Club to provide interaction among the new and old companies in the area on an informal basis with pleasant surroundings.

By 1984, the trends indicated the emergence and concentration of small firms in small units to one to ten employees. Asda opened two superstores, one on the Isle of Dogs in 1983 and one in Beckton in 1986. More and more firms moved to Docklands and by 2001, 35,000 people were working at Canary Wharf alone.

Jobs for the Future

The population of Docklands and surrounding Boroughs could grow by a staggering 160,000 within the first decade of the new Millennium, with a substantial rise at Canary Wharf. There will be jobs across the skills spectrum, including commodity dealers, foreign exchange cashiers, clerks, drivers, secretaries, fitters; cooks, merchants, lawyers, reporters, salespersons, etc. The area has a proud history and as a result, proud people. In the early 19th century the docks were built and the Isle of Dogs became the centre of technical excellence. The new companies should be committed to working with the local community to ensure that the opportunities are shared by all. They should support education, training and employment initiatives to bridge the gap between old skills and new ones. Employers would then tap into the latest talent here to allow everybody to succeed.

Setbacks and Problems

The regeneration of Docklands is not solely about land development; it is most importantly about the people too. For some time in the eighties it was clear those who came to live and work in Docklands did not accept readily the special efforts made for the local people. Local people were to be given every possible encouragement to involve themselves in the new opportunities being created there, so that they could really benefit from the many changes taking place. After all, they were in their territory.

The developers were changing their roads, changing the views from their windows and changing the social make-up of the area. All the building works going on day and night were creating a nuisance. The LDDC tried to justify these changes on the grounds that they would lead to something much better and an improved way of life. They tried to ensure that these improvements are shared with the community through opening up opportunities in skill training, employment and housing. It was not an easy or successful task. Changes brought tensions. Local working class people required not only new skills, but also new ways of presenting themselves to the incoming high-tech employers. The old and new communities could not adjust in order to live together in harmony. There were setbacks and problems, demonstrations and protests but the LDDC could see no sensible alternatives.

Little Communication

By 1987 nearly 4 million square ft (400,00 m2) of new developments had got under way in London Docklands. This represented a massive about turn in the perception of the area and equally large injection of capital from the private sector into Docklands. But there was still little communication between the LDDC and local people. Initially the LDDC took a much more robust approach to getting development moving and acted as a bulldozer. Local people had justifiable worries because they were not being told much. Even after six years of LDDC operation they were still not being told enough.

On the Canary Wharf giant project, the LDDC's biggest gamble, the Corporation never had any doubt that it would happen because of the level of activity that had gone on in the Isle of Dogs. They considered it "criminal" if the LDDC hadn't gone for it and, had instead followed the local people's "downside option". This included a much-reduced scale of development and housing for local people. The option had smaller benefits to local authorities and a much longer timescale for the smaller scale development of Canary Wharf.

Confrontation with Local People

The confrontational attitudes of local groups toward the LDDC were understandable. The Corporation's efforts were directed at fostering property development. The teaching of new skills to local workers who worked for generations in the docks, which smacked dangerously of re-education, and is not be undertaken by the faint of heart, did not receive the attention it should perhaps have had. The Corporation pointed out that this was a classic chicken and egg situation. Is it better to get new businesses rolling first, and new jobs, or to attend to social problems like re-training? Most people would argue to do both would be best, but the LDDC claimed it was difficult with limited resources and public funding.

Increase in Docklands Population

The number of people living in Docklands in 1994 had increased by 66% since the LDDC began its redevelopment programme. About 65,000 lived within the region, compared with around 39,000 in 1981. Experts predicted that by the time developments have been completed in the 21st century around 125,000 people would be resident, a population the size of Oxford. The figures were in a report "Key Facts and Figures" produced by the Corporation. Its report was a round up of information including details on residential, commercial and industrial developments, private investments, government grants, tourism, population, employment and housing.

There was a change in employment opportunities in the area. In 1981 around 27,000 people worked there, including 1450 in banking/ finance, 650 in energy and water and 4250 in distribution, repairs, hotel and catering. By 1992 the number of jobs had reached 51,500 including 16,400 in banking/finance and 8,400 in distribution etc. The water and electricity boards employed fewer people. Regeneration experts predicted between 155,000 to 217,000 jobs in Docklands by the year 2020.

Grants for Community Groups

More than 80 Docklands groups shared LDDC grants more than £1 million in some years. The grants were used to subsidise running costs and staff salaries, help finance fundraising and purchase new equipment. Community groups throughout the urban redevelopment area benefited with funds exceeding £1 million going to nearly 50 organisations in the three Docklands boroughs of Tower Hamlets, Newham and Southwark.

Activities backed by the grants included education and training, childcare, youth activities, sport, the arts and support for the homeless and work with ethnic minorities. In the early 1990s the LDDC realised that helping to maintain a network of activities and services available to the Docklands community was an important task in the regeneration game. The grants were subject to the Department of the Environment guidelines, which restricted funding to individual groups to a maximum of three years. The rule was also that the grants were to be complemented by funding from other sources. Unfortunately, the LDDC did not offer grants for independent research into their own regeneration activities and most of their records were disposed of into two large skips shortly before the 1992 General Elections, when it was thought that there would be a change of government to the left.

The old and new Dockland communities could not initially adjust, so that they can live together in harmony. There were setbacks and problems in the early 1980s, demonstrations and protests led by local MP's and GLC leaders, but the LDDC could see no sensible alternatives.

In 1986 Islanders interrupted a speech by the Governor of the Bank of England by driving sheep and carrying beehives to the site of Canary Wharf. They were protesting against the proposed Docklands light Railway, which they claimed would destroy the Mudshute Farm.

The Influence of Riverside Taverns and New Pubs

Prospect of Whitby

Three hundred years ago if a pirate was found in Wapping Execution Dock at the wrong end of a hangman's rope, the chances are he would have been tormented by the onlookers lining the balcony on the Prospect of Whitby. Today, London's oldest riverside pub is more likely to be filled with weary stockbrokers and businessmen rather than bloodthirsty people, but its history and influence locally still live on. First called "The Devil's Tavern" back in 1543 it only changed to the Prospect of Whitby in 1790 taking the name of a ship bringing coal from Whitby in Yorkshire, which moored outside the pub.

Perched on the Thames and hemmed in by Docklands' budding developments, it has always been more of a famous waterside landmark almost isolated in Wapping's narrow back streets. But for those prepared to find out about its glorious past, it soon becomes clear that the Prospect of Whitby has more fame than beer alone. Judge Jeffreys of "Bloody Assizes" fame in the 18th century, as well as Samuel Pepys the diarist, both savoured its food. Pepys recorded that typical dishes of the period included a barrel of oysters, a bash of rabbits, a lamb and a rare chine of beef, a great dish of roasted fowl, a good calf's head with dumplings, tart, fruit, cheese and plenty of wine of all sorts. Sitting in the room in which he used to dine, you will still find that today's menu, although more sedate, is no less varied, and the specialities may include, amongst other things, a young shark.

The Town of Ramsgate

This historic 17th century Wapping tavern was described unfairly by Macaulay as a 'mean' alehouse. But the 'Hanging ' Judge Jeffreys discovered this to his cost when he was captured here by a lynch mob as he tried to escape to Europe on a collier! There is also an irony at this pub, when one considers that many of the Judge's victims were hanged at nearby Execution Dock. These were generally pirates sentenced to death mainly for crime on the high seas. Lashed to posts in the back garden of the pub, they were left to drown by the rising tide. Apparently as late as the 1890s people could still recall such watery tales!

Formerly known as "The Red Cow" after a famous red-headed barmaid, the pub was renamed in the middle of the 19th century by the fishermen from Ramsgate who sold their catch from the Old Wapping Stairs to the west of the tiny building. Towered over by the adjoining converted Olivers Wharves with its rich City's dwellers, the long and dark pub has a magnetic atmosphere for business men and local people alike, despite the shivering feeling of its vaults where convicts were once chained before their deportation to Australia!

Great Expectations of the Grapes

Another haunt for Docklands business people is a tiny riverside pub in Limehouse. "It had not a straight floor and hardly a straight line, but it had outlasted and would yet outlast many a better trimmed building". Charles Dickens wrote of the Six Jolly Fellowship Porters in his book of Our Mutual Friend. The Pub's real name was the Grapes, and it is still there in Narrow Street just as Dickens - who knew it well - described it in the 19th century. Recently refurbished by Taylor Walker, it is good to see a brewer sensitive to protecting authenticity and heritage, from the new rear balcony overhanging the Thames to the antique furniture provided throughout the pub. It is well worth a visit on an evening for the real ale and fish dishes in the upstairs restaurant. The adjacent 18th century Captain's houses have also attracted well known politicians and media people who were sympathetic to Docklands regeneration in the critical period of the early eighties.

The Gun

Formerly the haunt of dockers and watermen and 17th century pirates, this charming old pub, now the meeting place of businessmen is tucked away in the residential street of Coldharbour on the east side of the Isle of Dogs. The surrounding 19th century houses were the residences of ship captains and dock company officials, set at a precarious angle to the river's edge, the quaint pub has a roguish sort of atmosphere, possibly bearing the images of the original pirate clientele! It is reported to be the meeting place of Lord Nelson and Lady Hamilton. Although recently renovated, the original features are intact. More recently it has acquired a spectacular view of the Dome and also Blackwall Reach of the river. There are three separate bars; the favourite is the middle one, which leads out on to the river balcony.

Pubs on Isle of Dogs

The East End of London is celebrated for its pub culture. Pubs mean different things to different people and there's many a tale to be told about each one. On the Isle of Dogs there was a pub on almost every corner before the Blitz. One of them, The Ferry House, dates back to the time when the only way to cross the Thames was by ferryboat. Most pubs were built when the Island was industrialised. The Anchor and Hope and the Blacksmith's Arms were among the first to appear in the 19th century, at the northern end of West Ferry Road, followed by a succession of pubs right round the Island, including others that have disappeared, like the Pride of the Isle, the Great Eastern, the Ironmongers Arms, the Princess of Wales, the London, the Manchester and the Prince Albert. The working day for dockers, shipbuilders and factory workers was long and dirty, and the pub was the place for a thirst-quenching pint. It was also the place for entertainment, (professional or home-grown) and was used as a meeting place for unions, football clubs and loan clubs.

Not all Island pubs are as our grandparents saw them, especially on the inside. They perhaps wouldn't even recognise The Waterfront, newly built on the dockside, as a pub at all. It is the first pub of the new era on the Isle of Dogs, and more are expected to be built; not that they can replace the old ones, for there will never be another like Charlie Browns, that famous landmark in West India Dock Road, now demolished to make way for the Docklands highway and which was once a bizarre museum of souvenirs from all over the world, deposited by sailors whose ships came into the docks.

Top. The Grapes pub with Dicken's connection at Limehouse.

Bottom. The Prospect of Whitby is believed to be the oldest pub in London.

Top.
The beautiful Hayes Galleria, overlooking the Thames at Bermondsey, has a new pub, wine bars and restaurants.

Left.
The new Cat and Canary Pub at CanaryWharf facing the converted Grade 1 listed Warehouses at North Quay. It is very near the Meridian Line shown by the white laser line from Greenwich.

Docklands Tales

From Canary Wharf on the Isle of Dogs to Butlers Wharf in Bermondsey, Dockland names tell many tales. The derivation of the name "Wapping", Dockland's oldest district, is not clear with theories suggesting an Anglo Saxon Wappa, a ship's rope called Wapp, or the Old English wapol, meaning bubble or froth, not unlike the current property demand in the area, where two bedroom flats could cost over £300,000! Further east, Shadwell probably combines the Old English sceald (shallow) with wella (spring or stream). Limehouse refers to the 13th century kilns, which produced lime for buildings in London using stones from the Kent quarries. Ratcliffe means red cliff, but could also refer to a Lancastrian, a follower of the House of Lancaster in the Wars of the Roses. Tower Hamlets goes back many centuries and relates to the small settlements east of the Tower of London, including St Katharine's and Wapping..

The origin of the name Isle of Dogs is not clear and there is no hard evidence to prove the relevant theories. It is said that when Henry Viii occupied the Royal Palace at Greenwich his hunting dogs were exercised on the Island. Sailors in passing ships, who gave the Isle its name, heard the barking of these dogs. In the 18th century, the village of Millwall on the western side of the island became well known for its rows of windmills - from whence the area takes its name. The dark inhospitable place, described by Pepes in the 17th century, probably explains the name Black Wall for Blackwall. Barratt's Pierhead Lock high rise apartments near the Blue Bridge was once part of Yarrow's boatyard at Folly Point, famed during the 19th century for its fast torpedo boats, while nearby Compass Point was the site of Dudgeons boatyard, which built equally nippy sailing boats during the American Civil War.

Commemorating Famous Names

Many famous names still remain. Cubitt Wharf commemorates William Cubitt, the 19th century developer and builder who drained the land and built most of the east side of the island and gave his name to Cubitt Town. He also built at Hays Wharf and Regent Street. His brother Thomas designed and built for the rich at Belgravia, Victoria and Pimlico. Virginia Wharf, on the Greenwich Meridian, just like the earlier Jamestown Harbour development at Blackwall Basin marks the embarkation in 1606 of three ships, *Susan, Constant, Godspeed* and *Discovery* to found the American colony of Virginia. The old Blackwall Dock, visited by Pepes in 1661, also witnessed the departure of Frobisher (1577) and Hudson (1607) in their attempt to find a north-west passage to India! Although Burrells Wharf, on the south west corner of the island, was named after the last occupants of the old warehouses, Burrell & Co, who used the site for the manufacture of colour and pigments. Its new block names of Charthouse, Shipway and Taff Rail refer to the famous Victorian engineer Isambard Kingdom Brunel's achievement in building the steamship, *Great Eastern*, at the Scott Russell boatyard and launched after 13 attempts down the slipway extent to the side of Burrell's riverside found in 1982. The plaque has been preserved.

Street Names Reveal Stories

Docklands' street names often reveal fascinating stories. Take Ratcliff's Senrab Street, named in 1883 after the property owner Willoughby Barnes but spelt backwards because of the existence of a Barnes Street. Harbinger Close and Hesperus Crescent on the Isle of Dogs recall the Orient Line sailing ships plying the Australian route. The strangely named street names of Chipka and Plevena are linked to the Russian-Turkish War of 1877-88. Stainsby Road is named after the 1860s MP Paynton Piggott Stainsby Conant. There are Scottish influences in Docklands. The Earl of Strathmore owned some parts of Shadwell and hence Glamis Road, while Glengall connection on the Isle of Dogs stems from both Cubitt's original land purchase, and from the marriage of the Mellish family's daughter to the second Earl of Glengall, whose forbears included Bacon Cahir, hence the street title.

Area's Fragrant History

Many coined names for the new developments are obvious, such as Tobacco Dock and the Rum and Wine Closes of Wapping built over the old London Docks and the wine vaults. At Shad Thames, south of the Thames, spicy new blocks of Cinnamon and Tamarind Courts, Spice Quay, etc. give a whiff of the area's fragrant history. In the Surrey Docks, Swedish Quays and Finland Street relate to the Baltic timber trade, or Canada and Columba Wharf with North American grain import to London. The beautifully converted New Concordia Wharf near Tower Bridge was named after Concordia, Kansas City, Missouri, where the grain came from. The first mention of a Mr Butler on the site of Butler's wharf has been found in the General Rates book of 1794 when he was in partnership with a Mr Holland leasing a group of warehouses at the north end of St Saviour's Dock. Even the romantic sounding name of Silvertown simply refers to the 1850s rubber and telegraph works of SW Silver & Co in the Royal Docks.

Docklands Plaques

There are 23 plaques in Docklands recalling famous inhabitants and achievements; seventeen in Wapping, mainly the City fringes, four in Shad Thames, two on the Isle of Dogs and on in the Surrey Quays. The plaques reflect the two major historical aspects of maritime London and World War II Blitz. During the latter, historic buildings were lost. On the Isle of Dogs the most famous plaque commemorates the launching of the *Great Eastern* ship by Brunel. In Limehouse, the Reverend St John Groser, the priest and social reformer, is remembered in Butler Row. Docklands best maritime plaque is by the river in King Edward VII Memorial Park, Shadwell, commemorating the great seafarers Sir Hugh Willoughby, Sir Martin Frobisher, Stephen and William Borough and other navigators who, in the second half of the 16th century, set sail from this reach of the Thames near Ratcliff Cross to explore the Northern Seas. Other famous people of Docklands include John Newton, born in Wapping in 1725, who captained a slave ship before becoming a leading speaker against slavery and found time to write the hymn "Amazing Grace".

THE MUSEUM OF DOCKLANDS

Housing memories of East Enders and Dock History

Evidence of Dockers' LIfe
Following the closure of the docks, the Docklands area was littered with the tangible evidence of the dockers life industry including river craft, dock machinery and warehousing, largely unchanged since the time of Dickens. For the Museum of London the findings were treasure troves. The artefacts were all just lying around waiting either to be scrapped or rescued. There were cranes, handcarts and huge number of other items rusting away. There was also an enormous archive of material including photographs and paintings, which have been kept by the Port of London Authority (PLA), with details of everything from the construction of the docks to the cost of individual lock gates.

Royals Warehouse Temporary Home
Formally handed over to the Museum of London by the PLA in 1987, the Docklands Museum was initially housed in the W Warehouse, an old listed East India Company tobacco warehouse on the north side of the Royal Victoria Dock. The items exhibited over fifty dock crafts, including rigging, cooperage, whaling and ship repairing. What was surprising was the sheer antiquity of design of machinery was after all in use up to the last twenty years of the docks. Even as man landed on the moon, London dockers were still shovelling sugar with spoon-shaped shovels, making barrels and corking wine bottles by hand, using hand barrows and beam scales of a design which went back at least in to the early 18th century, carrying Trinidadian sugar on their backs down "Blood Alley" so called because escaping grains rubbed the porters shoulders raw. The Museum's photographic archive backed up by each of these exhibits with some contemporary images of the work in progress.

Permanent Home in Sugar Warehouse
The question, which was asked in the 1980s, was where precisely this collection should be permanently housed for thousands of visitors to seek weekly. The sugar warehouses on the North Quay were the first choice but nothing was decided until just before the demise of the LDDC in 1998, when the listed sugar warehouse was allocated. A lottery grant of £11 million was at the same time given for the Museum to provide an exciting glimpse of the local way of life now irrevocably lost. It is going to be an interactive museum with a working portrait of life and work in the docks, including a floating collection of tugs, lighters and launches. Some of the industries represented in the Museum are among the oldest and longest established in Britain. For example, a steam press has come from a ship-repairing firm in Blackwall, which had been working on its site for 400 years until it shut down in 1986. The Museum is as much part of London's history as the Houses of Parliament and should attract possibly as many visitors.

Galleries on Port of London
No1 sugar warehouse on the North Quay houses in 2002 the modern Museum of Docklands to tell the 2000 year old story of the Port of London. Two galleries look at the coming of the wet docks early in the 19th century. Then there is a gallery devoted to London's mid-Victorian sailor town that gives a taste of the dubious delights of Limehouse and Ratcliff History. A fourth major gallery, called the First Port of the Empire, shows the old Port in all its manifestations and social/economic history from the 1830s to 1930s.

The Docklands at War floor shows the impact of bombing and devastation on the local communities in the 1940s. It also covers the secret construction of the Mulberry Harbour for the Allied D-Day landing in 1944. A story is told about Pluto, the pipeline which supplied oil across the English Channel to the invading armies.

Re-building Docklands Gallery
A sixth gallery deals with the re-building of the docks in the 1940s and 1950s called New Port - New City and finally covers the shift downriver to Tilbury and Essex, and the closure of the upper docks in London. Then follows an exhibition on the regeneration of Docklands with the coming of the London Docklands Development Corporation (LDDC) in 1981 and the changes that took place during the last two decades of the 20th century.

PLA Archives
The museum also houses the Port of London Authority (PLA) archives and 40,000 black and white photographs taken by mostly unknown photographers. Many hours of taped interviews with former dockworkers are also available.

The state of the art museum is housed on North Quay in a superb Grade I listed warehouse described by the Royal Commission as one of the great monuments to European economic power of the 19th and 20th century. It houses the world's biggest collection of port-related artefacts with renovated cranes, tugs and barges outside to recreate the atmosphere of the old working dock. The museum is expected to attract at least a quarter of million visitors a year, swelling the ranks of more than 2 million tourists visiting Docklands annually.

National Maritime Exhibition - A view of the All Hands Gallery at the National Maritime Museum, Greenwich.

RUN UP your own signal to the fleet or load your own canon below decks. You can do this and experience many more seafaring tasks in the National Maritime Museum's first interactive gallery in the new Leopold Muller Education Centre which was opened as a result of the late Czechoslovakian millionaire's generosity.

Experience seafaring tasks in the interactive gallery in the new Leopold Muller Education Centre.

HALF AHEAD – and watch your stern! Felicity Natoli and Sandy Mead take the controls on a modern bridge, while below a young visitor tries supplying a ship in port with a giant box of tea.

Gallery teachers take the controls on a modern ship bridge while below a young visitor tries loading a ship in port with a box of tea. Modern controls on a ship bridge and model crane.

Maritime Museum All Hands Exhibition -The All Hands Gallery at the National Museum was launched in an effort to attract the interest of young visitors. Youngsters of seven to eleven year olds can, for example, develop seafaring knowledge by exploring models of tea chests operating cranes, firing guns and steering a vessel into a dock, supervised by experienced teachers. The gallery is divided into two main sections, the first dealing with life of seafarers and the second tackling maritime skills. The popular diver's chamber teaches children how to perform simple operations under water. The pride of the place is a 53 metre long model of the 1813 battleship Cornwallis, which fought for Britain against the War of Independence by America.

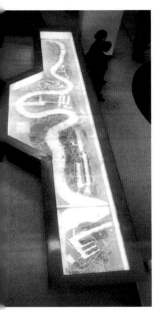

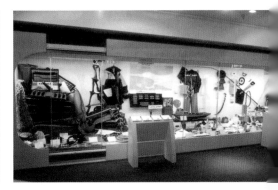

Port's Past at Science Museum, South Kensington - Left An old model of the Port of London showing the locations of the enclosed docks from Tower Bridge to Tilbury, c 1938. Top left A mural captures a loading scene from the Dockland's past. Top right Artifacts and memorabilia of the old Port of London. Science Museum Exhibition -There is a permanent Port of London exhibition at the Science Museum, South Kensington, London. The exhibits are centred around the large model of the Port as it was until 1969 when containerisation led to the upriver docks to be closed. There are many illustrations that provide the working of the docks and how they changed over the past forty years.

TO ALL SEAMEN

YOU WILL BE WELCOME AT THESE
CHURCHES NEAR THE DOCKS

Museum of Docklands The industrial collections of the museum cover over fifty trades, including spinning, iron casting and watch making. A large variety of tools and equipment which were used by dockers are also among the collections on show. The bottom illustrations show the exterior and interior of the museum historic building on the North Quay of the Isle of Dogs.

Jack the Ripper and Kray Brothers of Whitechapel

Murder Tales in East London

Torrid tales of crime and social deprivation were the seamier side of life in bygone East London. Conditions in Victorian London showed violence and squalor, which characterised the poorer parts of the capital, much of it in the East End. This was an era when a convicted rapist would get a three-month sentence, while a young boy would be jailed for a week for stealing a piece of firewood. The tales include stories of the plague, Jack the Ripper of 1888, the Kray Twins of 1966, Sweeney Todd, hung men and executions of pirates in Wapping during the 17th century.

The murder of a tavern keeper and his family in 1811 enraged people in the East End. A sailor, accused by the police on the flimsiest of evidence of being the killer, hung himself while in custody. The mob felt cheated, snatched the body and paraded it through Stepney and Wapping before burying it in Cable Street in a shallow grave with a stake hammered through the heart!

Three Months that Shook the World

More than a century after five grizzly murders in the old district of Whitechapel and its slums, the story of the killer known as Jack the Rippers continues to fascinate, the more so, since he has never been identified and "advertised". Jack the Ripper committed his murders at Whitechapel on Docklands' doorstep and a stone's throw from the present News International Printing Works at Wapping. Between 1 September and 9 November 1888, the mutilated bodies of five women were discovered in Hanbury Street, Durward Street and Mitre Square. They were prostitutes, named Mary Ann Nichols, Annie Chapman, Elizabeth Stride, Kathy Eddowes and Mary Jane Kelly. The killer was never found but his nickname, taken from an absurd letter to the Times newspaper, has not been forgotten.

The first body of Mary Nichols was found by a constable on the beat in Buck's Row at half past three in the morning. An incision had been made from under the lower right rib, curving down to her pubes and up again to the left of the stomach. The body was disembowelled and the intestines lifted out and draped over the right shoulder. The throat had also been cut with a clean sweep. A week later, Annie Chapman's identically mutilated corpse was discovered and great panic gripped Londoners in horror. On 30 September the Ripper struck twice on one night, killing his victims 40 minutes of each other, even though their bodies were found two miles apart. Kathy Eddowes had her nose and ears cut off, her uterus and one of her kidneys was missing. A piece of the kidney was sent the following morning to the police detective along with a note: "The other piece I fride and ate. It was very nise" wrote Jack with poor spelling.

Accusations were pointed at a number of people. The evidence argued that the killer was a doctor or a surgeon. Others said he was a butcher, so the police duly questioned all the butchers at nearby Smithfield in the City. A pro-Jewish scribble: "The Jews are not to be put upon" was found daubed in human blood. Other theories stated that Jack was Sir William Gull, personal physician to Queen Victoria. But really nobody knew and the myth continues in the 21st century. Mary Kelly's eviscerated body was discovered on 9 November and people held their breath for the next tragedy, but it never came. The Ripper had since disappeared forever.

The Kray Brothers of Whitechapel

In the early 1990S a kind of nostalgia spread around Reg and Ron Kray, the brothers who were serving their 25th year in prison for assorted crimes of violence, racketeering and murder. These earned them notoriety and wealth in the 1960s and have since spawned a cult, which has produced films and books of varying qualities. Reg Kray was particularly keen to feed the sentimental ideas that he and his twin brother were just your friendly, neighbourhood gangsters who helped old ladies across the street in between getting rid of their enemies. In 1993 in his latest book, "Villains we have Known", is a disorganised catalogue of the colourful characters, hoodlums and rogues who had supporting roles or walk on parts of East London during the Krays' reign. These include names such as Big Pat Connolly, Jack Spot and Frankie Fraser who will already be familiar to those who know at least part of the Kray's story.

On the Trail of the Ripper

As part of the historic walks in London, visitors can go on a "Jack the Ripper Murder Trail", with experienced guides, starting from the underground station at Whitechapel. The walkers are whisked past the busy high street and led down a long dark alley and then follow the roads until they reach the place where the first murder was committed in Bucks Row. The Ten Bells public house is in the middle of the Ripper's territory and you can stop here to quench your thirst. You can also examine old newspaper cuttings on the pub walls or sample the Ripper's Tipple - a red cocktail kept in a dusty green bottle behind the bar. The tour lasts about two hours and covers four of the murder sites. It has been reported that some walkers have fainted on this murder trail!

It's August 31st 1888 and the East End of London is about to be rocked by the discovery of a young prostitute whose body has been mutilated almost beyond recognition.

This is the beginning of Jack the Ripper's reign of terror during which, four more prostitutes were to meet their deaths in the most gruesome and evil of ways.

But who was the killer? Who was Jack the Ripper? Was he really Queen Victoria's grandson, Clarence? Where did he come from and where did he go to?

Come with us down the dark, dank streets of London a century ago and maybe you too will feel the spirit of the Ripper as he stalks his next victim.

Nous sommes le 31 août 1888. L'Angleterre va bientôt être secouée par une découverte macabre : une jeune prostituée dont le corps, affreusement mutilé, est à peine reconnaissable. Ce meurtre est signé Jack l'Eventreur, qui sèmera la terreur en assassinant quatre autres prostituées dans des conditions particulièrement atroces. Mais qui commit ces crimes abjects ? Qui était Jack l'Eventreur? Etait-ce Clarence, le petit-fils de la reine Victoria ? D'où venait-il, et qu'est-il advenu de lui? Pour le savoir, venez explorer les ruelles sombres et humides du Londres de l'époque victorienne, et sentez planer sur vous l'ombre de Jack l'Eventreur.

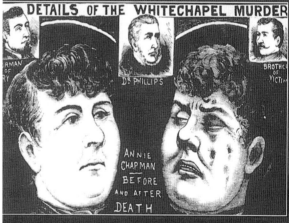

Engravings of Jack the Ripper's murders at Whitechapel in 1888 during three months that shook the world!

The murder of a tavern keeper and his family in 1811 enraged people in the East End.

Reports of Jack the Ripper's murders of 1888 in Police News.

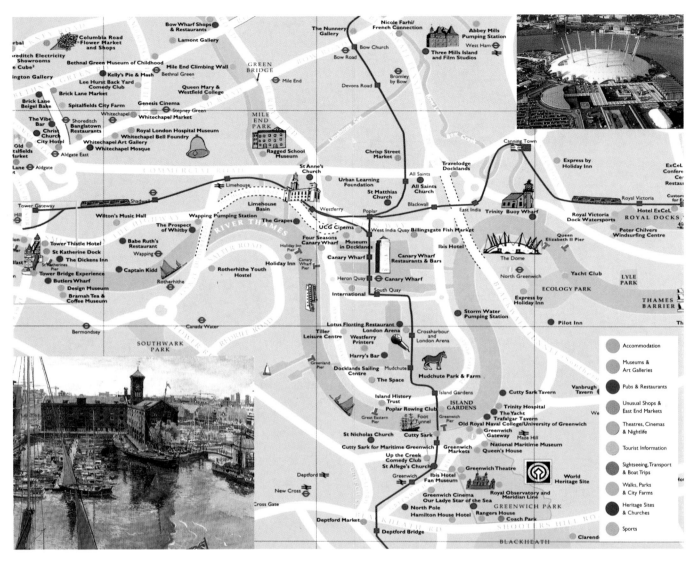

Map legend:
- Accommodation
- Museums & Art Galleries
- Pubs & Restaurants
- Unusual Shops & East End Markets
- Theatres, Cinemas & Nightlife
- Tourist Information
- Sightseeing, Transport & Boat Trips
- Walks, Parks & City Farms
- Heritage Sites & Churches
- Sports

Millions of British people and visitors from all over the globe are making tracks to Canary Wharf and London Docklands. The historic water city, once a run-down part of London, has been transformed into a fiesta of new culture and environment. The area provides a world stage and a showcase to present the progress made in this large expanse of East London in recent years and shines with international opportunities which remain for the advancement of private enterprise and business.

Barclays Bank has taken out one million sq ft space at this 30 storey tower on the north side of Churchill Place, the third of the squares on the Wharf. It is one of the largest buildings and features five south facing atrias.

Aerial view of Canary Wharf looking north west showing the construction of new towers and the DLR station at Heron Quays in May 2002. Building close and over live railway lines is always a challenge - especially when the DLR trains that run on these lines have no drivers!

The international Morgan Stanley finance company has increased its presence at the Wharf with a new building next to Heron Quays DLR station. Skimmer, Owing and Merrill designed the 13-storey building.

The 200,000 sq ft building on the north side of Canada Square and to the east of HSBC tower is the new home of Waitrose Superstore and a Reebok gymnasium. Waitrose has the bottom two floors and Reebok the top three.

The headquarters of the Northern Trust company on the West Side of Heron Quays, designed by Cesar Pelli.

The one million sq. ft 30 storey tower is the new home of Lehman Brothers and lies on the West Side of Heron Quays, between the Jubilee and DLR stations. Cesar Pelf, the architect for Canary Wharf Tower, designed the building.

McGraw Hill international publishing company has a new 500,000 sq ft building at Canada Square to the east of Citigroup Tower. The 12 storey headquarter overlooks the Square to the north and Jubilee Park to the south.

Adjacent to the Jubilee Line station eastern entrance and overlooking Jubilee Park, the 30-storey stainless steel and glass is being partly occupied by a law firm.

The 32-storey tower is at the centre of five new buildings at Heron Quays and is the new offices for a firm of lawyers and other businesses.

151

LDDC FAREWELL TO ISLANDERS

Funding to support Local Community

First Call for the Quango

It started with a morning phone call to Mr Nigel Broakes one Saturday in October 1980 and it finished exactly seventeen years later in October when the London Docklands Development Corporation (LDDC) handed over its pride and joy, the Isle of Dogs to the London Borough of Tower Hamlets. The call from Mr Michael Heseltine, Minister for the Environment, in the newly elected Conservative Government, was the signal for the full assault on the dereliction, decay and despondency that was the remains of a once greatest port on earth.

Mr Heseltine wanted to form development corporations for the docklands in London and Liverpool and he wanted a seasoned property developer, Nigel Broakes as Chairman for the regeneration team that would be sent into action to turn dismay into dramatic show in East London. Mr Broakes looked up the A-Z map of London and found London really stopped at Tower Bridge, but despite this he decided to accept the appointment of the LDDC's chairman designate. He recruited the East Ender, Mr Bob Mellish and they appointed Mr Reg Ward, the first Chief Executive, who was a dreamer and a visionary. In July 1981 Parliament passed the act for the formation of the LDDC, despite a Select Committee declaration that the regeneration of Docklands would be a draconian measure!

The first pioneers were Limehouse Studios, who occupied one of the sheds where the Canary Wharf Tower now stands. Asda Stores were seeking more supermarkets in the South East and Northern & Shell, the magazine publishers, brought their staff from Covent Garden in buses to inspect the first new office dockside building on the east side of the Isle of Dogs. Because of the newly gained Enterprise Zone status given to the Isle, the first firms got bonuses of 100 per cent tax allowances.

Farewell Funding for Local people

With new jobs replacing the 5000 lost when the West India and Millwall Docks closed in 1980, the local residents who had opposed the arrival of the LDDC, after few years began to see some benefits. It appeared that the sceptical response from the locals, who didn't like their new quango, matched their dislike for the Docklands Councils too! The first phone call produced a knighthood for Sir Nigel Broakes and his stint at the LDDC ended in 1984, when another property developer, Sir Christopher Benson, took over.

For an island that started with a medieval chapel and a row boat ferry across the Thames to Greenwich, the Docklands Light Railway has provided the greatest benefit from the recent regeneration of the Isle of Dogs. Hi-tech railways provide locals and thousands of new residents and commuters who pour daily into the area with lifeline links to the rest of London. However the local islanders have lost their community benefits with the demise of the LDDC in March 1998. It took about 15 months of discussions and back-biting to get it agreed, but the Farewell Funding deal between the LDDC, Tower Hamlets Council and the communities covering the Isle of Dogs was announced in hurry, confusion and recrimination in October 1997. While the main participants and their hangers on hit the media with their versions of the deal, it was not very clear what the exact details were. It was claimed by the Islander's leader that the LDDC had failed to secure the future of its regeneration programmes. The local community who have borne the brunt of living for 17 years on Europe's largest building site have not been treated properly.

Farewell Funding is a lumpsum endowment paying enough interest to enable the voluntary sector to continue to provide vital additional community needs and to have the income to maintain many recently provided amenities on the island.

Final Endowment

The final deal tempered by Government Ministers gave over £1 million to support local voluntary community work, despite needs report funded by the LDDC, which recommended an endowment of £6.4 million as vital if the LDDC was to leave the area without damaging the social regeneration. It was commented by the Community leaders that they were disappointed with the Government Ministers who had allowed this deal to go through after all the support they had shown for the Community in their fight to gain ongoing benefits from 16 years of regeneration in the Isle of Dogs. It was predicted that there would be a shortfall of £300,000 a year and the Government seems to be under the impression that the business community will somehow bridge this enormous funding gap. It was clearly pointed out by the leaders that they will not and why should they; after all it was not their responsibility.

Funds for Tower Hamlets

It should be pointed out that the Business Rates Revenue from the glittering office buildings on the Isle of Dogs is now likely to put £50 million per year in Government coffers. 22% will be filtered back to Tower Hamlets Council from Whitehall; an increase of 10% would solve the problem once and for all for the shortfall in future funding. But cash-strapped Government said no extra cash will be provided for the Islanders because they have had a decade of building works.

Other Fundings For Future

There have been community Farewell Funding deals in other districts of Docklands which have been transformed over the past 17 years, but it has been the Isle of Dogs that has borne the brunt of the £4billion worth of office and transport construction over the past years and still has major works stretching for the next decade or so. In the Surrey Quays the LDDC and Southwark did community deals and arranged land swops to fund them. Wapping problems were surmounted by ongoing maintenance deals with the continued success of an early community trust fund set up by a grateful News International, Rupert Murdoch's empire. Beckton's deal was pivotal on community provision, land deals and estate maintenance.

THE FUTURE OF DOCKLANDS

New Commercial and Culture Centre of Britain

Premier Business and Communication Centre

The Isle of Dogs has already established itself as London's new business district and premier communication centre, with most of the national newspapers operating there. The centre can provide 21st century modern purpose built premises within easy reach of the City and West End to attract the new breed of television station which will probably arise in the wake of the digital revolution. It is becoming a great tourist quarter for London, where people, live, work, visit and play. Several top hotels have been built and more are to come. The completion of the Jubilee Line makes Canary Wharf within 10-15 minutes of the West End and almost most certainly makes people even more enthusiastic to work in Docklands. In two decades the Isle of Dogs would look substantially different. Some of the cheap and cheerful stylish office structures towards Millwall Dock will probably be demolished and replaced with high rise office buildings. Canary Wharf's three towers would be becoming increasingly the commercial and cultural centre, not only for London but also for the South East and Great Britain.

International Companies such as Texaco, American Express, HSBC, American Bank, Citigroup, Morgan Stanley and Ogilvy and Mather have been attracted by its high quality and open environment. Practically all the national newspapers have made their homes here.

The Royals Challenge

The Royals, with their magnificent stretches of water, now have rail and air transport links, are in the process of development. The challenge will be to spread the benefits into the whole of North Woolwich and south of the Thames, particularly Woolwich. A new road link between Docklands and south of the river is essential. The Blackwall Tunnel is working to well over capacity. Docklands also needs to become involved and connected to the Channel ports and the Channel Tunnel. The Thames Gateway Crossing (Galleons Reach) is needed to make full benefits of the Docklands success. Using the historic and the new, Docklands will reflect and consolidate the international standing of London for the forseeable future.

Canary Wharf Gleaming Towers

Canary Wharf has continued to sprout gleaming new towers at a frightening pace, and there are more planned with firms signed up and in a rush to move to the former Docklands of East London. The City Group Centre to the south east of the main tower was opened in October 2000, before its new 42 floor sees a Pelli-designed tower completed during 2001. A similar size creation alongside was also racing to finish first for its HSBC tenants. In the year 2000, 6.5million sq ft of office and retail accommodation was under construction in the area to add to nearly 4.8 sq. ft built before the property crash of the early 1990s. This included 5 new buildings on the former Heron Quay, plus more to the east of the main tower. By the end of 2000, 35,000 people were working in the area against a target of 50,000 in 2003 and 90,000 in 2005, helped not least by the new transport to the area via Jubilee Line extension. Canary Wharf Group, the company which designs, finances, manages and maintains the whole estate entered the FTSE 100 in 2000.

World Class Capital's Prosperity

East London is today a vital part of London and is entitled to claim a share in the world class capital's prosperity. The huge investment in infrastructure is not only for the benefit of Canary Wharf but for the residents of both north and south of the river. All areas of the East End are benefiting from the new Docklands Light Railway, the Jubilee Line extension and London City Airport. The regeneration of Docklands in terms of jobs, housing and commercial offices for the whole of London has happened at an alarming pace. The benefits to the local communities are still evolving and will continue to do so. The statistics include over 24,000 new homes in Docklands, refurbishment of 8,000 social housing units, 25 million square feet of commercial office development and 72,000 jobs in 1997 compared to 27,000 in 1981. The forecast job growth in the Docklands Borough is from 450,000 in 1995 to 610,000 in 2010.

East London Gateway to Europe

The imbalance between West and East London is being addressed for the first time in centuries. London could not continue to be the centre of the world commerce and compete with the rest of Europe without the innovative, imaginative and energetic efforts of Docklands. It is 12 times the size of the City of London. The centre of gravity of the capital has moved eastward over the past few decades. With the Channel Tunnel Rail Link, London City and Stanstead Airports, as well as much improved highways, East London will be the gateway to Continental Europe and has a bright future during the 21st century. This destiny will not be deflected by critics whatever their motivation.

Future Development

As Canary Wharf continues to grow the 40,000 people already working there is forecast to double within a few years, the next big thing on the Isle of Dogs is the development of South Quay and Millharbour. Now known as the Millennium Quarter, the 50-acre site has been subject to master planning and construction exercise by Tower Hamlets Council, developing a planning framework governing the scale and height of development, infrastructure and open spaces. The applications have included two high-rise commercial buildings, 17 and 42 storeys, a 15-storey residential block. The World Trade Centre has its own building on South Quay. British Waterways Board, currently responsible for the docks, have a strategy for the Isle of Dogs. This includes a water-taxi service, covering a maritime route connecting Greenwich with the new Museum of Docklands on the North Quay of the former West India Import Dock, a new marina, cruising and residential moorings, and a floating retail attraction on Millwall Inner Dock.

A view of New Providence Wharf riverside apartments and the 400 bedroom hotel on the eastern side of the Isle of Dogs, c2002.

Redevelopment of the London Arena site into residential apartments, including affordable homes and shops, c2003

The breathtaking views from the penthouses on the South side of the Thames c1999, around a bend in the river from Tower Bridge and the city (left) to Wapping (centre) and up to Canary Wharf Tower (right). The need for building imaginative bridges is clearly demonstrated.

The £5.2 Billion Channel Tunnel Rail Link will cut the London to Paris rail journey to 2 hrs 20 minutes when completed around 2007. Built in two sections, it has major station at Stratford, a short distance North from Canary Wharf.

Will the East London River Crossing when built at Blackwell or Gallions Reach look like this bridge?

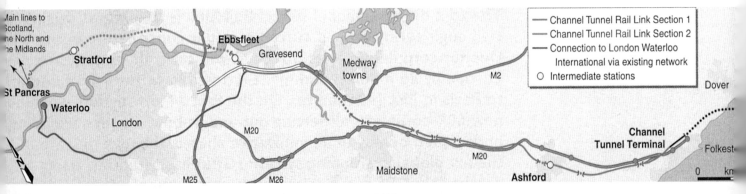

A Shopping mall provides services for office workers who occupy the buildings surrounding Churchill Place, on the east side of Canary Wharf Estate. The design includes a large glass atrium roof that sheds natural light into the space below and outdoor facilities surround the greenery. Similar tall office buildings are on the way for the riverside, south west of the estate.

Heron Quays on the south side of Canary Wharf estate has been the site of of five major buildings. Jubilee Place has a retail mall under the park and connects with the glass dommed JLE Stations and DLR Station. The 32 Storey tower in the middle of the picture was designed by Cesar Pelli. Heron Quays is to be the site of Canary Wharf Crosssrail Station when built.

Opening of Campus by Ken Livingstone

The new Mayor of London, Ken Livingstone, officially opened London's first new University campus for 50 years on Tuesday 4th July 2000. Built on the north bank of the Royal Albert Dock, the new £40 million Docklands Campus of the University of East London (UEL) brings higher education to a previously neglected area of the Capital. The Campus, complete with lecture theatres, laboratories and canteen facilities will eventually serve 5000 students with onsite accommodation for nearly 400 of them in brightly painted "hatbox" shaped circular halls of residence. Despite its modern design and the fact that UEL is one of the country's newest universities the Campus offers traditional student pursuit. The Dock is acquiring a 2000 metre Olympic-rowing lake which students are allowed to use.

Training for Local People

Noise from the London City Airport opposite the Campus means that windows have to remain shut. The architects have designed environmentally friendly ventilation and heating system. Other innovations built into the four-acre site include a Muslim prayer room, fitness centre and 28 business start-up units where fledgling enterprises can capitalise on the research work being undertaken at the University. Faculties that have moved from the University's existing Campuses in Barking and Stratford include Engineering, Design, Fashion, Culture studies and Media and Communication studies. It is claimed that the Departments who had chosen to come to this Campus came because of what they could bring to the redevelopment of East London. Plans for the Campus were first mooted in 1992 and funding has been provided by the University, the Department for the Environment, Transport and Regions and the now defunct London Docklands Development Corporation. The Docklands Light Railway serves the Campus. It offers skills and training for members of the local community at a range of undergraduate and postgraduate studies. Ken Livingstone on his first full day of work following his inauguration as London Mayor was guest of honour at the official opening of the Campus, arriving with the other guests on a specially chartered DLR service. The guests included former Minister Stephen Norris, Sir Terence Conran, local MPs, Diane Abbot and Stephen Tims. There were five mayors also present from the local boroughs.

The Campus buildings are partly traditional and partly resemble a business park. They are cloistered and turreted but also tinned roof. The cost of construction is half of what some buildings in Cambridge would cost. The coloured round towers of the residential accommodation are clearly visible as a feature of the site. There is a huge car park for staff and students at the Campus. The Campus has a public right of way running through the main square and along the dockside by the International Rowing Course. The waterside walkway gives excellent views of the Royal Docks and the London City Airport south of the campus on the other side of the Albert Dock. The main entrance to the Campus is on foot from Cyprus station of Docklands Light Railway.

ExCeL International Exhibition Centre

East of Canary Wharf a building larger than the Millennium Dome was completed near the end of the year 2000. Its aim is to replace Earls Court and Olympia Exhibition Centres in West London. Located on the north quay of the Royal Victoria Dock and somehow resembles the old buildings which were used for loading and unloading cargoes, the centre is in a vast area of the Royal Docks. It is called ExCeL Centre, which is a £500 million-exhibition centre and is bigger than the National Exhibition Centre in Birmingham. The first phase of the building opened in November 2000, its aim is to replace its West End rivals as London's leading exhibition centre. If it succeeds it will shift the centre of gravity of the capital.

International Business

There is a 1500 capacity night club and supposedly a perfect lively Covent Garden style atmosphere for meeting old friends and making new ones, claimed by the developers. It has an arrangement for the earthly delights that offset the drudgery of large corporate events. Its ambition is to be a space station for international business in the outer docks to hold big, trade shows that oil the wheels of commerce. It is hoped to do it more efficiently than any other venue, having two halls the size of many football pitches which can be sub-divided, or opened up and are ringed with a three-lane truck route whence stands and exhibits can be offloaded at incredible speed. Its promoters make much of its integral digital system. It will compete for consumer shows, attended by the general public - the Boat Show is and an obvious target, with all the surrounding water.

Competition with West End

The centre will have to persuade punters that the Jubilee Line or the Beckton Branch of the DLR is as convenient as the District and Piccadilly Lines to the West of London. Possibly more helpful will be the fact that ExCel has a parking capacity for 5000 cars and is handy for the M25. Beyond its share size its architecture is nothing special. It has the look of a superstore, which symbolises the regeneration of Docklands. At its entrance it has half a glass pyramid, in short, it looks an industrial building. The exhibition halls have views towards the city and the truck route occupies the point. At first floor level you enjoy the waterfront view. There is a spine road, which runs down through the centre.

Penthouse Conference Centre

There is also a penthouse conference centre where again the opportunity for views is available. It could equally well be in the attraction of a hotel. However this description does not obscure the epic scale, Excel is the sort of thing you might find in the wide open spaces of America. And it is only the yawning emptiness of the Royal Docks that makes it possible. If it succeeds we will see the next great shift in the Capital's evolution eastward.

Views of University of East London Docklands Campus in the Royal Docks completed in September 1999 and formally opened by Mr Ken Livingstone, Mayor of London on 4 July 2000. The round shaped buildings overlooking the Albert Dock are the residential accommodation for students.

The need for a new Exhibition centre in the Capital was identified many years ago by the Association of Exhibition Organisers and others. The response is the ExCel Centre on the north side of the Royal Victoria Dock opened in November 2000 and connected by a footbridge to the south side. ExCel is not only London's newest, but the UK's most advanced events venue.

Located on the north side of the Royal Victoria Dock and connected by a footbridge to the south, ExCeL is not only London's newest but the UK's most advanced events venue.

ExCel Exhibition Centre. The giant centre includes 65,000 square metres of exhibition space, 9,000 square metres of seminar area and extensive conference and banqueting facilities. It has secured the boat show winning it from Olympia.

Page numbers in *italic* refer to subjects within illustration captions.

Acknowledgments

I gratefully acknowledge the debt I owe to previous writers, photographers, estate agents and other individuals, who so kindly assisted in the preparation of this book in all its stages. My institution, the University of East London, deserves a special thank you for its support of the research work.

For the supply of information, I am grateful to many people and organisations including he former London Docklands Development Corporation, Docklands News, Docklands Magazine Tourist East, Port of London Magazine, the Museum of Docklands, New Civil Engineer, the Builder, Dock and Harbour Authority Journal, Geomex Ltd, Butlers Wharf, Canary Wharf Company, Olympia & York, Rogue Magazine, Docklands Light Railway, Carlton Smith, Knight Rutley, Thames Line, Tobacco Dock Company, Savills, Cluttons and Chesterton.

For the supply of excellent photographs and aerials I am most grateful to Mr George Iaccabesco, Managing Director of Canary Wharf Group and to his assistant Deanne Siggins whose help and co-operation are much appreciated. I am also grateful for the co-operation and help of Mr Tom Samson and Paul Proctor of Realistic Stafford Studios who supplied some aerial photographs.

I would like to thank sincerely Marie Francis for her valuable work in typing the whole manuscript many times, with skill and care. I am grateful to Terence O'Connell for his loyal support and general assistance. Special thanks are due to Tom Juffs for his help, enthusiasm and unstinting support for all the books. I am grateful to Dr Paul Smith and Professor Reg Schofield for their encouragement. I also thank Linda Day and Joy O'Neill for typing and help, John Noble for preparing the index and proof reading, Sheila Johnson for adminstration and Dave Hobson of Lipscomb printers. Many thanks are due to Steve Cook of Stadium graphics for the excellent scanning of photographs and illustrations.

I am deeply grateful to my wife Irene for her loyalty and forbearance over many years during the writing of my fourteen books. Thanks are due to George Cossey for his kind reviews and to Jason Kingsley for the support of the University research effort..

Finally, I would like to tender my sincere thanks to the readers of my books worldwide, to whose kindly letters and encouragement the latest publication owes much.

Internationally Acknowledged
BOOKS ON DOCKLANDS & LONDON

Author: Professor S K Al Naib, University of East London

"London Canary Wharf and Docklands" Social, Economic and Environmental, Lipscomb Printers Ltd, First Printing June 2003 ISBN 1-874536 988 **(in colour)**
London Canary Wharf and Docklands is an independent research publication on London's great urban regeneration and the people who build, live and work in Europe's fastest growing new city within a city. The book reports and reflects the developments over the past few decades in the 8.5 square miles of London's waterside. Prior to regeneration, the area was a decaying leftover from a glorious trading post, which was a depressing and dying monument.
The book has four main themes in unfolding the story of Docklands and Canary Wharf. The first outlines the background and significant events in the history of the area. The second concentrates on the formation of the London Docklands Development Corporation that helped bring Canary Wharf into existence. The third theme is the construction of the largest project in Europe and its impact on the London property and financial centre. The fourth theme is concerned with a variety of physical, environmental, social and economic changes, which were derived from the regeneration to benefit the whole of London and Docklands area.

"London Dockland Guide" Visitors Pictorial Panorama, The KPC Group, Kent. First Printing August 1996. ISBN 1-874536-03-1. **(in colour)**
An historical journey of discovery through 200 years of London Docklands life and work, including urban regeneration, Docklands stories, heritage walks and Great Britain Millennium Exhibition. See London as it was and take a magical tour along the Thames and Old Docks. Enjoy the earliest engravings and photographs of the river and London life. Fascinating footage of London as only the legendary East Enders can remember it. Admire the scenes and read about the Good Old Days and the New Docklands. The indispensable guide to the wandering visitor or Londoner, with over 300 photographs, including colour illustrations and many easy to read maps.

"Discover London Docklands" A to Z Illustrated Guide, Ashmead Press, London, June 1992, Second Printing October 1992, Third Printing March 1993. Fourth Edition March 1994, Fifth Edition October 1995, Sixth Edition August 1996, Seventh Edition 1998. ISBN 1-874536-00-7.
This authoritative work is a comprehensive illustrated guide to modern London Docklands. It deals with all buildings of note from Wapping to the Royal Docks accompanied by a concise history. The construction of Canary Wharf, the Limehouse Link Road and the proposed Jubilee Line Extension are described. It serves as a unique reference for business people, local and government departments, visitors, commercial developers and other organisations. It is useful for use in schools and colleges in the teaching of architecture, engineering, geography, planning, design and technology, history and art. Sections describe the conservation areas and their maintenance which is of fundamental importance to all those who live, work or visit the dynamic area.

"London Illustrated" Guide to London's Greatest Attractions, River Thames Landmarks and Royal Palaces. The KPC Group, Kent, First Printing April 1994. ISBN 1-874536-01-5.**(in Colour).**
This unique and comprehensive illustrated guide is designed to help Londoners and tourists to enjoy the sights and pleasures of London. It covers the capital's history and heritage from the Roman relics to the famous Tower and the latest City skyscrapers, with many maps and photographs. A wealth of information is provided on notable buildings, royal palaces, museums and galleries, shopping arcades, entertainment, sports, street markets and annual events. Attention has been given to River Thames Landmarks and their dramatic changes over the past quarter century. The intention is to present the old scenes as an expression of the history of the city over many centuries and to bring about the London of 21st century - not only changing its outward appearance through new buildings and development but providing the vibrant environment to make it the greatest city in the world. (First printing of 5000 copies)

"London Docklands" Past, Present and Future, Ashmead Press, London, March 1990, Second Printing May 1991, Third Printing March 1993. Fourth Edition March 1994, Fifth Edition October 1994, Sixth Edition October 1995, Seventh Edition October 1996, Eight Edition January 1998, Ninth Edition July 2001. ISBN 0-901987-81-6.
This authoritative book traces the history, heritage and regeneration of London Docklands from 18th century into the 21st century. It begins by outlining the historical background and construction in the Port of London, draws together some of the surviving engineering and architectural features and finally attempts to provide a summary of current development and future building. It is a record of one of the most glorious chapters in the history of Britain, the English speaking nations and worldwide trade.

"Dockland" Historical Survey, NELP/GLC, London, March 1986. Second Printing December 1986 and Third Printing March 1988. ISBN 0-901987-80-8.

`Dockland' is recognised as a major unique reference book on the architectural, engineering and social aspects of London's port for two centuries. It is a factual guide for those who want to know about the heritage of the area with authoritative text on every aspect of life in the area. It brings together the experiences of dockers, civil engineers, architects industrial archaeologists and marine historians to provide a vivid portrait of dockland from the 19th century to 1970. The detailed gazetteer of sites and bibliography make the book an essential reference for those with a professional interest in Docklands as well as a fascinating read for anyone eager to learn about its history.

"European Docklands" Past, Present and Future, Ashmead Press, London, March 1991. ISBN 0-901 987-82-4.
This unique book is an illustrated account of history, heritage and regeneration in a number of enchanting docklands in Belgium, Denmark, France, Holland, Sweden and Germany. By working together with an international team of expert architects and engineers, it was possible to produce this fascinating book. It is suitable for use in schools and colleges to study and compare the construction, history and development of representative European docklands and the way in which their futures will reflect the past of these historically important areas.

"London Millenium Guide", Education, Entertainment and Aspirations Lipscomb Press, First Printing July 1999, ISBN 1874536-201**(in colour)**
The Millennium Experience 2000 brought Britain together around the most ambitious and exciting programme of Millennium celebrations in the world. The Experience included the Millennium Dome at Greenwich and the Millennium Festival of Great Britain. There were major exhibits designed to provide education, entertainment and aspiration. This colourful London guide, including Docklands is a truly astonishing collection bringing to life 2000 years of the Capital's history and the new millennium celebrations. Chapters have been added on cultural, environmental and educational activities for the ever increasing interests of schools, colleges and general public. There are easy to read maps and extensive colour photographs spanning from the Romans to the Millennium.

"London and Docklands Walks" The Great Explorer. Lipscomb Press, First Printing July 2000 ISBN 1844536 252 **(in colour)**
"London and Docklands Walks" is the long awaited follow up to the successful and fascinating seven books on London and Docklands. Published with both Londoners and tourists in mind the book is mainly an evocative illustrated record of the last four decades of the area through many guided walks. It features in colour with maps, the images of the historical City and distinctive features of new developments. It contains over three hundred illustrations depicting social and environmental changes that have shaped the great Capital city. The book will appeal to everyone who has an interest in the changing face of 21st century London.

"London Water Heritage"A Portrait in Words and Pictures. First Printing January 2001 ISBN 1874536 406 **(in colour)**
London enjoys a rich and varied water inheritance from her historic past. Evidence of how Londoners have been shaping their river and water environment can be traced hundreds of years even before the coming of the Romans. It is this inheritance which has been commemorated in this book. The text and colour photographs show the story of water issues which have and will continue to confront Londoners as they enter the 21st century. No other natural resource is as vital to human existence. Water is the "life-blood" from which all else flows. This book provides a fascinating guide for the general public, schools and colleges, private and public corporations and anyone interested in this unique heritage and its influence far beyond the life of Londoners.

"Encyclopedia of London Docklands" Modern & Historic (Forthcoming) ISBN 18745 33 333
Now recognised as the greatest regeneration in the world, the encyclopedia provides the most complete context possible for understanding the two-century story of London Docklands. It gathers the research work of nearly three decades to produce a reference of over 500 entries, ranging from short descriptions of developments to lengthy essays on broad topics.
The book is a ground-breaking compendium of information about the ever growing new city. It opens with a historical chapter as a perspective into the past culture, followed by a comprehensive study of the modern world of Docklands and those conditions which have shaped the area over the past few decades. It covers a range of diverse topics, providing readers and researchers with a firm understanding of the breadth of the regeneration and its influence throughout the world.

For information contact UEL on 020 8223 2531/2530/2478.